# Plutarch's
# LIVES

# Plutarch's LIVES

*ALAN WARDMAN*

*PAUL ELEK LONDON*

© 1974 Alan Wardman

*Published in Great Britain by*

Elek Books Limited
54–8 Caledonian Road, London N1 9RN

ISBN 0 236 17622 6

*Printed in Great Britain by*
*A. Wheaton & Co., Exeter*

There was among them Plutarch's *Lives*, which I read abundantly, and I still think that time spent to great advantage.

BENJAMIN FRANKLIN.

The heroes of Livy are the most insipid of all beings, real or imaginary, the heroes of Plutarch always excepted.

MACAULAY.

# Contents

# Contents

# Author's Note

References to the *Lives* are based on the text of Lindskog-Ziegler. Where the wider context is relevant, chapter numbers only are given; otherwise references are to chapter numbers and sub-sections. References to the *Moralia* are by number and letter (e.g. 327A).

I have tried to keep the notes fairly brief. In general they are intended to supply more illustrative material from Plutarch or to indicate a modern work as a starting-point for further reading.

In transliterating Greek words I have usually chosen the form of a proper name which is more familiar in English (as, Pericles, not Perikles). I have also written 'politicus', not 'politikos', as it seemed that the former would be less remote to readers without Greek. I have however used 'k' for the adverbial form (viz. *politikōs*), as also for words like *dēmotikos*.

# *Abbreviations of the* Lives

| | | | |
|---|---|---|---|
| Aem. | Aemilius | Tib. Gracch. | Tiberius Gracchus |
| Ages. | Agesilaus | Luc. | Lucullus |
| Alc. | Alcibiades | Lyc. | Lycurgus |
| Alex. | Alexander | Lys. | Lysander |
| Ant. | Antony | Marc. | Marcellus |
| Arist. | Aristeides | Mar. | Marius |
| Art. | Artaxerxes | Nic. | Nicias |
| Brut. | Brutus | Pel. | Pelopidas |
| Caes. | Caesar | Per. | Pericles |
| Cam. | Camillus | Philop. | Philopoemen |
| Cato i | Cato the elder | Phoc. | Phocion |
| Cato ii | Cato the younger | Pomp. | Pompeius |
| Cic. | Cicero | Publ. | Publicola |
| Cim. | Cimon | Rom. | Romulus |
| Cleom. | Cleomenes | Sert. | Sertorius |
| Cor. | Coriolanus | Sol. | Solon |
| Crass. | Crassus | Them. | Themistocles |
| Demetr. | Demetrius | Thes. | Theseus |
| Dem. | Demosthenes | Tim. | Timoleon |
| Fab. | Fabius | Tit. | Titus |
| C. Gracch. | Caius Gracchus | | |

The abbreviation *Comp.* refers to the Comparison (*sunkrisis*) which
follows most pairs of *Lives*.

# English Titles of Works in the Moralia

# Introduction

My purpose in this book is to offer a conspectus of Plutarch's moral
and political interests in the *Lives*, in the hope that it may be of use
both to those who read Plutarch because they wish to and to those
for whom he is required reading. I suspect that readers in the latter
class are now in the majority; and they can themselves be separated
into two main groups. On the one hand there are students of Greek
and Roman history, for whom Plutarch is a late, secondary source,
valued because he transmits information from earlier writers whose
works are lost. Secondly, some of the *Lives* are indispensable as the
source-material of Shakespeare's Roman plays, and our understanding of Shakespeare is deepened by some acquaintance with Amyot
and North. Neither the historian nor the literary scholar is likely to
value Plutarch much for his own sake, since it is easy to forget that
he did not write to provide the historian with facts or the dramatist
with his theme. I hope that both groups, though their priorities are
different, will find it an advantage to have a critical exposition of
the *Lives* from another point of view.

Furthermore, the reader of one *Life* or a small periodized number
is not in a position to know how far the *Coriolanus*, for example, or
the fifth-century Greek *Lives* are typical of the whole corpus. Yet
we cannot hope to understand what Plutarch has to say about a
particular character unless we know whether he approaches other
characters in the same way. I have therefore attempted to collect
and discuss the more important ideas which govern Plutarch's
evaluation of biographical material. Even though the *Lives* are
easier reading than the *Moralia*, they cannot be followed by the
unaided light of common sense; it is essential to have an informed
idea about the kind of biography they represent. I have used the
*Lives* as the main source of illumination, and I have drawn also on

several treatises among the *Moralia*. It is misleading to divide Plutarch's works into essays, speeches, dialogues and biographies, since he is often concerned with one and the same theme – the conduct of man in politics.

I share the view that Plutarch's independence of judgment has usually been under-estimated; and I assume that where a theme or idea recurs in several *Lives*, we have a guide to a dominant interest of Plutarch's own. In discussing different topics I have usually adopted a convenient or 'received' translation of the relevant Greek terms and have given the words in transliterated form, as a reminder that they are more or less opaque to the translator. In one case – the word 'politicus' – I have perhaps over-used the transliterated form, as it can refer to the activity of the hero both as leader and as citizen.

The first four chapters discuss the form of the biographies and the nature of Plutarch's interest in political behaviour and character. The remaining chapters provide some background information on his adaptation of historical methods and on the value he attaches to 'political philosophy' and rhetoric. I have not included anything on Plutarch's own life, since the bare facts are easily accessible and we now have an admirable survey of the prosopographical background.[1] Lastly, I should point out that by the term *Lives* I mean all the surviving biographies; one ought, strictly, to speak of the *Parallel Lives* as distinct from the *Aratus*, the *Artaxerxes* and the two extant *Lives* of Roman emperors, the *Galba* and *Otho*. But they all seem to have enough in common to justify a general treatment.

[1] C. P. Jones, *Plutarch and Rome*, Oxford (1971).

# I

# *The Form and Purpose of the 'Lives'*

Most, if not all, of the heroes in the *Lives* were known to Plutarch through the writings of Greek and Roman historians, though he claims the right to omit some facts which historians would have to mention, and to use other material from various sources. The course of a narrative is usually governed by the outline of events which historians would find important; and, broadly speaking, the *Lives*, though obviously not historians' history, are to be regarded as an offshoot of ancient historiography. But the special concern of the *Lives* is with character, the preoccupation which affects their form in numerous ways. Yet historians had not ignored character; and it is useful for the student of Plutarchan biography to begin by considering the extent to which historians had used character-descriptions (section 1 of this chapter). Historical writing, however, was not the only ancestor of this kind of biography; some of the earliest attempts at what is recognizable as biography were in the form of encomia on great men. The study in section 2 compares and contrasts the encomiast's approach to his subject with that of Plutarch. *one who writes speeches of praise*

The other question, why did Plutarch write the *Lives*, needs to be treated as embracing several distinct topics. Firstly we can isolate and examine Plutarch's own meditations on this subject; hence section 3 is an analytical account of Plutarch's theory, as we may call it. But the writer's own views of his activity are often one-sided; we have to go by our own sense of what he has actually achieved and check the writer's theory by his practice, as it appears to us (section 4). Lastly, we can use some of the hints in the *Lives* to arrive at a conclusion about the kind of readership Plutarch had in mind. We do not know the precise identity of more than a few readers but we can make a guess at some characteristics of the reader whom Plutarch would have thought desirable and sought to influence.

## 1.1 BIOGRAPHY AND HISTORIOGRAPHY

Plutarch's *Lives* are an outstanding achievement in the field of biographical writing. But although Plutarch was a prolific writer, he did not invent the idea of biography; we should never forget that he is a late author (he was born ca. 46 AD, in Chaeronea, Boeotia, and died ca. 126 AD), indebted to his predecessors in many subjects. It is, however, difficult for us to see where exactly Plutarch stands in relation to this literary form, because the works of many earlier writers have either not survived at all or are in such a fragmentary state that it would be rash to pass critical judgment on their nature and quality. Leo, in his classic study – *Die Griechisch-Römische Biographie nach ihrer literarischen Form* – put forward the theory that Plutarchan biography was descended from a Peripatetic tradition of writing about men of action, whereas Suetonius, in the *Caesares*, adapted the 'Alexandrian' technique of describing the lives of literary men by rubrics or headings. Leo's book has a lasting place in studies of biography, even though his theory does not square with the Euripides Life by Satyrus; this clearly does not use a rubric method for the life of a literary man. More recently Dihle has discussed two factors which he thinks crucial; firstly, the importance of Socrates, as a figure who was described by means of events from everyday life; and, secondly, the influence of Aristotelian ethics and psychology, which passed on a method of interpreting character to later biographers. Yet we are hampered in our attempt to understand the origins of Plutarchan biography by the loss of much Hellenistic literature. On the other hand, we can be sure that sketches of character had not been neglected by historians proper. Now Plutarch took many of his facts and emphases from historians; furthermore, he sought to assess the true worth of public men, those who were politically important; and it will therefore be useful to start by comparing Plutarchan biography with the kind of character-study to be found in historians. In this way we can come to a better understanding of Plutarch's own distinction between lives and histories (*Alex.* 1.2).

2

We no longer have all the *Lives* composed by Plutarch; indeed, among those which have not survived is the *Epameinondas*, the record of a hero who was probably among the statesmen most admired by the biographer. Although the absence of this particular *Life* is a serious handicap to the student of Plutarch, the biographies are sufficient in number to enable us to see that there is a clear underlying pattern. Most of them are arranged in pairs, the story of a Greek being followed (usually) by the account of a Roman, though this is not to imply that the Greek subject was always prior in the author's conception. The two *Lives* are followed by a comparison (*sunkrisis*) in which the author meditates on the various qualities of the heroes. A few pairs have no such comparison; and it is an open question whether these comparisons are missing because they were not transcribed or because the author, for some reason, failed to write them. At any rate, the comparative assessment is in principle an integral part of Plutarchan biography, and translations which omit them are, in effect, depriving the reader of an essential part of any given *Life*.

Without exception, the heroes of the *Lives* were public men whose activities, used by Plutarch as a clue to their character, had a decisive effect on some important historical events of their own lifetime. Whether he is justified or not, Plutarch thinks that outstanding men determine the course of historical events; thus the Athenian victory at Salamis is seen as the expression of Themistocles' character in the world of action, and the liberation of Greece in the second century BC is attributed, not to Roman policy as a whole, but to the character of one particular Roman, Titus Flamininus. The character of the heroes cannot be divorced from their historical significance. Furthermore, it is clear that Plutarch came to know and assess the characters of his heroes through the medium of historical writing; historians' narratives supplied him with the basic framework and the basic facts which he examined in order to elicit the character. A glance at any one *Life* is enough to demonstrate that the debt to historians is considerable and even when they are not named precisely they are often referred to by general expressions like 'some [writers] say'. It is, of course, undeniable that the historians' material has been supplemented; but it remains true that over half the biographer's capital has been borrowed from those whose prime interest was in historical writing. Wide though this last term may be, one must realize that there is a sense in which Thucydides, Herodotus and Phylarchus are all (however they differ as historians) engaged in one kind of literary activity, while Plutarch is concerned with another.

The heroes, then, were men who had influenced the making of history, men whose name and fame were for the most part transmitted to Plutarch by writers of history. The student of the *Lives* cannot escape from the fact that one of the first questions he must consider is the relationship between Plutarchan biography and Greco-Roman historiography. The form of the *Lives*, to use a convenient phrase, is dependent on the various types of historical writing. This is not merely a chronological dependence in the sense that the biographer could not have begun his task without the prior achievement of historians. It is also a dependence on method, in part at least; for biography annexed certain practices which had already been suggested or deployed in historical writing.

This view may surprise those who are familiar with the remarks in *Alex.* 1.2, where Plutarch apparently makes a sharp distinction between history and biography.[1] After appealing to his readers not to be captious if they find omissions in the *Lives* of Alexander and Caesar – his justification is the sheer number of events – he says: 'We are not writing histories (*historias*) but lives; it is not always the case that virtue (*aretē*) or badness (*kakia*) is disclosed by the most glorious actions.[2] Indeed it often happens that a minor incident, a saying and a jest show up character (*ēthos*) more clearly than battles with numerous casualties, armies facing each other and cities under siege.' The statement has often been taken as the foundation-document of biography contrasted with historical writing. Although it is not to be taken quite so weightily, the passage does deserve close attention for two reasons. Firstly, we can legitimately ask whether Plutarch's remarks here are prompted by the immediate task in hand or whether they represent his considered opinion on biography as a whole; this question will be discussed later under the heading of historical methods.[3] Secondly, we can ask what precisely is said to be the difference between history and biography and whether it is justified or not in the light of our knowledge of the tradition.

To say, as we have, that Plutarch distinguishes between history and biography is a fair way of rendering the passage, though it is

4

something of an over-simplification. In fact Plutarch has no word for biography but 'lives', which suggests that he sees a difference not between modes of enquiry but between finished products, the life of a person as compared with the history of people or a war. Elsewhere he uses the word *historia* (in the sense of enquiry) when he speaks of the difficulties which confront the biographer of Theseus (*Thes.* 1.5). This is the natural Greek for enquiry, it is true, but it is above all the term sanctioned by usage for historical investigation, as we would call it. Plutarch also uses the term in *Nic.* 1.5, where he justifies looking into works other than written histories by the idea that his is not a useless *historia* but one designed to shed light on the character of Nicias. Thus the evidence of language indicates that in some respects at least biography is thought of as yet another mode of that general enquiry into the past called history.

Yet it is clear that some kind of contrast is envisaged in *Alex.* 1. If biography and history share a common mode of enquiry, perhaps the difference is held to reside in their purposes; perhaps the final cause of historical writing is quite other than the final cause of biography. If so, since biography is explicitly intended to bring out character, Plutarch may be implying that history does not concern itself with character at all.

If Plutarch means his remark to be interpreted in this way, he is to be criticized for hasty and impatient writing. And, secondly, even what *we* know of the Greek and Roman historians, let alone what was known to Plutarch, suggests that he would have been unlikely to hold the view that character is no concern of the historian. A glance at some of the historians used and venerated by Plutarch will show that this is so. Admittedly, the reader of Thucydides does not carry away the impression that this historian is positively interested in character; yet a closer reading of his work, as has recently been argued,[4] may indicate that Thucydides did become more concerned with this subject as his work progressed. Even if this case is debatable, there can be no doubt about Xenophon, who was also admired by Plutarch. Xenophon, of course, is mainly concerned to put a subject like the death of Theramenes in its historical setting, as an event which happened during the tyrannical rule of the Thirty at Athens. Yet he cannot resist quoting two remarks made by Theramenes shortly before he died; he admits that they are not in themselves important, but they have impressed him as evidence of an admirable attitude in the face of adversity and imminent death. More elaborate are the character-sketches of the dead Greek commanders which are to be found in the *Anabasis* and which provide a wealth of detail about such figures as Clearchus and Menon.[5]

Yet in these cases, even when character does appear as a dominant interest, it can be said that it is only incidental to other interests. The character of Menon does not appear, however dimly, in and through the main narrative; it comes in a kind of moral appendix, which offers evidence about his character that cannot be found elsewhere in the story. So the classic Greek historians, Plutarch may have thought, dwelt on character as an interesting supplement to their main fare. However, the later Greek historians had shown more and more awareness of the possibilities in this field. The study of character, in Polybius' view,[6] contributes to the value of history; and the same point is made in the work of Dionysius of Halicarnassus, whose history of Rome was used by Plutarch in the composition of more than one *Life*. Dionysius explicitly recognizes that it is incumbent on the historian to discuss the characters of some men; thus he says of Publicola,[7] 'I should not omit the most remarkable of all his glories, something that has not yet been mentioned, for I think it is above all fitting for writers of history not only to report the achievements in war of great leaders or their beneficial acts of policy, but also to indicate the quality of their lives, whether they were moderate and controlled and true to their inherited customs.' He then goes on to describe the qualities of Publicola, such as his readiness to be content with little, a quality which has not yet been presented through the narrative.

It seems right to conclude that description of character was not *as such* alien to writers of history. In fact, given that many of them had a moral purpose in writing, some degree of character-study would only add to the reader's edification. It seems, too, that attention to character had become more pronounced among historians since the time of Thucydides. Plutarch's study of character differs from that made by historians in that he pursues this objective throughout his narrative; whereas historians' character-study tends to appear as the subject of an incidental digression, occasioned very often by the fact that the historian's account has reached the year in which a great man died. Furthermore, when a historian sketches a character in this way, he often makes use of facts about the man which have not already been referred to in the narrative.[8]

If we turn to consider the means whereby Plutarch brings character[9] out, these may seem at first sight to reflect a method that is remote from the procedures of a historian. Plutarch speaks of 'minor events, sayings and jests'. His biographies are not restricted to this material, but it occurs in sufficient quantity to justify the prominence which he gives it here. A good example of a 'minor event' is the story of Timocleia[10] in the *Alexander*; at the siege of Thebes a Theban woman called Timocleia was assaulted by one of the Macedonians and killed him in retaliation. When questioned by Alexander, she told him that she was the sister of a man who had fought against Philip at the battle of Chaeronea. The incident, as related by Plutarch, illustrates the woman's virtue (*aretē*) and her frankness of speech (*parrhēsia*) to the king who might be expected to treat her as an enemy. Instead, Alexander is said to have admired what she had done and her courage in telling him the truth; the king's response to virtue in others is presented as a testimony to his own virtue. The incident occupies about half the space which Plutarch devotes to the fall of Thebes and shows that what is not worthwhile for the historian can be a substantial resource for the biographer.

However, the *Lives* are not composed of 'minor events' alone and it would not be right to conclude that the biographer always uses material of a different order from the historian. The biographer makes use of 'minor events' partly because they may be novel to those already familiar with the historical record, partly as a means of attaining brevity. Plutarch does seem to have looked for evidence that would hit off a character succinctly. Clearly, this purpose would be well served by evidence in the form of sayings and jests. The scale of Plutarchan biography does not admit the long speeches which are in part used by historians to indicate character. Instead of using a speech, he can aptly include a saying to illustrate *in petto* a hero's rhetorical capabilities, since oratorical power, though not an ultimate good for Plutarch, is a necessary means to political action; and it also reflects Plutarch's own preference for trenchant discourse rather than long-winded speech.

Plutarch's expressed liking for jests as evidence of character is

7

surprising to those who are acquainted with his seriousness, not to say solemnity, as a writer. In order to understand him we must take into account the opposition between what is serious (*spoudaion*) and what is play (*paidia*). Plutarch is convinced that man is revealed by what he does or says at those times when he does not seem to be engaged in serious actions, such as defending his country or persuading the assembly. He has in mind Plato's idea, that men's amusements are a guide to their natures (*phuseis*);[11] that the good educator will take the trouble to see how people behave at symposia as well as how they conduct themselves during military training. Thus, what we have called 'jest', for convenience in translation, covers more than the idea of a verbal joke, though the ability to joke is regarded as important if it appears as an unpremeditated response.[12] It also refers to such things as the proper management of dinners and symposia, a talent for which Aemilius is praised (*Aem.* 28.7–8).

By his insistence on these means Plutarch widens the gap between the biographer and the historian. Yet the effect of any one *Life* on the reader does not quite match the expectations aroused by the theory. There is never a vast abundance of 'minor events, sayings and jests', partly because he follows, broadly, the emphasis already created by the historian. Thus his *Aristeides* is mostly concerned with the hero's participation in the battle of Plataea;[13] his *Galba* is not so much a life, as we would understand it, as a study of the episode which attracts the historian, the emperor's brief reign and sudden downfall. Plutarch in fact was making use of methods with great potentialities which he was not able to exploit to the full. There are several reasons for this; it is never easy to discover 'minor events' and so forth when the subjects are long since dead and have already been consecrated by history. Again, one of his reasons for writing *Lives* was to put before his readers models of political action in the widest sense; it follows that he naturally devotes considerable space to such events as Cicero's handling of the Catilinarian conspiracy, because it is historically important and shows Cicero as a political leader. Hence some of his interests lead him towards the public figure, the hero as he is on duty in battle and political debate, while the resources of the biographical method are capable of providing a quite different form of biography, which can discard the official uniform and show the human being.

If we judge Plutarch by the effects produced by his method, we have to admit that he has achieved a sort of compendious history rather than an independent biography. Some of his ideas seem at first to entice him away from the emphases of the historian, but he is soon obliged to return to them. His closeness to the historian can be illustrated yet again by the use he makes of the digression. The formal prescriptions of Greek and Roman historiography allowed the writer some scope for straying from his main subject. The purpose was to provide a respite for the reader; but though digressions were allowed they had to be short (digressions on the Herodotean scale were felt to be objectionable and formless) and they must not be directed to fanciful or mythological subjects. The historian must confine himself to a true account even in his digressions; the description of a country's geography would be a good example and was often incorporated.[14]

Plutarch's use of digressions tends to conform to the historian's pattern, even when he is writing on subjects that are concerned with character and have moral implications. In *Cor.* 11 he discourses on the moral significance of proper names[15] and concludes by saying : 'but this is a subject proper for another kind of enquiry.' If his interest is avowedly in the field of morals and character, why does he feel that an apology is necessary? It can only be that he is, so to say, genre-conscious; and the genre by which he is still constricted is historiography. We notice this odd constraint on his part in passages where we would least expect it. In the *Dion* (21) Plutarch describes the heroic behaviour of Thestē, the sister of the elder Dionysius, and ends his account with the words : 'this is a digression not without its uses.' He means by 'use' that the tale of Thestē is full of relevance for the student of character; but, since character purports to be his central theme, why should he make this half-apologetic conclusion? I can only assume that, in spite of his other protestations, he still feels bound by the historian's rule. He is unfolding a story like a historian and his allegiance to this story means that some comments on character are not ranked independently but come in as asides, resembling therefore the digressions made by historians. It is true that he does not always conclude his digressions in this way; but he has a significant number of this kind, which suggests that his biographies have not entirely freed themselves from the modes of historical writing.

9

Thus the form of Plutarchan biography is closer to historiography than his utterance in *Alex.* 1 would, at first, have us believe. It is easy to forget his closeness to historical writing because he naturally speaks of his method with a view to making us aware of the differences between history and biography. Yet we soon become aware that the *effect* of 'minor events, sayings and jests', so far as they are used, is to achieve a shortened form of history. If I have stressed his closeness to history in this account, the reason is that it can easily be overlooked. Elsewhere, at *Mor.* 347A, Plutarch writes as though the main aim of historians was to achieve vividness (*enargeia*), the quality of making the reader feel present at the scene described. This is a quality for which he admires Thucydides (*Nic.* 1.1) and disavows as his own objective. Anyone who compares his version of Marcellus at Syracuse with that of Livy, or Livy's account of how the Romans received the news of Trasimene with the laconic mention in the *Fabius* (3.5–6), will be inclined to agree.[16] Plutarch, as we shall see, considered that he had good reasons for not attempting this particular effect. But we should not forget that his stress on the differences between biography and history conceals the fact that there is a close relationship between his *Lives* and their sources in written history; which is other than the indebtedness of a secondary writer to his original, but not less important.

## 1.2 BIOGRAPHY AND ENCOMIUM

The *Lives*, then, are indebted to written history and to the increasing importance which historians had attached to character. But character-description, particularly in the early days of historical writing, had only been a marginal interest. Studies of character were developed by those who wished to display their rhetorical prowess as well as to commend a great man to contemporary society. The eulogy or encomium is to be regarded as a distant forbear of Plutarchan biography. Otherwise there seems to me to be little in common between the two forms, though it has been said that there is a good deal of encomium still present in Plutarchan biography;[17] a brief study of some features of encomia will enable us to see that Plutarch's purpose is not as straightforward as that of the encomiast and that he presents character in a different way.

A remarkable passage in Polybius draws our attention to a sharp distinction between history and encomium.[18] He says that he has already written a separate work in three books on Philopoemen, in which he has described his early upbringing and his most distinguished actions. 'Clearly, in the present narrative, it will be fitting to remove the details about his early upbringing and his ambitions as a young man, and add details to supplement the brief account in that work of his mature achievements, in order to observe what is appropriate to each kind of writing. My earlier treatment, being encomiastic, required a defence of his actions and an amplification of them; but the historian's approach dispenses both praise and blame; it demands a true account, together with the evidence and the reasons for particular actions.'

Although we no longer have Polybius' encomium on Philopoemen and it does not seem possible to do more than guess at the contents, we could not wish for a clearer statement about the two genres. The first thing to strike the reader is that Polybius draws a contrast between history and encomium, not between history and biography or lives. In a sense this is natural enough, as he wishes to refer the reader to his own encomium. Yet the fact that he wrote an encomium, not a work which he might have called a life, does suggest that it was not yet the received custom to write lives of contemporary politicians. The encomium seemed to be the proper medium, which shows that the subject-matter was not politically neutral but was handled persuasively in order to allot praise to Philopoemen and to uplift the audience.

In the second place we should notice the remark that 'history dispenses both praise and blame'. Polybius means this to be contrasted with the encomium, in which only praise is feasible, or, if the hero *is* blamed, the note of criticism is subdued. Which of the two has the closer resemblance to Plutarchan biography, we may ask? Superficially, it seems that Plutarch's benevolent attitude to most of the heroes puts him in the encomiast's camp. But this impression will not survive a comparative reading of those *Lives* where the biographer has used an encomium as one of his sources. In the *Philopoemen* he was, in part at least, indebted to Polybius' lost work; and in the *Agesilaus* he makes explicit references to Xenophon's panegyric on the Spartan king. A passage from *Ages.-Pomp. comp* 3 is particularly instructive; in comparing the military

11

conquests of Pompey and Agesilaus, Plutarch says: 'not even Xenophon, I think, would put the victories of Agesilaus on the same plane, even though he had, as it were, the special privilege of writing and saying what he wanted about the man because of his other fine achievements.' The language shows that Plutarch is aware of the exaggeration to be found in the encomiast and implies that Plutarch himself does not see the military career of Agesilaus in the same bright colours. It is true that Plutarch finds much to admire in the Spartan king; but he ventures to criticize his attitude towards Lysander (*Ages.* 8.6), a subject on which Xenophon is silent. We can conclude that Plutarchan biography is closer to the function of history, as seen by Polybius; for though Plutarch's tendency is to admire, he does not hesitate to point out those short-comings in a career which, in his view, impair it as a political model.

Another difference between history and encomium, according to Polybius, turns on the question of telling the truth. This major obligation upon the historian does not (it is implied) have to weigh at all upon the encomiast. Clearly he is expected to omit or to amplify if it suits him to do so. Polybius does not consider that there is any impropriety here, for he assumes that the genres have different rules. But if we were to suppose that an encomiast who merely tells the truth is as unworthy of his trade as a historian would be if he were to suppress or distort the truth, we would be putting words into Polybius' mouth. For, although he allows the encomiast scope to amplify, he clearly expects that the subject will be meritorious in the first place. He means that his praise of Philopoemen did no more than add legitimately to the deserts of one whose greatness was undeniable. Now Plutarchan biography, in this respect also, seems nearer to history as Polybius conceives it than to encomium. Plutarch's omissions are made partly in order to achieve brevity, not in order to leave dark acts out of the record. And if by amplification we mean the use of rhetorical figures to adorn the plain fact, this too is alien to Plutarch. He does have passages in which he discourses at length on a particular action or remark, as for instance at *Per.* 38.4–39 where he quotes Pericles' famous remark on his death-bed, that no Athenian had put on black because of him. But the discourse is used to put across Plutarch's own views and theories; he enhances the value that he detects in Pericles' words, not by virtuosity of language, but by expounding his own moral ideas. The enthusiasm of an encomiast is present, but it is an enthusiasm rooted in his own conviction of the truth.

Numerous features of the encomium imply a scheme of values quite different from those of Plutarch. The encomiast finds material for praise in the greatness of his hero's country, as Isocrates congratulates Evagoras and Xenophon praises Agesilaus for being a Spartan. Plutarch, however, does not make much, if anything, out of a hero's country of origin; virtue (*aretē*) in his view is a 'self-sufficient plant'[19] and ought therefore to appear in small lands as well as in great cities. This is his theory, which is of course belied to some extent by the heroes he has actually described, nearly all of whom were born into cities of political importance. But for Plutarch this is an accidental fact, a piece of chance (*tuchē*) about the hero, which does not disclose character as action does.[20] In this sense he tries repeatedly to discriminate between chance and action. His point is that the sum of biographical facts is divisible into passive and active events, as we may call them; passive events happen to the individual through the agency and purpose of other men, and only help to disclose character when the reaction to these happenings exhibits purpose. In this sense Cicero's exile is a passive event, though his reaction to it can be used as evidence of character. Active events, on the other hand, are the successful expression of an individual's purpose in the world of political action. For example, Dion and Brutus resembled each other purposively, in that both men conceived the plan of liberating their countries from tyranny; there is, too, an accidental similarity, for both men died before their aims could be carried out as they wished (*Dion* 2).

In much the same way Plutarch makes very little of noble birth, which is a favourite introductory topic in encomium. For Plutarch this too is extraneous, like the possession of wealth. At times he even seems to dwell, with approval almost, on those cases where a hero has external handicaps which an encomiast would find distressing or prefer to omit. He mentions the services performed by various distinguished members of Coriolanus' clan to Roman history. But what he lays stress on is that Coriolanus was brought up by his widowed mother: 'he demonstrates that loss of a parent, while it does have other grave disadvantages, is not an impediment to becoming a great man, one superior to the many.' (*Cor.* 1.2)

13

In the main part of its narrative the form of Xenophon's *Agesilaus* has some degree of similarity with a Plutarchan *Life*. The author makes use of a chronological sequence to relate the actions of Agesilaus and deduce from them the presence of particular virtues. The system of dating is rudimentary and imprecise but nevertheless forms the backbone of the story. The encomiast, however, is more explicit than the biographer; he seldom shrinks from expounding the virtue-significance of a particular exploit, whereas Plutarch leaves some tales without a moral coda, presumably because he is confident that the reader can follow the pointers of the narrative. Yet, towards the end of the *Agesilaus*,[21] Xenophon turns to a different system; instead of relating the events and deducing the virtues from them, he now recapitulates the virtues without the particular instances. Thus he here begins with Agesilaus' piety towards the gods and goes on to the justice of Agesilaus, and so on. This technique, which is used to elaborate effect, has no real parallel in Plutarch, though it is true that near the beginnings of some *Lives* there are references to the main virtues of the pair in question. Xenophon says that he has adopted this practice in order to make his panegyric more easily remembered. The encomiast's use of summary is therefore an aide-mémoire and seems to owe its relevance to the fact that the encomiast is addressing an audience on a contemporary or near-contemporary theme. The headings assist the reader to see the meaning in facts with which he is familiar, because they are contemporary knowledge; the first part of the discourse has acted as a formal reminder. The summary or heading could serve no such purpose for Plutarch, whose subjects were too removed in time, whereas the encomiast can use his audience's knowledge to impart an immediacy of emotional tone to his speech. The heroes of the *Lives* are in a sense present to the reader, but only because it is the author's belief that examples of virtue, whenever they occurred, are useful here and now.

A typical encomium, if we can allow ourselves to conceive of such a thing, seems to differ from a Plutarchan *Life* in several important respects. The encomiast's net has a wider mesh than Plutarch's and he therefore incorporates into his account all events which can be exploited in the hero's favour; good luck (part of what I referred to above as passive events) adds to the subject's stature in a way that is foreign to Plutarch, though he plays with the idea in his *Aemilius* and *Timoleon*. Both the encomiast and Plutarch are admirers of what is fine (*kalon*), but the panegyrist's conception of this is limited by a narrower sense of patriotism. The more successful the hero's country, the more this adds to his own magnificence; whereas Plutarch indicates that the worth of political life is not to be measured by the degree of imperialist power. The grandeur of the Roman heroes varies with other factors than the expansion of Rome's rule over the world. Thirdly, we have noticed that encomium, being often a persuasive harangue on a contemporary subject, can depend on the audience's familiarity with the subject. This fact is used by the encomiasts to spread a sense of urgency and relevance throughout the discourse. Plutarch, of course, is insistent that the *Lives* do have relevance as examples, but the sense of proximity in time is absent from them. A final difference turns on the question of style and presentation. Here the encomiast's point of view is shown most clearly in the *Evagoras*,[22] where Isocrates exploits to the full two allied ideas; one, that it is difficult for the writer to match in words the exploits of the man of action, the other, that the man of action depends on the writer for the survival of his glory. In this conception of his task, the writer's skill is exalted as the driving force which takes Achilles along with it. But Plutarch remains doggedly faithful to one of his cherished convictions, that action is superior to theory or talk (*logos*); in his view the writer therefore is a subordinate, who is privileged to mediate a career but must not suppose that artistry and fine words are needed to embellish the tale of virtue, which seems to act directly upon us whether it is expressed elegantly or not.

Yet these differences should not obscure an important similarity between encomium and Plutarchan biography. Both are concerned with putting the history of events into the perspective of the individual and both assume that the record of the actions is a guide to what they see as character. Particular actions are made to disclose particular virtues. The validity of this procedure does not appear to be questioned, either by the encomiasts or by Plutarch. For an expression of doubt we have to go, perhaps surprisingly, to Polybius, who discusses the whole subject because of contradictory views about Hannibal. Polybius' argument is designed to question the assumption that office discloses the man, because, so he maintains, men who hold political office may be obliged to act out of character through force of circumstances or the influence exerted by their friends.[23] The cruelty which the Romans saw in Hannibal can perhaps be explained as the defect of a subordinate which has been unfairly ascribed to the commander. So too with his reputed avarice; it is possible that Hannibal was held responsible for what was committed by those under his command. Thus Polybius suggests that the careers of politicians are not an open index to their characters. If we make the mistake of supposing that they are, we shall find ourselves faced with apparent contradictions in one and the same character. Agathocles, for instance, won power by bloody means but later used it beneficently and kindly; Polybius, it seems, would have us select only one as the true Agathocles and explain the other as a man compelled by events or ruled by friends. These are prudent reservations on the subject of reading politicians' characters from their *res gestae*. Nothing like them is to be found in the pages of Plutarch, who seems, rather, to be confident that actions will readily give up their secrets of character to him. Perhaps the reason is that he does not think of politics in the same way as Polybius does, as a mixture of fine actions and expedient actions. The Polybian statesman will aim first at what his country needs – if this is not only expedient but fine, then so much the better; Plutarch, on the other hand, assumes that political life is only good when men perform fine actions. He admits that his heroes should adapt to changing circumstances, but only to an extent; they should remain loyal to their nature and carry through a consistent policy. He thinks that duplicity and cunning are, on the whole, the attributes of those who are false politicians, those whose goal is power or glory for its own sake, not as a means to virtue. If Polybius is prescribing for power-politics, then Plutarch is writing of political life as measured by his ideal and transformed by his own eagerness to admire.

In this account I have drawn attention to the differences between the encomiast's and Plutarch's presentation of character. There is some indebtedness on the part of Plutarch but it is perhaps a coincidence that a chronological core is common to both. On the other hand, Plutarchan biography seems to have more in common with the historian's approach to character as defined by Polybius.

We cannot end this comparative study without taking note of the fact that character as seen by the encomiast is merely one version of the rhetorician's approach to character. The encomium is a particular medium for that rhetorical prowess which is only interested in presenting character in order to achieve its own various ends, which do not necessarily keep company with the respect for moral truth that governs Plutarch's narratives. Thus, in Plutarch's view Agesilaus is an instance of virtue, but this does not mean that Plutarch is blind to the partiality of sources like Xenophon. The orator, however, whether he is composing a paean or making a political speech, has immediate designs upon his audience. We have stressed the importance of this to the encomiast; and much the same factor can be detected in other fields of oratory, as for instance with Aeschines' presentation of Timarchus.[24] Aeschines' aim is to discredit Timarchus as a politician and he therefore dwells on his immorality as a private citizen, assuming that the man who has offended against the laws in that way will not be reliable as a political adviser. The speaker can or does assume that the laws of his society form an accepted standard by which character can be presented and judged. Thus, in political as well as in epideictic oratory, the description of character is largely controlled by contemporary knowledge and contemporary needs. Plutarch is not subject to this pressure of the moment; he is, rather, free to impose his own laws, so to say, his own assumptions about character, and leaves it to his readers to reflect upon his judgments. They are not persuaded or moved but informed of the facts from which the character is taken. Such would seem to be Plutarch's idea of his function as a biographer. It is fair to add that if he makes few attempts on his readers through the insinuations of verbal art, he does however make direct statements of his own beliefs which the reader is expected to share.

There is, finally, a difference between Plutarch and the encomiasts in their attitudes to the death of a great man. The encomiasts, if possible, exploit the idea that the hero has died in the fullness of his achievement, acknowledged by his countrymen, and rewarded by them for his services. But very few of the *Lives* have this rather naïve motif; only two heroes seem to be qualified for this kind of encomiastic treatment, Timoleon and Aemilius, and even the latter's hour of triumph is darkened by private misfortune. A simple regard for the truth made it difficult, if not impossible, for Plutarch to indulge in idealizing portraiture of a hero's death.

The failure of a Dion or the inglorious end of a Philopoemen were not facts that he wished to run away from. Indeed many of Plutarch's heroes did not come to a grand or peaceful end; some, like Caesar and the Gracchi, were assassinated; others, like Marius, show by their conduct that they have not come to terms with ambition. But for one who sets out to encourage us to virtue (*aretē*), the life that ends ingloriously can present something of a problem, for virtue unrewarded or even penalized will cast doubts on the value of pursuing it. Plutarch, therefore, reminds us of a principle which he cherishes, that virtue cannot be vanquished by fortune, even though a man like Phocion is put to death by an ungrateful country.[25] Again, to take our minds off the indignity of virtue finding an unjust reward, he dwells with some satisfaction on the punishment of those who clearly do not have virtue but who have contrived the downfall of good men. The reader is shown that Demades, the scurrilous opponent of Demosthenes, does not prosper. Philip V is punished for his treatment of Aratus' son, and Orodes pays for his cruelty to Crassus.[26] Thus the inglorious end of the good is presented, not as a failure of virtue to achieve what it ought, but as an accident caused by the mischievousness of phenomena; on the other hand, the deaths of the bad are seen as the just reward for their misbehaviour. In these ways Plutarch reminds the readers of his moral purpose; but there is some inconsistency here, since for him the deaths of bad men are morally commensurate with their lives (they are a proof of the gods' aversion) whereas the undeserved death of a good man does not call in question the gods' approval of virtue. That remains an unchallenged article of faith.

## 1.3 THE PURPOSE OF THE 'LIVES': PLUTARCH'S VIEWS

The question, why did Plutarch write the *Lives*, can only be answered by considering a few items of internal evidence. In the first place there are Plutarch's own explicit comments on his writing, which are found at the beginning of some *Lives*; there are, too, various hints of a more oblique kind which allow us to draw conclusions about the kind of audience Plutarch had in mind. The evidence is neither certain nor abundant; thus we do not know *for certain* the date at which Plutarch started to compose and so the cultural significance of the date is bound to escape us.[27] Nor do we know anything about the reactions of contemporaries as the *Lives* appeared, whether Greeks felt proud of the parallelism imposed on the two peoples or whether some Romans were inclined to regard it as yet another piece of Greek impertinence. The evidence is not merely internal but, often, incidental or casual; such as it is, it can be used to set forth Plutarch's own theory and to provide suggestions about the readers whom he would have wished to attract.

An obvious guide to Plutarch's ideas about his purpose is to be found in the opening pages of the *Aemilius*. He tells us that he began writing *Lives* because of others, but that he persisted in the task because he came to like it and found it helpful to himself. It was a means of making himself better by looking at the virtues (*aretai*) of great men as in a mirror and shaping himself by this association with the best. We do not know exactly what stimulus was offered by others, though one is tempted to conjecture that they were eminent Romans bent on encouraging a revival of things Greek. But it does seem certain that we should take Plutarch's remarks about his own self-improvement seriously. The *Demosthenes* confirms this impression; the ostensible subject of the opening chapters is the difficulty that confronts a writer on great subjects, when he is handicapped by residence in a small town and does not have immediate access to the libraries or traditions of a large city. Good biography, he suggests, must be harder to compose in Chaeronea than in Rome or Athens; but though the other arts can only prosper in metropolitan centres, virtue (*aretē*), which is the greatest art of all, should be able to flourish anywhere. The inhabitant of a small town should not blame his country but himself, if he falls short of living as he should. The company imposed on one by the needs of daily life may not always be morally acceptable; but its influence can be amended by the ideal company selected by the writer from among the great heroes of the past. Thus biography of the kind devised by Plutarch is an aid to the good life or the attainment of virtue (*aretē*); and the good life can be lived in Chaeronea or Aegina as well as in important places, since one does not need to be born in a famous country in order to achieve true fame (*Dem.* 1.1).

I am sure that Plutarch is perfectly sincere in this view, but it seems that his enthusiasm for virtue (*aretē*) has run away with him. For the most part his subject is virtue as shown in public life (political *aretē*), which is bound to be more impressive when the city is Athens or Rome rather than a small provincial town. All his heroes come from cities which in their day were politically important; furthermore it is difficult to suppose that Plutarch could even have begun to write the lives of great men from unimportant places.[28] Why, then, does he assert that true happiness (*eudaimonia*) is not dependent on being born into a prosperous and important community? He means to remind us that virtue is the property of the individual's character, that we must distinguish between external importance (conferred, for instance, by holding high office) and true quality, which can only be ascribed after careful scrutiny of a man's career. He wishes to abstract all that can be regarded as fortunate or adventitious, as though he could then confront us with the mere man, equipped solely with his virtue (*aretē*). What he loses sight of is the idea emphasized by Aristotle, that certain virtues can only be practised if the medium is adequate to express them; the political talents of a Churchill would have been wasted had he been ruler of a remote island.[29] Plutarch, for his part, does not (theoretically, at any rate) attach much importance to this question of scale. He thinks that there is a sense in which political virtue, if exhibited at Chaeronea, is not merely commensurate with but equal to political virtue at Rome, since the virtues can be held up for examination without the localities. We should add to this the consideration that he has the understandable pride of a provincial who has become famous and has chosen to reside in his home town. If men like him continue to do this, instead of flocking to the big cities, they must improve the state of things at home.

This desire for self-improvement (which aims at being more useful and effective in politics, however local) was a powerful motive, leading Plutarch to continue what others had prompted him to begin. Yet he did not go back to a heroic past because he was dissatisfied with the present. It is tempting for us to think that Plutarch was so motivated, if only because we readily compare the Greece of the late first century AD with the earlier periods of greater freedom[30] in Greek politics, and suppose that the comparison must have been as obvious and as disagreeable to Plutarch as to ourselves. If we do make this supposition, we are forgetting that Plutarch is too good-natured and generous to be a hostile critic of any age or period, including his own; and though he sometimes reflects, almost with sadness, that complete virtue is difficult to attain, he is essentially an optimist about the possibility of attaining some, if not all, virtue – *aretē*, he says, is a plant that can take root anywhere. The models of the past can therefore be repeated or imitated in the present. There is more truth in the view that the case-histories of particular *Lives* were, so to say, imposed on Plutarch, simply because he had to take the subjects offered by the historians of Greece and Rome and was not free to cast about for a subject like Gibbon. Political biography of this type would have to include studies of Pericles and Themistocles, because they were of the first importance to historians. To think along these lines, however, would be to restrict the biographer's sense of freedom, to forget that he at least *regards* himself as free to choose his subjects.[31] We shall do better to realize that with Plutarch the study of the past is not escapism or a necessity; to remember that Plutarch the philosopher justifies his choice of subjects by reflecting on the roles of perception and reason.

The distinction between the two forms an essential part of the introductions to the *Pericles* and the *Aemilius*. The *Pericles* (1.2) asserts that human beings have by nature a fund of curiosity, a love of learning which should be expended on its proper object. Perception (*aisthēsis*) cannot pick and choose among phenomena; whether these are useful or not, it is obliged in the nature of things to take notice of whatever meets with our attention. But reason does not suffer from this subjection to all objects, regardless of their value; we are free, by using our reason, to examine what we approve of and, furthermore, to nourish ourselves on what is best. The physical eye, that is, might well prefer certain colours to others, on the valid grounds that they stimulate vision, but it is not able to select those colours when it wishes and to exclude others. But the eye of the mind (the metaphor, though not Plutarchan, represents his thought) does have this freedom to choose objects that will be beneficial; and the right way to employ one's reason is in the study of actions performed by those with virtue (*aretē*). It is, I think, through some such reason that Plutarch would justify writing about past heroes rather than contemporaries, since the former can only be known by

21

reason – we cannot avoid our neighbours and contemporaries in the way that we can choose to study a Pericles – and the range of objects is thereby widened as well as being dependent on our choice. A similar point is made, though less explicitly, in the *Aemilius* (1.4), where Democritus is criticized for saying that we should 'pray for well-shaped images'.[32] Here Plutarch is vexed by the pride of place allotted to perception in a system such as Epicureanism; and he is, I think, challenging the assumption that perception is capable of dealing with man's true good, even if it could be lucky enough to have nothing but beneficial images for its objects. In his view, as he says in the *Pericles*, perception is at the mercy of phenomena; and so he goes on to contrast this vain hope expressed by Democritus with the acts of choice and avoidance whereby the mind selects from the best examples of the past that which constitutes its true moral nourishment. An exercise like the composition of the *Lives*, being a mode of reason, is bound to enlarge our vision and present us with more objects of the proper kind than are likely to be available in the narrow circle of our acquaintance.

So far I have discussed the different values put on perception and reason as a means of suggesting that Plutarch would think it quite natural to look towards the past for his subjects. Reason enjoys a freedom which perception lacks and can therefore be used to compensate for the shortcomings of the present. But the natural appetite for knowledge, which is the initial driving-force of reason, must be fed on the highest objects; it would be easy to trivialize our desire for knowledge in the way that some people direct their affections on to pets instead of humans (*Per.* 1.1). The highest object, says Plutarch, is virtue (*aretē*), for it represents the best that man is capable of as a social being and is advantageous to those who see it operate, whether they witness it in daily life or are informed by biography. It is advantageous to others because it immediately provokes our admiration and inspires us to emulate what we have been shown. Now we might divert this natural appetite for knowledge to inferior objects which would not be as satisfying. What would be wrong, for instance, if we were to use up our curiosity in admiring works of art in the modern sense, such as beautiful poems, statues or paintings? According to Plutarch, we may admire the achievement, but not the artist, for the good artist has to devote so much time to his art that he is unable to perfect himself as a citizen – he cannot be a good man. This view is expressed with great force in the *Pericles* (2.1): 'no young person, who has natural talent for the good, wants to be a Pheidias on seeing the sculptor's Zeus at Pisa, or a Polycleitus on seeing his Hera at Argos . . .' Both the artist (in the modern sense) and the good man of action do things which are fine (*kala*); but in the latter case the fineness of an action is an expression of the doer's quality of mind, whereas the fineness of an artefact is derived from the artist's mastery of the medium.

The fact that fine art and fine action are so contrasted depends on an assumption that is not always made explicit in Plutarch's writings; I refer to the assumption that virtue (*aretē*) is an art (*technē*), the highest art within the reach of human nature, since it produces the highest good for man, the good life. This is not an assumption which Plutarch even questions or explores; he has inherited the idea from such sources as Platonic dialogues in which it clearly is a live issue and gives rise to debatable questions. But for Plutarch, as for others of his age who were philosophically minded, the idea has come to enjoy the status of a hallowed principle, invoked but no longer discussed.

As we are investigating Plutarch's purpose, it is necessary to look more closely at his ideas on the subject of imitation (*mimēsis*) since thereby we can appreciate what he was likely to think of his function as a writer. The artist, whether he is a poet, sculptor or painter, imitates something; his success in calling forth our sense of wonder depends on the extent to which the work of art resembles the original. He is not, *qua* artist, dedicated to the improvement of his audience, but exploits his control over a medium to give pleasure, for instance the pleasure of recognizing that a picture is a likeness of one we know. The artist, however, has no all-controlling purpose (*proairesis*)[33] of the kind that is thought to lie behind the actions of a good life. He may paint a picture of a good man or a bad man; as long as we recognize, in the one case Achilles, in the other Thersites, his aim as artist has been fulfilled. This is a part of the artist's activity which seems to Plutarch to be particularly dangerous, since people may assume, just because a picture is a good likeness, that it represents something good or fine which we may therefore take as a model for action. He will not allow us to say, of Thersites' picture, 'That is fine,' but he thinks we ought to use some form of words such as, 'That picture is finely done'. We should not suppose that other Greeks would agree about this form of words, against which Plutarch is warning us; Plutarch, however, wants us to be prim and use the adverb, in order to remind ourselves that in art it is mastery of the medium that is the all-important factor.

What, then, of the biographer? Does he not stand between the original and the audience in the same way as the artist? We might then argue that the biographer's art, his style and presentation, is of vital importance; that only by means of such art could an instance of virtue be successfully commended to readers later in time. Plutarch, however, does not adopt this solution. He repeats, in a number of places, his conviction that action is superior to theory and rejects the sophistic maxim that the hero would be nullified without the writer. In his view, it seems, Achilles does not need Homer; Callisthenes, as historian of Alexander, does not so much bestow fame on the hero as record his achievements. The hero is first in time and precedes in value. Plutarch's enthusiasm for fine action as opposed to fine words is in a way admirable, a sensible protest against the tiresome claims of those who wrote variations on the theme that the pen is mightier than the sword. On the other hand, his theory entails a disregard of style that seems to be a major injustice to the art of the biographer. In his view (at least, according to *Per.* 2) the instance of virtue acts directly upon the audience, whereas in art (e.g. poetry or sculpture) imitation through a medium plays a part in affecting the audience. Biographical facts, so to say, are good and true, and excite the wonder of the audience, which comprehends the purpose (*proairesis*) behind the action and is inspired to act similarly. Plutarch's idea of the difference between art and biography can therefore be expressed as follows; we may admire the art without wishing to be either the artist or his subject; whereas we cannot but want to be and act like the subjects studied by biography.[34] Thus Plutarch's theory leads him to put little or no value on his own function as a literary artist. If we speak, as people often do, of Plutarch's art as a biographer, we are talking about an impression that Plutarch did not deliberately cultivate. I do not find myself tempted to think of Plutarch as a biographical artist at all, either in terms of his prose style or of his ability to compose events and sayings with a

24

harmonious sense of before and after. This is a minority view but it seems to accord with Plutarch's objectives as a teacher and moralist; yet his disparagement of the writer's art is poor theory, since the *way* in which we speak or write about past instances of virtue affects the question of how important we think they are. There is much in the sophist's claim that the good man would be left nowhere without the good writer. Plutarch finds such an idea offensive because he sees the good life as consisting of action, not words; and, besides, we should not forget that his heroes were well-known and familiar to him. One is more likely to lay stress on the importance of the writer when the subject has not yet been canonized by others writers, or seems to call forth a spirit of paradoxical expectancy. Plutarch, of course, supposes that the audience has by nature a disposition for virtue, as a result of which there is an immediate attraction to the particular instance and a desire to emulate.

His point of view about the status of art needs to be taken into account when we read the curious work *The Glory of Athens*.[35] It is tempting to dismiss this as a juvenile rhetorical piece, because it asserts the superiority of Athens' men of action, her generals and statesmen, to her painters and poets, and because we now think of Athenian art and poetry as having a permanent value which we do not ascribe to the achievements of Athenian politicians. The mode in which this thesis is presented is indeed rhetorical, but this does not mean that we should scorn the underlying thought as trivial in Plutarch's view. It seems, rather, to be in agreement with what is said and implied in theoretical passages of the *Lives*, though these are written more soberly. This is not to say that Plutarch did not admire the great writers of the past for their literary qualities. As we have seen, he praises Thucydides for the quality of vividness (*enargeia*) which makes the reader affected by his narrative and feel that he is almost taking part in the events described. But this quality is said to be beyond Plutarch's reach; and few, I think, would point with confidence to any part of the *Lives* and say that it is moving in this way. Vividness, however, is not merely an unattainable classic ideal; it is, on Plutarch's theory, a quality that is not required by the biographer's function, because virtue (*aretē*) is held to call directly to those with the aptitude to listen and follow.

The comparison between biography and painting, which occurs

in the programme-statement at *Alex.* 1, should not lead us to suppose that the two activities are comparable in respect of their goals. Here Plutarch merely compares the painter's concentration on certain features and his subordination of others in order to justify his own practice of looking for signs of the soul. More representative of his thought are the passages where he writes of poetry as 'speaking painting' and of painting as 'silent poetry'[36] – for the point is that both aim at vividness through different media. The *Cimon* (2.2) indicates that painting and sculpture are in a sense inferior to biography; for the image of the character, as rendered by biography, is a finer thing than the copy of the body and face which is offered by the portrait-painter. This idea was something of an orator's commonplace, for Cicero exploits it in his speech for Archias.[37] Plutarch, however, uses the idea not just for effect, but because it is well adapted to his general theory.

We have seen that, according to the theory, Plutarch's purpose is to put before his readers instances of virtue, introducing them to a more reasonable world than the society in which they live. The writer's part is disparaged or belittled, so much so that it is hard to conceive that Plutarch regarded himself as an artist. It remains to point out that the biographer's function is incomplete unless it provides us with some instances of careers that were outstandingly bad (*Demetr.* 1).[38] Just as the doctor knows what is health and what is not-health, so too the biographer and the student must have a knowledge of opposites; it is important to see what must be avoided as well as to have examples of conduct to be followed. Plutarch insists here that his purpose is not just to amuse his readers – the misuse of ability, as evidenced by the careers of Antony and Demetrius, is felt to be shocking – but to show, briefly, some instances of not-virtue. His purpose will be adequately fulfilled if he provides one or two examples; for the whole burden of his writings is to illustrate the grandeur of which man is capable, because he thinks that what represents the best in man is most characteristically human. We could not imagine him setting out to compose a biographical corpus which would be equally divided between heroes and villains. The villains, so to say, are something of an afterthought; and their presence is justified because virtue (*aretē*) is held to be an art (*technē*), which embraces the study of opposites.

## 1.4 THE PURPOSE OF THE 'LIVES': THE THEORY AT WORK

According to the theory we have just outlined, we would expect to find a broad division between those *Lives*, the majority, which describe examples or paradigms of virtue, and others (certainly the *Demetrius* and *Antony*) which record the careers of those without virtue. This distinction is borne out by a reading of the *Lives*, though as it stands it is too simply expressed and needs to be refined. Indeed we soon notice that a *Life* is not just the tale of a single character, to the exclusion of all others; there is always a principal subject, a Themistocles or an Aristeides, who is characterized directly (usually by eliciting his qualities from his actions) and also by comparison with others. There are two sorts of comparison *within* the framework of a *Life* (to leave on one side for the time being a discussion of the concluding formal comparisons, the (*sunkriseis*); a particular hero may be compared with contemporaries who are either lacking in virtue (*aretē*) or have none at all – or he may suggest a comparison with another hero who is also the subject of a biography, a feature which is most noticeable in the *Lives* of fifth-century Greeks and the Romans of the first century BC. A good character, that is, invites some comment on his bad or good contemporaries. I shall indicate the ways in which Plutarch uses this device of juxtaposition in order to bring out his special interests in biography.

I shall start by taking those cases where a particular biography mentions another hero who is also the subject of a *Life*, since this will enable us to see whether the heroes are equal in value or whether some instances of virtue are superior to others. Plutarch often stresses the complementariness of contemporaries, as he is eager to put before us the idea that political activity, with which he is mainly concerned, should be a school of cooperation rather than a struggle of rivals each aiming at his own dominance. In the *Philopoemen* (8.5–7) he makes a comparison between Philopoemen and Aratus;[39] Aratus was less active in war and achieved his successes through diplomacy and friendship, whereas Philopoemen was a capable general and improved the morale of the Achaeans by winning military victories. The comparison is not intended to show a preference for one hero as against the other. The general theme, at this point of the narrative, is the liberating of the Greek states from subjection to the influence of the tyrannical power of Macedon. Plutarch does not here mention the fact that Aratus asked the Macedonian government to interfere in Peloponnesian affairs. He is, rather, thinking of both men, Aratus and Philopoemen, as *in general* opponents of Macedonia and protectors of Greek freedom; Aratus' success as a politician is seen as having the same objective as the generalship of Philopoemen. They are juxtaposed, therefore, not to suggest to the reader a choice or scale of preference, but to show that different virtues can contribute towards the same end; the two virtues are complementary and have in common a fine (*kalon*) objective. The two did not actually cooperate but are regarded as though they did.

The point is made, perhaps more forcibly still, with Marcellus and Fabius, of whom Poseidonius[40] had said that one was the sword, while the other was the shield of Rome. The two Romans are depicted as having different natures; the fiery, aggressive spirit of Marcellus, exemplified by his readiness to fight in single combat with a Gallic chief, is a contrast to the caution of Fabius. Again, there is no suggestion that the virtue of the one hero is superior to the other. Both are regarded as complementary and both are necessary to Rome in her struggle against Hannibal; Poseidonius had said that the mixture of these virtues had saved Rome, and Plutarch here (*Fab.* 19.4–6) confirms this. There is indeed a suggestion that Marcellus' energy and enthusiasm finally exposed him to Hannibal's wiles, a trap which Fabius was careful to avoid. Plutarch does not yet open his mind on the subject of the general exposing himself to personal danger,[41] nor does he allow himself to digress on the different military policies which Rome adopted towards the Carthaginian army in Italy. He chooses, instead, to emphasize that here is a case of one virtue cooperating with another, different virtue, in pursuit of a common goal.

The need for the virtues to cooperate is a subject to which Plutarch returns in the *Pelopidas* (3), where he contrasts and compares Pelopidas and Epameinondas, the riches of the one with the relative poverty[42] of the other, the outdoor pursuits of Pelopidas with the philosophical tastes of Epameinondas. Plutarch is understandably proud of his Boeotian compatriots of the fourth century and enthuses about their achievement of Theban independence.

But, after stating the contrast between them, he dwells with pleasure on the thought that they were not political rivals but fought for the same purpose. A good reason for their cooperation, *we* would say, was political only; the position of Thebes at this time was such that her politicians had every reason for combining in order to make their country emerge as a leading city-state. Plutarch, however, writes without reference to this aspect of the political situation. But there is no mistaking his view about the importance of cooperating; according to him, these two Boeotians were genuine 'fellow-officers and fellow-generals', united in their services to Thebes by their virtue and untroubled by envy of each other's achievements. He draws a contrast between them and the politicians of fifth-century Athens, Aristeides and Themistocles, Cimon and Pericles, Nicias and Alcibiades,[43] whose virtues did not combine in the amicable style of Pelopidas and Epameinondas. As I said before, the political reasons for this alleged difference are not looked into; instead, Plutarch once more preaches a sermon on the text that the particular virtues of heroes in the same society find their proper outlet in working together. In a sense then he is recommending to his readers the virtues of public or political men, while having a hygienic dislike for the cut-and-thrust of political life.

These instances of cooperation were welcome to Plutarch. But he knew that they were rarer than he would have wished; and because of this he does not flinch from mentioning the cases of heroes whose virtues were not dedicated to a common end. A passage in the *Cleomenes* (16)[44] deserves pride of place in this account because it is so revealing. In his narrative Plutarch has reached the point at which the Achaeans were getting ready to agree to Cleomenes' suggestion that he should be their leader. The effect on Greek politics was disastrous, since Aratus, either through distrust or envy of Cleomenes, decided to ask the Macedonians back into the Peloponnese. To Plutarch this is all wrong; Aratus the Sicyonian and Cleomenes the Spartan, who had tried to restore the good old system of Lycurgus, should have been on the same side, defending the Greek states against Macedonian aggression, because that was the fine thing to do. One would suppose therefore that Aratus' failure to cooperate with Cleomenes might be regarded as a deficiency in his virtue (*aretē*). Now it is certainly true that the incident calls forth some moral indignation on the writer's part, but he makes it plain that he is not thereby turning against one who is the subject of another *Life*. 'I write this not as an accusation against Aratus – in many ways he was both Greek and great – but from a sense of pity for the weakness of human nature. Even with characters like his, which are preeminent in virtue (*aretē*), human nature cannot accomplish what is fine (*kalon*) without there being some fault to find.' What threatened to be a criticism of the individual has become a lament about the imperfection of human nature in general. The reader has been reminded that where possible eminent individuals should cooperate in policies which Plutarch calls fine; but he has been able to record Aratus' failure without feeling called upon to question whether Aratus has virtue. This interesting passage also makes clear that Plutarch's judgment of virtue is not based on whether a politician acts in the interest of his country in the narrow sense of expediency; what matters to him is the doing of fine actions, such as the pursuit of political independence for the Greek states.

Plutarch's sense of pity for human failings should be kept in mind when we are reading or discussing other *Lives* which record the conflicts or disagreements of great contemporaries. His criticisms are not always explicit or they are given in a muted form. One such case is the opposition between Phocion and Demosthenes. Demosthenes, though Plutarch does not hide his faults, is admired for his policy of resistance to Macedonia. Phocion, however, had a different objective, to keep Athens out of military conflict with the greater power – and his aims could well be described as those of a quietist or appeaser. Plutarch alludes to this at *Dem.* 14.1, where he refers to Phocion as the 'advocate of a policy that was not praised. He appeared to be a Macedonizer'. Plutarch *might* have drawn a contrast between the objectives of the two Athenian politicians; if Demosthenes' policy was fine, as Plutarch says, one could not then say the same of Phocion's. Perhaps Plutarch alludes indirectly to this point in the phrase I have quoted; but he certainly does not intend us to turn our admiration for Demosthenes to the discredit of Phocion, for he goes on to say that the courage and justice of Phocion made him the equal of the fifth-century worthies. Plutarch is generous and kind-hearted as a writer, aware that complete virtue is difficult to attain and anxious to commend the instances he can discover without condemning a person for his inadequacies.

This is not to say that all the heroes who have virtue (*aretē*) are for that reason regarded as equal. Some comparisons are used by Plutarch as a way of bringing out differences in virtue; an example is the comparison between Pericles and Nicias (*Nic.* 3.1): 'Pericles ruled the city through true virtue[45] and his power as a speaker. He did not need any dressing-up or persuasive touch to handle the people, whereas Nicias, who was deficient in the qualities of Pericles but had money, used his wealth to manipulate the people . . .' The virtue which is missing in Nicias is the ability as a political leader to adhere to a policy and assert it effectively against the confused objections of the Athenian assembly. In this respect Nicias is inferior to a Pericles, though it is not denied that he does have virtues; but he falls short of being a leader ('politicus').[46] A similar point occurs in the *Marius* (28), where the Roman general is contrasted with his political opponent, Metellus,[47] the subject of a *Life* which has not survived. Marius is portrayed as a brave general who did not fear the enemy, but as a politician he acted out of character ('against his nature'), showing a lack of courage before the Roman mob. Thus the disciplinarian of Rome's armies failed to become the leader of the electorate. His contrast, Metellus, is described as one who 'made war on those who tried to seduce the people not with the best policies but with a view to pleasing them'. In this picture there is some reference to the disagreements of the two Romans over social policies; there is, too, something in the way of a contrast between the aristocrat and the new man Marius; but the important point is to bring out Marius' defection from his former self, by setting this against the steadfastness of Metellus (*Marius* 28–29). As with Nicias, we have to take into account Plutarch's presuppositions about the good statesman in order to understand his approach to Marius here.

We can therefore think of virtue (*aretē*) in two ways: either it refers to a particular virtue, such as the caution of a Fabius or the courage of a Pelopidas; or it has a more general reference, to the quality of the hero as a political leader. Probably both features of virtue (*aretē*) are relevant to the comparison between Lysander and Callicratidas who is, admittedly, not the subject of a *Life*, but might well have been had his career not ended in disaster at Arginusae. It is clear from *Lys.* 5–6 that Callicratidas had more of the particular virtues for which Sparta was famous than Lysander; when he replaced Lysander as admiral, the allied peoples admired his virtue – they thought it was like the beauty of a heroic statue – but were baffled because he simply did not look the part. His virtue was too archaic for his position as ruler of the Spartan forces, and he lacked the diplomatic resourcefulness of Lysander. Thus he would not resort to the intrigue that was needed in order to persuade the Persian gate-keeper to admit him to see Cyrus. Here Plutarch has divided sympathies; he is drawn towards the unaffected justice of Callicratidas; yet, on the other hand, his main subject is virtue as shown in practical politics and he believes that the political art calls for something of Lysander's flexibility, provided that the purpose is good and is not demeaned.

In these internal comparisons with other heroes there are several themes present. Plutarch wishes that heroes like his would cooperate politically, exemplifying the unanimity of the Theban pair; and he writes with some regret and despondency about the divisions between Caesar, Pompey and Crassus.[48] On the whole, he does not exalt one man's particular virtue in order to decry another, but he does at times state a preference for a leader as having more political skill of a general kind. Even adverse criticism is expressed with caution, respectfully, for the differences between heroes are minor inequalities after all; and it is said to be difficult to have virtue entire.

The same cannot be said of the differences between heroes and those who do not have virtue (*aretē*), men who are either lacking in a particular virtue or are unscrupulous in their politics. Such men differ from the mass of people in that circumstances show them up as 'conspicuous for badness' (*kakia*);[49] if they were not in office they would be obscure and ordinary, unlike the hero whose virtue appears even when he does not hold power. Plutarch tends to make a good deal of this possibility of contrast; we are tempted to think of it as a dramatic device for setting the hero against his opposites, and such can well be its effect on the modern reader of the *Lives*. But I doubt whether Plutarch sought for these contrasts as a deliberate artistic effect, since his theories would not lead him to place much value on presenting virtue in terms of literary art.

A simple example of this contrast is provided by the *Aemilius*. The Roman hero is a man with numerous virtues who also makes a success of his public life; to have virtue is rare but to have it and succeed, like an Aemilius or a Timoleon, is rarer still, for Plutarch thinks of virtue as often dogged by misfortune, from which it is on occasion rescued by the biographer.[50] The counter to Aemilius[51] is the Macedonian Perseus, who lacks virtue politically, as the leader of a state, because he tries to cheat his Illyrian ally of the promised subsidy. He thinks of money as an end instead of as a means and is therefore characterized as cheeseparing and avaricious. Later, after his defeat at Pydna, he shows that he is cowardly, for he humbles himself before the victor and so, in Aemilius' eyes, degrades the victor's achievement. He asks Aemilius to spare him the indignity of appearing in his triumph at Rome (*Aem.* 34.3); but this is regarded as further proof of unmanliness and cowardice, since Perseus did have it in his power to choose death instead of dishonour. As this comment follows closely upon the description of Perseus humiliated in the Roman triumph, it shows that we are not meant to pity the loser in his hour of misery, but rather to draw the moral that he has shown lack of courage. As the Roman puts it : 'When men are unsuccessful their virtue is treated with respect even by the enemy, but cowardice, even if it succeeds, is of all things the most contemptible to Romans.' (*Aem.* 26.12) This absence of sympathy for the defeated seems a harsh doctrine, but the reason is that even now virtue can shine through, when the victor will feel disposed to exonerate his opponent and hold the luck of events responsible. One has only to think of Phocion's steadfastness when sentenced to a death he did not deserve.[52]

In some *Lives* the hero is contrasted with several other figures. One cannot, for instance, read the *Dion* without noticing a number of these counter-heroes. Perhaps the obvious one is the tyrant Dionysius himself, whose way of life and political objectives are the opposite of Dion's. Yet an even more interesting figure is the politician Heracleides,[53] who had been exiled by the tyrants and joined Dion's liberating movement after attempting to bring an expedition of his own. 'He had no stability of purpose, but was easily swayed in all matters; least of all was he reliable in any political partnership involving office and glory.' (*Dion* 32.3) Thus Heracleides does not seem to have particular failings, such as lack of courage, though Plutarch might well have discoursed on his injustice. Both here, and in later chapters, Heracleides appears as the example of a false leader, who does not act for the best purpose but flatters the electorate because that is the easy way to discredit Dion. There is a contrast, then, between the true politician Dion (though it should be remembered that he does have the failing of ungraciousness[54]) and on the other hand the tyrant Dionysius and the demagogue Heracleides. I shall return to these types of false statesmen in the next chapter.

The result of these comparisons within *Lives* is that the gallery of portraits is much larger than the theory might lead us to expect. The heroes themselves are described in most detail; but any one *Life* offers brief outlines of other figures, whether these are accounted good or bad by Plutarchan standards. Yet the theoretical statement of *Demetr.* 1 seems to make most of the distinction between men with virtue and those, like Demetrius and Antony, who are 'conspicuous for badness' (*kakia*). We may then ask, in what respect are Demetrius and Antony so lacking? Are they to be reckoned in the number of tyrants and demagogues like Dionysius and Heracleides? And we may go on to consider whether any other pairs of *Lives* should be regarded as similar, in the light of Plutarch's remark (*Demetr.* 1) that he proposes to give 'a pair or two' of this kind.

We cannot say that Demetrius and Antony are out-and-out bad characters. It is obvious, for instance, that Antony is not without virtue; he is described as courageous, is said to have a general's prescience and behaves well in adversity, when he is 'most like a good man'.[55] Probably the clue to a reading of these two outcasts is to be found in a sentence in the introduction to the *Demetrius*. 'Both were similarly addicted to sex and drink; they were both soldiering men, with extravagant expensive ways, disrespectful to others . . .' We might say that these faults are not so bad, for it is possible to imagine a more serious indictment. There is a sense in which a Dionysius and a Heracleides are worse, for they seem to have little, if anything, of a positive kind to set against their nefarious political purposes. But the faults outlined in this passage are especially objectionable to Plutarch. He has no time for the statesman who may be a sexual profligate and comments adversely about this side of Cimon's life (*Cim.* 4.9). He is an enemy of extravagance and luxury, since for him the good life can be lived without vast resources of wealth; a state does not have to be rich in order to be good. By referring to them as 'soldiering men' he means to

34

criticize Demetrius and Antony for having, not the common touch,[56] which is sometimes needed by the politician, but for sharing the tastes of the rank-and-file for rough-housing and exuberant pranks. By disrespect (*hubris*) he means such things as Antony's treatment of Octavia (*Ant.* 53) or Demetrius' licentious behaviour on the acropolis at Athens. This list of faults brings out the puritanism of Plutarch, it is true; his justification for finding these actions so offensive would be that they all denote a lack of restraint or want of measure.

Demetrius and Antony exhibit, too, a failing of a more general kind, which reflects adversely upon their standing as political leaders. They seem to have no clear and certain purpose of the sort that Plutarch would approve, but they are swayed by a pursuit of glory which is not a true end of action, though it can assist the doing of fine actions. Demetrius mistakes titles and honours[57] for the substance – doing what is fine – that men with virtue ought to have as their objective; and the same point can be made of the grandiose titles bestowed by Antony on his family at Alexandria. Again, Antony's failure as a general when he was defeated at Actium bears some resemblance to Pompey's defeat at Pharsalus.[58] Both generals are described by Plutarch as men acting without judgment, prevailed upon by others to follow a mistaken course of action. Yet this alleged absence of judgment, though a serious fault in Pompey, does not form part of a condemnation of the whole career. To Plutarch it seems almost inexplicable and he expresses his amazement at some length (*Ages.-Pomp. comp.* 4). Antony's failure, however, is presented as more in keeping with the character that is already known; his flight at Actium is merely another instance of a habitual dependence, not on rational choice, but on Cleopatra.

Clearly, the reader is confronted with Demetrius and Antony as examples of what to avoid. But in some ways, I suggest, they are nearer to the pattern of virtue than many of those disreputable figures like tyrants and demagogues who are sketched incidentally. We can accept Plutarch's view that they are 'conspicuous for badness' (*kakia*) only if we remember that they had an aptitude for virtue which has gone far more wrong than right. But it is not clear that we can say with confidence that any other pair of extant *Lives* is designed to give this impression of the subjects. Many other heroes have serious flaws; there is the anger of Coriolanus,[59] the cupidity of Crassus, Marius' all-devouring obsession with power; but these men are characterized by a certain fixity of purpose which is missing in the two unfortunates who have been condemned by a preface as well as by their *Lives*. It is, too, a question of more or less; in other cases there is much to admire, so that the blemishes, while they are mentioned and explained, do not take away from the exemplary value of their careers. But with Antony and Demetrius the distribution is the other way; it is in this sense that they are meant to serve as a caution, not that they are entirely perverted.

In this extended comment upon the theory as it affects a practical reading of the *Lives*, I have so far concentrated on good and bad characters, filled out with biographical details. But character, for Plutarch, is not merely man as he is recorded in his actions. It is a shorthand for registering ideas about virtue and for discussing what virtue is. By Plutarch's time it was common practice for philosophers to explain what they meant or recommended by virtue, by referring to well-known instances of virtuous action. Authority and precedent had replaced that argumentative enquiry into first principles which makes the Platonic dialogues of lasting interest. Thus the introduction to the *Pelopidas* (1–2) is an account of what is and is not to be regarded as courage (*andreia*); but it makes little use of general definitions on their own and the difficulties which these can beget. Instead we are given a number of examples of courage, or what resembles it, which are a way of giving a lesson or a principle in concentrated form. We are told, for example, that the Sybarites were not surprised at Spartan valour in battle, as, in their view, the Spartan way of life was too grim to bear. This is, for Plutarch, a natural statement for Sybarites to make but it implies several wrong principles; a mistaken view about the good life, which is not hedonistic, and the error of supposing that readiness to face death is always a sign of courage. The argument (if one can call it that) is conducted by means of famous instances and sayings. Of course even Platonic dialogues make use of instances in this way; the difference is that with Plutarch the instances have begun to crowd the argument out. The reader who takes this point will not be baffled by the superficial difference between the *Moralia* and the *Lives*, for, although there seems at first to be a gap between the philosophical essayist and the biographer, there is nevertheless throughout the same reliance on teaching by example. The *Lives* therefore are, for Plutarch, moral philosophy in another genre, and it is no surprise to find that many instances used in the *Lives* occur also in the *Moralia.*

1.5   THE AUDIENCE

We would understand much more about the Greek and Roman world of Plutarch's time if we knew the reactions of some of his contemporaries to the *Lives.* But because this information is lacking, we cannot do more than guess at the kind of reader for whom Plutarch would have wished; for he hoped not only to improve himself but to exhort others to take part in public life by profiting from the lessons of the past as he interpreted it. There are a few indications which can be used to suggest the taste and background of his first public; we know the names of a few individuals (though they are remote and colourless compared with what we know of the writer himself), and we can take note of the adverse remarks, which occur throughout the *Lives*, on 'the many' and their views. By analysing these we shall see that Plutarchan biography was not, in the first place, designed as a *popular* work, without qualification. Provided we bear this in mind, there is no harm in thinking of the *Lives* as popular history, as long as we do not extend the idea uncritically to the time when they first appeared.[60]

It is usual to speak of Plutarch's wide acquaintance as comprising his 'Greek friends' and his 'Roman friends'.[61] This is a useful distinction as long as we remember that it does not refer primarily to a difference of language or culture. By 'Roman friends' is meant above all those who had held official posts in the imperial administration; men like Mestrius Florus, who probably helped Plutarch with his *Galba* and *Otho*, and the Avidii brothers, to whom Plutarch dedicated some essays in the *Moralia.* Several such Romans were known to Plutarch; but we cannot be sure how well he knew them or whether he thought they might benefit from the *Lives.*

The most interesting Roman friend of all was Sosius Senecio, who was twice consul (in AD 99 and 107) and was a close adviser of the emperor Trajan. Hence his official career was remarkably successful, the more so if he was of Greek origin, as has recently been suggested.[62] According to Plutarch, he was responsible for suggesting the compilation known as the *Table Talk*, a collection of arguments in some of which he takes part. But, more important still, he is the principal dedicatee of the *Lives*; his name occurs in three of the *Lives*, and it is possible that he is to be included among those who are said to have prompted Plutarch to write biography (*Aem.* 1).

If we knew more about the relationship between Sosius and Plutarch, we might be able to judge whether the writer hoped to influence official administrators and careerists in the imperial service. The sceptical may be inclined to discount the fact that the *Lives* are dedicated to Sosius; what can be more natural, or more suspicious, than that a provincial Greek should cultivate the acquaintance of an influential administrator? The conversations in which Sosius is a participant may be so many fictions, a sop to the author's snobbery and a vain compliment to the administrator's apparent acquaintance with Greek learning and culture. It is possible to dismiss the evidence in this way (though difficult, if we believe that Sosius came from Greece) but I do not think we are justified in so doing. Plutarch's tone, in the passages where he refers to Sosius, is not that of a flatterer, nor would flattery accord with our general impression of Plutarch's character; he warns us against flattery in a special treatise as well as throughout the *Lives*.[63] Nor do I see any reason for supposing that Sosius did not, in some sense, take part in those discussions in which he appears in the *Table Talk* essay. We cannot be sure that he is a fiction here as we can be certain that some of the characters in Cicero's dialogues, though authentic persons, are accredited with speeches which they did not in fact deliver.[64] Besides, we do know that at this time many upper-class Romans showed a serious interest in all things Greek and in Greek philosophy in particular. Plutarch refers to other eminent Romans such as L. Mestrius Florus and Iunius Arulenus Rusticus; he says of the former that he had a 'philosophical nature'; we do not need Plutarch's word to convince us that Rusticus might aptly be described in that way.[65]

The sincerity of the dedication to Sosius need not be doubted and we may suppose, whatever his origin, that his knowledge of Greek thought was considerable. Plutarch begins the *Dion* (1) with an allusion to Simonides[66] and an analogy that do not suggest that he is in any way writing down to the recipient. Both the manner and the matter of this introduction presuppose a reader who is on terms with Plutarch's trick of using a sophistic mode to convey what he regards as important truth. The analogical form and the allusions to poetry could well have been exploited by a sophistic orator; the thought, that the *Lives* of Dion and Brutus set forth the debt of Greece and Rome to Plato's Academy, is, for Plutarch, a cherished instance of the general truth that political action ought to be imbued with philosophy. But, even if we grant this much to Sosius' learning, are we entitled to say that Plutarch hoped or expected to influence men like Sosius? Would a Sosius be typical of those Roman readers whom Plutarch wished to educate? I think that Plutarch would have been embarrassed by the question put in this simple form. Sosius is, rather, the reader who already exemplifies by his life and achievement the kind of activity to which the *Lives* exhort us. He has been mellowed by philosophy, with an active political life of which any Greek or Roman might be proud. He is therefore typical of the fulfilment rather than the hope. He represents a type of Roman for whom philosophy and action are not incompatible; we may contrast him with the case of Agricola,[67] who was prevented from too enthusiastic a devotion to philosophy on the grounds that it was not suitable for a Roman. Plutarch does not expect that this sort of anxiety will afflict the Roman readers of *his* works. Yet, if this lesson about the relevance of philosophy had already been absorbed, what benefit might readers like Sosius derive from the *Lives*? Broadly, one can only think of a willingness to equate Greek and Roman political models; a readiness, that is, to extend the pantheon of Roman worthies by a critical, though not patronizing, comparison with Greeks. Greek political experience is presented as in some ways the equal of Roman and therefore enters into a common background.

Though he was the friend and associate of influential men, Plutarch had, of course, a wide circle of Greek friends in the home-lands, as we would expect of one who sought to dignify his home-town Chaeronea by continuing to live there. Perhaps he hoped that the *Lives* would be of use to some Romans who were experienced in politics and had intellectual interests. But his main objective was to stimulate his fellow-countrymen to a consciousness that they should take part in public life, even if this meant no more than the politics of the parish-pump. Throughout the *Lives* there are indications that the needs of the Greek reader are looked after more than those of the Roman. There are, for instance, several discussions about the significance to be found in Roman names, which are often translated, presumably for the benefit of those who have no Latin; the Roman triumph is explained in a way that is obviously intended to appeal to Greeks (*Marc.* 22); and the justification of Roman scrupulosity in religious matters (*Marc.* 5.7) is designed, along with other items, to present the Romans as good men as well as the conquerors they were known to be. As an expounder of Rome's achievement to Greek readers, Plutarch has an approach that is difficult to characterize, though we may try to summarize it by comparing him with Polybius and Dionysius of Halicarnassus. Plutarch does not have that triumphant sense of discovery which lends intellectual colour and excitement to Polybius' analysis of Roman customs in Book vi; nor does his work give off an air of guarded justification which seems, in Dionysius,[68] intended to lull the suspicions of a hostile audience. He uses material that would appeal to the apologist but does so in a matter-of-fact way. It is as though he supposed it to be by now an axiom that Greeks and Romans should be regarded as comparable; he does not give the impression that he is revealing to his compatriots, whether derisively or pompously, that they are as good as or better than the Romans. He seems, then, to take for granted that his Greek audience is reconciled to the rule of Rome, and he has other objectives than those of the apologist.

Our evidence for his Greek readers is virtually restricted to the *Aratus* and the *Precepts on Public Life*. The preface of the former is addressed to Polycrates of Sicyon, as the fellow-citizen and descendant of Aratus; his way of life and power (Plutarch means, presumably, the authority that comes from good conduct in office) are said to be no discredit to the third-century Achaean. Polycrates himself is said to be well-acquainted with the life of Aratus, so that for him the story will not be a novelty. It seems, rather, to be intended for his sons, Polycrates and Pythocles, who can use the book to supplement what they hear about Aratus from their father. The example of Aratus will be the more effective because it is in the family, which has not merely survived to Plutarch's time but is also influential in politics. This point is emphasized again at the close of the *Life* (*Arat.* 54) where we are told that the family of Philip V, whom Plutarch regards as not having virtue (*aretē*), was extinguished by the death of Perseus; by contrast with the line of Aratus, the tyrant's family has died out.

It is clear from this preface that Plutarch's aim is not just to supply the family of Polycrates with the documentation needed for a panegyric, since he draws a contrast between those who praise their great ancestors, as a way of masking their own inadequacy, and those who (like Polycrates) lives up to their forbears. For such a family the story of Aratus has value, because the members of it have the aptitude to imitate what is fine. Now the main form of this imitation must be to take part oneself in the political life of one's own community. Plutarch's message to his Greek readers is that they should live up to their connexion with Greek heroes of the past, by excelling in that activity which he commemorates. This reference to the survival of an illustrious family is a means of making the past come alive, as we see when Plutarch speaks of the Spartan Callicrates (*Ages.* 35.2), the honoured descendant of one who fought against Epameinondas; but here, in the *Aratus*, it is also a reminder that the present must live up to the examples of the past. That the political life is a prime obligation, is a lesson also inculcated by the *Precepts on Public Life*, a work addressed to Menemachus of Sardis. The recipient of this work, which uses many of the instances given in the *Lives*, is a young would-be politician, who has asked for instruction about the right principles of public life.[69]

The Greek readership of the *Lives*, ideally, would include those whose aptitude for politics would be called into action by the paradigms of virtue described by Plutarch. The author's aim is to assist the education of Greek youth; yet it seems that he does not have in mind this class as a whole, but rather that minority which is wealthy and leisured and is therefore able to attend the lectures of philosophers. There are various indications in the *Lives* that the reader is expected to be in the know about points of Greek philosophy; and the *Lives* often refer to erroneous views of 'the many', implying that the reader will not succumb to whatever particular vulgarity is at issue. In this sense the *Lives* were not, on their first appearance, a work of popularization.

Some of Plutarch's analogies employ terms of comparison that are, to say the least, unexpected and do not seem likely to make the unfamiliar more acceptable. He refers to a theory that the Spartan lawgiver deliberately imported the spirit of rivalry into his political arrangements (*Ages.* 5.5); 'Those who study nature (*phusis*) think that the heavens would be halted if strife were removed from the universe, that generation and motion would cease because all things would be in harmony; similarly, it is held, the Spartan lawgiver mixed into his constitution the spirit of rivalry and ambition; his aim was that the good should always have feelings of competition with one another, for he supposed that a system of reciprocal favours, without testing, was inactive and uncompetitive and should not be called concord.' Plutarch does not himself agree with this theory of ambition (*to philotimon*) but there is no reason to suppose that he owes the formulation to anyone else. To explain a political custom by referring to a cosmological theory that would not be accepted by everyone, is to make high demands on the attention and cultivation of one's readers. Though Plutarch thinks that this view of ambition is wrong, it is not because he would think it misleading to compare microcosm with macrocosm. Such forms of comparison occur to him naturally (cf. *Phoc.* 2) and they show that he does not expect his readers to be men who are interested in action without theory, even though he looks upon the political life as the highest form of action.

Analogies of this type, though not all that frequent, occur elsewhere. At *Lys.* 25.5 he compares the complexity of Lysander's scheme for changing the system of kingship at Sparta to a 'mathematical proposition, advancing through a series of difficult and intricate steps to its conclusion'. And at *Lyc.* 29 he compares Lycurgus' feeling of satisfaction over Sparta's new constitution with Plato's remarks on the contentment experienced by the god when he observed the formation of the cosmos and its first movement. I cannot think that these comments were meant to dazzle the reader with a sense of the writer's accomplishment and range in philosophical matters; they come in naturally, abstruse though they may seem to a modern, and imply that the author expects a high degree of philosophical learning among his readers.

Plutarch's ideal man differs from the many by his superiority in virtue (*aretē*); and his ideal reader, we may say, differs, even to start with, from the many, because he does not share their wrong views and interpretations which are mentioned from time to time. Thus, at *Crassus* 27.6 we are given a description of Crassus in defeat after the battle of Carrhae, with his head covered; 'to the many he was an example of fortune, but to men of intelligence he was an example of thoughtlessness and ambition, through which he was not satisfied with being the first among so many thousands but thought he lacked everything because he was judged to come behind two men' (i.e. Caesar and Pompey). No one, who has read so far in the *Crassus*, will suppose that only *now* is he enlightened about the moral significance of Crassus' career. The reader is himself one of the intelligent and knows, along with Plutarch, that the ups and downs of history yield lessons about character; the details of a career make the character known, whereas the many gape at the obvious difference between Crassus in success and Crassus defeated. They see the event as evidence of the power of fortune to move men up or down; but Plutarch and his readers know that while fortune does play a part in human affairs, the significant part is to be ascribed to the virtue and failings of men.

This distinction between the many and those with intelligence (or those who know) is of vital importance, and one does not have the impression that Plutarch expects his readers to be among the many. They will know, as the many do not, that anger is a form of pain (*Cor.* 21.1–2) and will follow his reason for comparing the angry man with a man in a state of fever.[70] They will not suppose that the ability to put up with insults and injuries is a weakness (*Cor.* 15.4). They will not think, as the many do, that cowardice is caused by luxury and an extravagant way of life; they know it is the mark of a 'bad, ignoble nature that follows wrong opinions' (*Art.* 24.9). The many make errors of judgment in interpreting the actions of a character. They think (for a time at least) that what is, in Fabius' case, genuine non-emotionalism (*apatheia*)[71] is sloth and idleness. To them the behaviour of Cornelia, the bereaved mother of the Gracchi, must be incomprehensible; they will think her mad because she can speak of her dead sons without weeping. But the lesson of Cornelia for the perceptive is quite different; her case shows what is the effect of 'a fine nature and a fine upbringing', in that they contribute to the mastery of pain. Also 'when virtue stumbles, fortune does not take away the ability to accept things reasonably.' (*C. Gracch.* 19.4)

43

Plutarch's reader is not likely to share these false views of the many, because they usually originate in a philosophical ignorance from which he is clearly exempt. But the life of a good politician, which is the career commended by Plutarch to his readers, has certain dangers precisely because politics brings the good man into association with the many. The main danger is that his training will not hold firm and that he will, under pressure, behave like the multitude. This point is in Plutarch's mind when he writes about Cicero's disappointing reaction to his exile from Rome and Italy.[72] He moaned and whined despondently, in a way that we would not have expected from one who asked his friends to call him, not an orator, but a philosopher; who should therefore know how to conduct himself in adversity. Here, then, seems to be proof that a good character can give way and put the same valuation on catastrophe as the many would. One ought to put up with exile in the spirit of Camillus or Metellus (*Cam.* 12.4 and *Mar.* 29) rather than show the anger of a Coriolanus (*Cor.* 21) or the despair of a Cicero. The reason for Cicero's collapse is as follows: 'Opinion is wonderfully clever at washing reason out of the soul, like a dye, and smearing on the emotions (*pathē*) of the many, because men in political life must associate and live with them – unless one is extremely careful and approaches the external world with the intention of joining in events without sharing in the emotions that are attached to these events.' (*Cic.* 32.7) This abstruse passage contains some of Plutarch's most cherished convictions. He thinks of political life as a form of philosophy made active among the wayward complications of events. The good politician has to deal in material that is to some extent intractable; and he has to value events as philosophy dictates, not according to popular opinion. But because he lives among the many he is exposed to their views and is at some risk of infection, however good his training.

One may detect a similar caution about the value to be ascribed to fame or reputation (*doxa*) by the man who aspires to be a good politician. Plutarch believes, and expects his readers to agree, that the right aim of political life is virtue (*aretē*), not the achievement of a glorious name. The perfect man would not need what is commonly known as a 'good reputation', though some is necessary to allow him entry on to the stage of action and to win him credibility (*Agis* 2). Virtue, then, is the goal to which the good aspire, whereas fame, we may suppose, is the value admired by the many; fame, like wealth, is no more than a means to the good, though vulgar opinion can give it pride of place. The fact that fame is to some extent considered necessary means that Plutarch can allow that ambition (*philotimia*) contributes to the life of virtue in a subordinate way. But as political life is spent among those who think that the holding of office is *as such* a good, there is a danger that ambition may get out of hand and be pursued for its own sake. A fair number of the *Lives* are to be read as salutary warnings about the over-valuing of ambition.

Plutarch assumes that his readers will not question his philosophical values though, at the same time, he warns them that the life of political action can tempt the right-minded to accept the false opinions of the many. Politics, for him, is philosophy in action, not just theory (798B). In the *Moralia*, as well as in the *Lives*, Plutarch likes to pick his moral instances from the careers of public men. Thus the reader is expected to share his view that control of one's temper is a surer index to courage than conquest of others in battle. One could teach the lesson by citing instances of self-control from the lives of philosophers; the lesson is taught more effectively by collecting examples of rulers and kings who checked their anger. 'Those who are not right-minded' allege that philosophers are lacking in bile and a collection of such instances would not therefore prove the point. I do not think that Plutarch here (457D–E) is addressing himself to 'those who are not right-minded' with a view to converting them; he is, rather, reminding his readers, who are already initiated, that instances from the life of action can here be a more complete proof. He confirms a thesis by argument from cases that would be accepted by the many, because even on their premises his view can be shown to be correct.

It was only natural that Plutarch should make the assumption that he is addressing readers who are philosophically educated and, further, prepared to accept *his* philosophy as the right one. He was convinced that a training in philosophy was of inestimable value to those who would embark on the life of action. In the second place he developed his interest in biography after a training in philosophy and he was therefore used to a tradition which studied certain historical events to see whether they confirmed particular theories. The *Lives* have many references to this sort of discussion. In the

*Aratus* (29.7–8) we have an account of the baffling symptoms of Aratus' behaviour; he seemed brave, to judge by his taking part in battles, but was subject to giddiness and loosening of the bowels in a way that might denote cowardice. 'Hence philosophers in the schools discussed the question whether palpitation of the heart and changing colour in the presence of danger are a sign of cowardice or some deficiency in the bodily mixture (*duskrasia*), such as an excess of cold. Aratus was always named as being a good general but who nevertheless experienced in battle the symptoms described.' This particular example shows that philosophers had discussed cowardice in relation to symptoms which might be caused by the constitution or make-up of a person and could therefore be discounted as evidence for the moral quality. The story about the death of Antigonus (*Cleom.* 30.4) seems also to be an example of philosophers' discussions about the relation between moral qualities and physical symptoms.

The *Pericles* has three instances which are relevant. Aspasia's relationship with Pericles is the subject of a fairly long digression, in which it is said that she 'provided philosophers with no small subject of debate' (24.2). Though we are not told exactly what the discussion was, it seems that Aspasia's ascendancy over Pericles was felt to be mysterious; philosophers asked what art or faculty did Aspasia have that enabled her (according to one version of events) to sway the policy of Pericles. The famous story of how Pericles raised an expedition's morale by showing his knowledge of eclipses was also related in the schools (35.2). This incident might have been used by philosophers for a variety of purposes; to show the dangers of superstition or demonstrate that a knowledge of science is useful (essential even) to the man of action who has to control the masses. The third instance is more clear-cut (38); according to Theophrastus,[73] Pericles, when suffering from the plague which soon caused his death, was found wearing an amulet provided by one of his women folk. Theophrastus used the incident in discussing the question whether character changes or not according to the symptoms and ailments of the body. If Pericles, the rational and good, acted so foolishly because of physical suffering, it might be possible to argue that distress of this kind can cause loss of virtue (*aretē*). Plutarch in fact goes on to another story which seems to him to show that Pericles at the end did have a consciousness of what *arete* truly consists in. He rejects, it appears, the interpretation of Theophrastus, but not the kind of question which the Peripatetic had raised.

Some of the questions which Plutarch discovered in historical instances were therefore suggested by the tradition, long-established in the philosophical schools, of citing well-known facts in arguments about general moral questions. Plutarch's professional formation made him value such discussions, and he clearly expects that his readers will be able to follow and understand interpretations of a philosophical cast. He thinks of his audience as knowledgeable, not as sharing the views of the many, though it should be noted that he does not adopt a hostile or contemptuous attitude to the mob like the mixture of fear and arrogance that show through Tacitus' account of mutinies.[74] When the many get on top politically, Plutarch comments, almost in a matter-of-fact way, that 'spirit' (*thumos*) has taken charge of reason (*Galba* 1.3). Even when the occasion is relaxed, as in the *Table Talk*, Plutarch insists that while the subject-matter should not be abstruse, it should be designed to be of moral value. Here his model is Plato in the *Symposium*, who there discusses the first good and the gods, not by cogent reasoning but by means of 'paradigms and instances from mythology' (614D).

The *Lives*, then, were intended for a minority, if not an élite; they imply a readership with sufficient leisure and social status to have spent time studying philosophy. Though the *Lives* are readable and often run fluently, they require an acquaintance with philosophy that makes it difficult to think of them as 'popular' in the sense that we would understand the idea. Of course, there are passages where the narrative seems to exist independently of a didactic or theoretical drive, and the biographer's interest in the story carries him along. But in general it is true to say that antiquity did not produce biographies in which the author enjoys the character described for its own sake – equivalents, at narrative length, to the sketches in Theophrastus,[75] which exhibit a sense of delight or astonishment at the oddities of a person. One reason for this is that historical and biographical facts had been at the service of philosophers in the schools; Socrates the man, so to say, was lost from view and was replaced by Socrates as an instance of how to control anger or govern a licentious disposition by means of reason.[76] Plutarch was not the man, either by background or

47

purpose, to create a non-didactic biography. Yet he sketched a theory which would account for a different form of biography; and he had talents that enabled him at times to write free and self-sustaining narrative, not wholly compatible with the desire to draw a moral.

# The 'Politicus' (1)

The next two chapters study the functions of man in politics, as Plutarch sees them. Firstly, he explicitly rejects certain forms of political action as improper; demagogy and tyranny are the two perversions which are to be contrasted with the actions of the figure commended by Plutarch, the man who is 'politicus' (section 1 of this chapter). The role of the 'politicus' in relation to the whole state is often expressed through the metaphors of harmony and medicine (section 2).

Although the heroes were men with great virtue (*aretē*), which usually, in Plutarch, refers to having one or more particular virtues, their true natures were often mistaken by contemporaries, sometimes from ignorance and sometimes from malice. The hero must therefore take thought about the impression he makes on his society, for this affects his credibility and persuasiveness as a man of action (section 3). Lastly, the greatness of the hero is itself apt to provoke a hostile reaction or fear on the part of equals and lesser mortals. It follows that envy is a universal factor in political life, as Plutarch sees it; and he is therefore interested in the various ways in which eminent statesmen have attempted to allay this kind of resentment (section 4).

## 2.1 THE 'POLITICUS', DEMAGOGUE AND TYRANT

One of Plutarch's main interests is the study of virtue (*aretē*), not as an isolated or self-regarding exercise, but as the means which makes society both good and cohesive. Political *aretē*, he says (*Arist.-Cato i comp.* 3.1), is the most complete virtue man can attain, and he adds that this view would be undisputed. Since many thinkers consider that the art of managing one's own family affairs successfully (creating sufficient wealth for one's own household) is no small part of this *aretē*, poverty, as Lycurgus saw, can be a more serious obstacle to the partnership of citizens than great wealth. If there are two men, equally just, one of whom becomes wealthy while the other does not, we should put the richer man first. Thus we can praise Cato for being as able at managing his own affairs as he was at leading the state; Aristeides, on the other hand, though noted for his justice, died in poverty. This is not to say that justice is *per se* useful to others only, that the just man is by definition bound to neglect his own financial interests. Rather one should say that in this respect the political activity of Aristeides was defective. There is no reason in the nature of political *aretē* why Aristeides should not have been both just and also procured a modest competence to provide his daughters with dowries.

Thus it appears that political *aretē* aims at the moral well-being of the whole community without excluding the prosperous management of one's own affairs. Although a community cannot exist at all unless all the members have – to an extent, at least – some degree of *aretē*, the *Lives* are a study of the outstanding examples of those who displayed great virtue by comparison with their contemporaries. Political actions cannot be fine or great until power and good fortune are combined with prudence and justice in the same person (*Dion* 1.3). This is Plutarch's way of putting the Platonist case that states will have no respite from their troubles until philosophers become kings. Whether an action is pure or not depends on the purpose (*proairesis*) of the agent, for Plutarch, as a student of character, is not content to enumerate fine actions but wishes also to be certain that acts worthy of a hero are the expression of a persisting quality of character. Similarly, the greatness of political actions is to be assessed by quality of mind, purpose and character, not by the size or external importance of the state. The good life, politically speaking, is not as such concerned with conquest and expansion but with order and civic harmony.[1]

The heroes of the *Lives* are often characterized as being by nature 'politici', a favourite term which Plutarch accords to people with great natural ability for public affairs. But ability by itself is not enough to make a man a 'politicus', since one must also have virtues (*aretai*) which do not come by nature alone, but from the training in social customs imparted by the state or by contact with the right philosophical education. Thus Agesilaus gets his virtues (such as his obedience and frugal ways) from the social framework in Sparta; Dion, on the other hand, is indebted to his association with Plato for developing an attitude of hostility towards tyranny.[2] It is therefore useful to examine the public functions of the Plutarchan 'politicus', whom we may describe as the perfect individual with the most perfect form of human *aretē*. The study will provide a slight corrective to what Plutarch says about his work in the *Demetrius* (1), where he explains that he proposes to add a pair or two of bad men in order that we may know what to avoid as well as having copious examples of what to follow. This statement encourages us to think of most of the heroes as models of *aretē*, while regarding Demetrius and Antony (along with, perhaps, Alcibiades and Coriolanus) as examples of badness (*kakia*).[3] As we have seen, the *Lives* are more complex than this suggests, since the good heroes are often good to a degree only and even the obvious bad men have some virtues. When we have examined the actions of the 'politicus' we shall see that the figures can be grouped differently.

An important key to this other arrangement is provided by a passage in the *Theseus* and *Romulus* (*Comp.* 2). 'Both men [Theseus and Romulus] were by nature "politici" but neither maintained throughout life the style of a king. Both of them changed; the one became more popular, the other tyrannical, making the same mistake from opposite passions (*pathē*). The ruler's first task is to keep his office intact; which is achieved as much by abstention from what is improper as by adhering closely to what is proper. The politician who gives way or tightens things up does not remain a king or ruler. He becomes a demagogue or despot and creates in his subjects hatred or contempt. However, the former [i.e. becoming popular] is thought to be a sign of leniency (*epieikeia*) and humanity, whereas the other is a mistake made by self-love and harshness.'

When Plutarch says that the ruler must keep his office intact, he is thinking of ruler, office and rulership in the ideal sense. The implication is that such rulers and their offices are good, whatever the overt political form of the society in which they are to be found. Secondly, we must remember that good rule is established for the benefit of rulers and ruled alike; so that when we are told that 'the office must be kept intact', this is not to say that rulers and ruled have different sets of interests. The ruler is to maintain the office because to do so is beneficial to society as a whole; thus the ruler is not thought of as a predator but as a good shepherd.

The above passage shows that we have to do with one good ruler (the 'politicus')[4] and two perversions, the demagogue[5] and tyrant. The last two are further described in that we are told of their subjects' attitudes to them; the tyrant is hated, the demagogue despised. What then is the attitude of the ruled to the 'politicus' proper? The present passage does not say but the answer is easily supplied from elsewhere in Plutarch. The ruled respect and cherish the virtue of the 'politicus' and have good will (*eunoia*) towards him, as he has good will towards them. We should add that the terms demagogue, though used pejoratively here, is not always so applied. *Dēmagōgos* meant simply 'leader of the people' (*dēmos*) and was a common Greek term in the fifth and fourth centuries BC for an eminent party-leader or politician in our sense. Both meanings, the neutral and the pejorative, occur in Plutarch and the sense is sometimes hard to judge. The difficulties of interpreting can be illustrated from the *Theseus*, the story of the king who is adduced by Plutarch as an example of the ruler who declines by seeking popularity. In the *Theseus* (14) we read: 'Theseus, because he wanted to be active and at the same time was acting demagogically, went to fight the Marathonian bull, which was inflicting great damage on the people of the Tetrapolis. He overcame it and put on a spectacle by driving it alive through the city; then he sacrificed it to Apollo at Delphinium.' It is difficult here to suppose that Plutarch considers that this was inappropriate action on the part of the king; certainly, to remove the pest could only be a benefit to the ruled and the ruler; but possibly the exhibition of the bull is disapproved of as a piece of popularity-mongering. One could agree that for Plutarch the act of *aretē* (e.g. slaying the bull) is enough to invite the good will of the ruled; but perhaps he means that to parade the monster is to flaunt one's achievement before the public in an immodest way. But all in all, it is hard to believe that the presence of the term in this passage is an adverse comment on the Athenian king. However, the arch-demagogue (in the pejorative sense) of the *Theseus* is not Theseus[6] himself, but his political opponent in later life, when he was absent from Athens among the Molossi. 'Menestheus . . . was the first, they say, to try his hand at demagogy and to court the favour of the people. He united the nobles and stimulated their anger against Theseus . . . and stirred up trouble among the many by saying falsely that they had only an illusion of freedom; in fact, he said, they had lost their homes and shrines, so that they now acknowledged only one lord and master, who was a foreigner, instead of the many good, true kings they used to have.' (*Thes.* 32) What is unusual about the demagogy of Menestheus is that he operates on both classes of the state, the rich and the poor alike. It is more common to find that the demagogue in the pejorative sense achieves his effect by working on the passions of the many. In other respects, however, Menestheus is typical; he does not speak truth to the people, nor does he advocate what is best, but that which will please them. He represents things as they are not, or values which are false, as when he decries Theseus for being a foreigner, whereas the true view of things will accept as ruler not the man with a good pedigree but the man of *aretē*.[7] Menestheus' aim is to seize power for his own sake, not to rule as a 'politicus' because to do so is owing to his *aretē*. This is not to say that the true 'politicus' does nothing at all about his credibility in the eyes of the masses; but he differs from the demagogue in that the latter advocates what is immediately pleasing to the masses, who are swayed by the passions and are often incapable of judgment.

The demagogue and the tyrant are perverted rulers who are contrasted by Plutarch with the true ruler. False though he is, the demagogue is still preferable to the tyrant. It is probably true to say that there are fewer tyrants than demagogues in the pages of Plutarch, but there are enough to compose a representative portrait. Peisistratus is described as follows (*Sol.* 29.3): 'He had something artful and ingratiating in his way of talking; he assisted the poor and was lenient and moderate towards his enemies. As for qualities which he did not have by nature, these he feigned and was believed to have them more than those who actually did. He was thought to be careful, law-abiding, a friend of equality, vexed with anyone who proposed changing the present state of affairs and might want a new arrangement. By these means he deceived the many.' The tyrant is a deceiver in a different way from the demagogue; the demagogue takes on the opinions and desires of the masses, whereas the tyrant only seems to, in order to reach his objective, which is to grasp power for himself. According to Plutarch, Peisistratus himself was not wholly bad; Solon acknowledged his virtues but deplored his eagerness to be first, a passion which should be removed. It is obvious that Plutarch regards tyranny as difficult to read for what it is, and this is as true in its later stages, when it is fully established, as it is before the tyrant has seized power, as is the case with Peisistratus.[8] The tyranny of the second Dionysius 'seemed humane to its subjects' (*Dion.* 7.5). But this was not because the tyrant had become virtuous; there was no genuine virtue such as leniency (*epieikeia*), but the edge of the tyranny had become blunted simply because the ruler was base. True 'politici', we can say, may at times have virtues that can be mistaken for faults by the masses, or can be easily misrepresented; thus it takes time for the caution of a Fabius to be accepted for the virtue that it is; tyrants, however, are adept at assuming virtues that they do not have and their faults can very readily be made to look like virtues.

The 'politicus', contrasted in this way with the two distorted figures, may well seem too scrupulous, unable to survive in real life. But Plutarch certainly thinks of him as having to make allowances for political conditions, so that he is not expected to act in a uniform way. 'The "politicus" is many-sided in handling events so that each will be managed in the best way . . .' (*Sol.-Publ. comp.* 4.5) What is meant here can be seen if we examine a character like Coriolanus, who is described as simple. Although simplicity of character is in one sense always a virtue, for action must be in accord with character, the simplicity of Coriolanus is of the wrong sort and leads to political troubles for himself and Rome. He chooses to ignore the needs of the people when they ask for their own officers to represent them, and is uncomprehending about their problems during the shortage of corn. Coriolanus' stubborn insistence on his own *aretē*, though genuine enough, is a source of error, since it dominates and does not bind; not that the 'politicus' should emulate Alcibiades, described as a man who would do anything. In the *Moralia* Alcibiades is mentioned as the 'greatest of the demagogues. At Athens he went in for wit, kept horses and led an urbane and elegant life. At Sparta he had his hair cut short, wore the *tribōn* and bathed in cold water; in Thrace he made war and drank, and when he came to Tissaphernes he took to luxury and idleness, putting on an act.' (52E) Such behaviour is for demagogues, not for the 'politicus', who will maintain the principles of his nature while all the time taking into account differences in circumstances. Probably the many-sidedness of the 'politicus' is shown most clearly in his assessment of the state's condition. It is difficult to legislate for a prosperous state, as Plato told the people of Cyrene – Lucullus came to Cyrene when that city was in con-fusion after a period of tyrannies and wars; and by reminding the inhabitants of this *vox Platonica* he made them amenable to the laws which he imposed on them at their request (*Luc.* 2.4). This would suggest that the 'politicus' is likely to succeed when the state has been 'humbled by fortune'. However, the opposite view is put forward in the *Phocion* (2): 'The masses (*dēmoi*) are thought to be more insolent towards good men when they [i.e. the masses] are enjoying good fortune, being elated by success and power. But the opposite happens. Disasters make people's character bitter, quick to be angry over trifles . . . The leader who reproaches people for their errors seems then to be criticizing them for their misfortunes; by speaking frankly he seems to show contempt.' Whatever the reason for this apparent inconsistency between the *Phocion* and the *Lucullus*, Plutarch goes on to give us a remarkable passage on the attitude, not devious but subtle, which the 'politicus' should adopt towards his people. 'Mathematicians say that the sun does not have the same movement as the heavens, nor a motion that is directly opposite. It proceeds in an oblique course . . . whereby the sum of things is maintained and is given the best mixtures. It is the same with political life. The note that is too high-pitched, in all things adverse to the people, will seem stern and harsh; and, again, so too it is dangerous to be swept along by the errors of the many and to acquiesce in their mistakes.' This fine image extols the 'politicus' as the source of light to his people; at the same time it shows that the ideal ruler must always take into account the conditions of the time, or else his virtue of frank speaking will seem contempt (when the people will think him tyrannical); again, if he does not speak frankly, he will seem to flatter and be hard to distinguish from a demagogue.

Thus the 'politicus', the tyrant and the demagogue are the three principal ruler-types in Plutarch's mind. Each has his own characteristic moral mode in relation to his subjects; all of them appear to be many-sided, though with the 'politicus' this many-sidedness is a necessity imposed upon him by the intractability of political matter, as Plutarch might put it. The demagogue's variety, however, is caused by his having no principles of his own, instead of which he adopts the various views of the many. The proper evaluation of the *Lives*, then, requires that we should bear in mind the threefold division between 'politicus', demagogue and tyrant. We shall then be able not merely to compare the better men with Antony and Demetrius, but to measure the hero's political *aretē* against the standing of lesser figures (one can instance Cleon as a demagogue and Dionysius as a tyrant) who do not deserve a biography by Plutarchan standards. What political *aretē* comprises will emerge more clearly as we study the function of the 'politicus' later in this chapter. At this point we must mention briefly two other ideas which can help us to understand the 'politicus'. Firstly, he is in a sense opposed to the general, as statesman is opposed to the leader of the armed forces. Most of Plutarch's heroes are military men and he does commemorate their soldierly virtues and their talents as commanders; but his attention is often directed to a study of what use they make of victory or defeat. To put it in terms suggested by the *Ethics* of Aristotle, generalship as an art is subordinate to the political art.[9] Generalship aims at victory over the enemy, but the political art uses generalship as a means of self-defence and employs its achievements for other purposes. The political art is different, too, in that it does not aim at victory over the citizens, but at persuading them.

In the second place it must be remembered that the 'politicus' is not merely a political leader; he is also a citizen and has to submit to being ruled as well as being able to rule others. The term 'politicus', that is, can be used of all citizens, not just of the eminent, describing that which pertains to citizens or is fitting for them to do. On the one hand a man does not stop being a 'politicus' merely because he is out of office; thus, he is entitled, by his *aretē*, to perform what the officers of state may not be carrying out. But the term 'politicus' is also used to refer to the activities of citizens and, above all, to the obligations of one citizen towards another as a member of the same community. This meaning will become clearer if we take some examples. Lucullus, who held no office at the time, persuaded Lucius Quintus, a demagogue, not to overthrow Sulla's laws, but checked a great sickness (civil war) at the outset – he acted '*politikōs* and safely'. Here the Greek adverb seems to have some such meaning as 'in the way a good citizen should act'. Although a translation so longwinded would be intolerable, one must draw attention to this kind of passage, if only because the significance of this adverbial form tends to disappear in translations. Yet the fact that Plutarch chose the words reflects his idea of what in one sense it means to be a 'politicus'.

There is a similar problem in *Sulla* 10. During the war between Marius and Sulla, Sulla passed a motion in the senate condemning his enemy to death. Then he put a price on Marius' head, 'neither mercifully nor *politikōs*, in that a short while before Sulla had put himself into Marius' power by entering his house and had been allowed to go unharmed'. Here Plutarch criticizes Sulla for failing to requite Marius with an act of citizenly decency. Yet again the translations obscure this point – thus 'acting neither generously nor, from a political point of view, wisely' suggests an almost Machiavellian standard of calculation which is foreign to Plutarch. Another version – 'neither gratefully nor politically' – is open to much the same objection. If we remember that the 'politicus' is a citizen as well as a politician, we shall be able to do justice to Plutarch's views here, however we translate the passage. He clearly does not mean us to think of a failure in self-interest so much as of a failure to do what is owing to the interests of citizens as fellows.

## 2.2 HARMONY AND MEDICINE

Political *aretē* may in theory comprise two activities, the arts of ruling and of being ruled. In practice, however, as might be expected, Plutarch is thinking mostly of the 'politicus' as ruler of his state. The purpose of his virtue is not to exert power for its own sake but to create or maintain the right conditions in which the community will prosper. He will be judged by the virtues permanently established in the community, such as 'internal security, gentleness and self-sufficiency accompanied by justice'; the ability to create a state that can conquer others is not commended as such

(*Lyc.-Numa comp.* 4.13). In order to describe the objectives of the 'politicus', Plutarch makes frequent use of two images, harmony and medicine. It was a commonplace of Greek thought to idealize political action as making a harmony or bringing about a state of health. Plutarch's use of these images is not, as far as I can see, particularly novel; but they are central to his thinking, and harmony in particular is important as it involves Plutarch's ideas on love (*erōs*).

Expressions containing the idea of harmony are apt to be uncongenial to translators and sometimes disappear. Thus, to take a small example, where Plutarch says of Aemilius (*Aem.* 4.4) 'he created harmony in the province', one translation reads 'he left the province in peace'. This involves a significant omission since Plutarch's word implies that different groups within the province were brought into unity. Indeed no one who consults the *Phocion* (2.8) can be mistaken about the vitality of the idea. 'Leadership brings about the safety of the state by making concessions to willing and obedient subjects; it grants the subjects' wishes, then asks them to do what is in the interest of the state, and people cooperate gently and usefully when they are not led by force all the time. But such leadership is troublesome and difficult; it has dignity which is difficult to blend with leniency. But if the blending takes place, what is achieved is the most concordant and musical mixture of all rhythms and harmonies, the very one by which the god is said to direct the universe; he does not apply force but guides necessity by persuasion and reason.' This passage shows the importance of the 'politicus', who is to the world of man in states what god is to the universe. Secondly, it shows that what is needed to produce a harmony is an acceptable combination of opposites. The 'politicus' himself, as a man of *aretē*, has dignity, as does his office. But both will overpower the people unless he introduces leniency. These are, so to say, virtues that do not usually coincide and the 'politicus' has to make them interpenetrate each other and exist together. When Lycurgus (*Lyc.* 7.5) is said to have 'harmonized and mixed' the state, we are looking at a large-scale example of the same activity. The Spartan state, with its kings, gerousia and assembly, consists of elements which may individually be inimical to one another. The proper balance, which was struck by the reformer, makes the virtues of each element cooperate with the others in such a way that the virtues of the parts come to be predicated of the state as a whole.

It is the same with individuals as with states and the elements that compose them. Phocion is contrasted with Chabrias whose nature was 'uneven and unmixed'. Chabrias, it appears, was in other ways sluggish and slow off the mark; but in the actual fighting he was over-enthusiastic and joined with his boldest troops in making risky attacks. By contrast Phocion was both 'safe and active', the qualities required in a harmonious general, whereas Chabrias had too much of the soldier to make him a good commander. Timoleon (*Tim.* 3.5) was 'evenly mixed'; in his wars he showed great intelligence as a young man and courage when he was older. In this case the evenness or harmony of the character is shown not by coincidence of opposite qualities, but by stressing a quality uncharacteristic of a certain time of life. In the war against Hannibal the single virtues of Fabius and Marcellus[10] – caution and energy – are successfully combined by the Romans. On the negative side Dion (*Dion* 52.6) suffers from a 'difficult mixture'; he had good objectives but his achievements lacked grace and his unsociable ways failed to give a persuasive aspect to his genuine greatness.

Thus the idea of harmony is closely connected with that of mixture, and the same conjunction can be observed in the *Table Talk* (620D), where the functions of the symposiarch are discussed. The symposiarch is an important figure for Plutarch, since a 'politicus' must know how to arrange entertainments as well as how to run states (*Aem.* 28.7). The purpose of the symposiarch is to produce a harmony (*sumphōnia*) among all present at the banquet. In order to do this he must have two opposite qualities, those of seriousness and play, properly blended within himself. He may find it useful to know (657B–D) the right proportions in which to mix wine and water. There are, Ariston says jokingly, different ratios in such mixtures, just as there are different ratios in musical concords.

Harmony is not merely an image but a goddess, as Plutarch shows when he writes of the sacred band at Thebes, which remained undefeated until the battle of Chaeronea. Pammenes, contemporary with Epameinondas, is said (by way of a joke with something of substance in it) to have criticized Homer's Nestor for arranging the Greeks by tribes and phratries.[11] The proper course (the argument runs) is to put lover by loved one, for an army united on the basis of lovers' friendship is invincible. Once again we notice that the harmony is a unity of opposites; both groups, lovers and loved alike, confront danger on behalf of the others; thus lovers act heroically out of affection for their friends while the loved are afraid to do anything disgraceful in the presence of their lovers. The Theban custom of encouraging this association, which is useful both in peace and in war, is wrongly attributed by the poets to Laius,[12] who ran off with Chrysippus, Pelops' son, and according to tradition became the founder of Greek pederasty. Plutarch rejects this view in favour of the notion that 'the law-givers wished to soften and relax the natural fieriness which was unmixed'. So they made extensive use of the *aulos* and established love (*erōs*) as a glorious institution in the palaestrae, 'mixing together the characters of the young'. The lawgivers rightly added Harmony, daughter of Ares and Aphrodite, to the city's pantheon : 'for where the warrior-element associates with that which has a share in persuasion and the graces, all the citizens come through Harmony to the most melodious and orderly form of society.' This form of love derives explicitly from Plato's notion of the lover as a friend possessed by god; indeed Plutarch ventures to think that the sacred band was so called because of Plato's description of the lover in the *Phaedrus*.[13] The love he is writing of has had the coarse facts of pederasty removed from it, because he sees love as a force which can unify the state politically. In similar terms he praises Spartan homosexual love in *Lyc.* 18.8; it is love seen through Platonist eyes, as a power which does not seek carnal indulgence but aims at the good of the loved object. Thus Agesilaus (*Ages.* 11.6) is portrayed as fighting against his desire to be kissed by the beautiful Megabates and Socrates' love for Alcibiades is contrasted with that of Anytus; Socrates is devoted to the well-being of Alcibiades (*Alc.* 4.3) whereas Anytus, who is presumably the wrong sort of lover, is hopelessly infatuated with Alcibiades and cannot do anything to make him a more orderly citizen.

Plutarch's sources provided him with a good deal of gossip about the sexual relationships of his heroes.[14] Thus Solon was said to have had a lover's relationship with Peisistratus; and Themistocles and Aristeides were alleged to have fallen out long before they disagreed politically, because they were rivals over the same boy. Plutarch reports but does not dwell on such matters with the relish of a Suetonius. The passages which typify his attitude are those quoted from the *Pelopidas* and the *Lycurgus*, where the power of love is expounded as a means of harmonizing different elements.

The love of man for woman is not the subject of a special eulogy in the *Lives*. Plutarch seems to take for granted that a lasting marriage is the arrangement which will benefit citizens and the state. He criticizes Cimon (*Cim.* 4.9) for having too many love affairs with women; and it is clear that one of Antony's many failings was his love for Cleopatra. 'Finally, as Plato says of the disobedient, licentious horse in the soul's team, he kicked aside all that was fine (*kalon*) and would help to save him . . . and sent for Cleopatra.' (*Ant.* 36.2) Antony's love is therefore totally unlike the idealized love of Theban or Spartan training, which is said by Plutarch to aim at what is fine and to produce a lasting friendship. In the *Amatorius*, however, which is Plutarch's version of Plato's *Symposium*, the writer does expressly idealize love between man and woman as preferable to a pederastic relationship. There is some disagreement here between the Plutarch of the *Lives* and the Plutarch of the *Moralia*; yet it is probably true to say that both in the *Lives* and in the *Amatorius* his main target is pederastic sexual indulgence. The idealized love of the Thebans and his eulogy of marriage are both to be contrasted with that form of pleasure-seeking.

In fact Plutarch took from Polemon a definition which includes both homosexual and heterosexual love : 'It is the service of the gods directed towards looking after and keeping safe the young.'[15] It is not surprising that Ariadne fell in love with Theseus who showed his *aretē* by his willingness to brave the Minotaur. One cannot find fault with Ariadne, says Plutarch, since her love for Theseus was clearly inspired by a god, so that she could assist the hero in his time of danger. There are here two separable ideas; one is that *aretē* is in itself likely to make people fall in love with it; the other is that the gods admire *aretē* and, by inspiring people with love for it, help it to prosper. Ariadne, who was compelled by the majesty of Theseus' *aretē*, deserved to receive the attentions of a god, and her later affair with Dionysus is to be read as a higher stage in the lover's ascent towards the divine. Polemon's definition is repeated in the *Alcibiades* (4.4), where the reference is to Socrates' love for Alcibiades.

Love, then, is a particular form of the harmony which Plutarch sees as one of the goods of the state. Harmony, as we have seen, is produced by creating a mixture (*krasis*) in the elements which make up the individual or the state. *Krasis* is also a technical term of Greek medicine; and the question arises whether the connexion between the two images – the 'politicus' as harmonizer and as doctor – is through the idea of *krasis*. The *krasis* of medicine is illustrated by a passage in the *Precepts on Public Life*, 824A: 'A sick body cannot begin to change towards health until the *krasis* in the healthy parts acquires strength and drives out that which is contrary to nature; and in the case of a people suffering from faction (a civil war that is not going to be totally destructive but will at some time stop) there must be an admixture of that which is healthy and free from the passions.' The word is the same but the idea seems different; for in this case the *krasis* of one part comes to exclude the other, whereas with harmony the *krasis* is achieved by allowing the qualities of one or more parts to mingle and then coexist.

It seems likely that the images are associated, if at all, not by any idea intrinsic to them but by an insistence on the gentleness of the doctor and the harmonizer. In Plutarch's terms 'political *aretē* consists, to a large extent, of stability and gentleness'. The harmonizer (cf. *Phoc.* 2 above) works gently by means of persuasion; and the doctor's function is often seen not as consisting in excision by surgery, but in persuading a patient to submit to a new regimen. Julius Caesar is said to have set out from his early years to overthrow Rome and achieve power for himself. One would not have thought this a course of action of which Plutarch would approve. Yet the age was corrupt and a change of the form of government was needed.[16] Once Caesar was successful and became sole ruler he turned out to be the 'gentlest of doctors'. Plutarch's view is aptly summarized in *Agis Cleom.-Gracchi comp.* 4.3, where he says 'it is not the sign of a good doctor or a good "politicus" to apply the knife unless it is absolutely necessary.' Thus the function of the 'politicus' is seen to depend on his own gentleness of character. His aim is to create a unified state, in which the citizens feel that the state as a whole is more important to them than their individual friends or enemies. An important means of achieving this is by means of *erōs* as a social custom, since lovers and loved will act heroically for the good of the whole community.

## 2.3 THE APPEARANCE OF THE 'POLITICUS'

So far we have seen how the ideal 'politicus' differs from those shadow-statesmen, the demagogue and the tyrant, and how, by *erōs* for example, he sets out to create a unified and harmonious state. To achieve his goal the 'politicus' must realize that he has to deal with a world of appearances; even if he knows what is in fact best as a policy or law, to the other members of the state it may seem a course to be avoided. Furthermore, although he has *aretē* (wholly or in part) his rivals and the many may misrepresent it deliberately or simply fail to recognize it. Thus Dion was traduced by Philistus, and Fabius' caution was not at first seen as a virtue but thought to be timidity or fear.[17] Now the effect of *aretē* on those who are by nature well-endowed is to make them go and pursue *aretē* likewise; but, evidently, this capability is not often found extensively among the contemporaries, whether rivals or subjects, of the 'politicus'. His function is made more difficult by the fact that his *aretē* may seem over-bearing or objectionable; and the symbols of high office (like the consul's *fasces*) will make his *aretē* seem even more remote. In short, the good 'politicus' will not be automatically loved by his people. He has to avoid the dangers of magnificence and he will only succeed by earning the good will (*eunoia*) of the many.

The term *onkos*, for which I have used 'magnificence', is central to Plutarch's ideas on this subject.[18] It has a variety of meanings and ranges from a reference to external pomp to a quality of mind, which is usually, though not always, bad. Thus Plutarch thinks of tragedy as having magnificence for two reasons; the language is elevated or highflown, so that it seems grand even though the sentiments of the characters of the playwright are morally and theologically unsound. Again, the outward show of tragedy is magnificent; the actors wear splendid clothes and masks, they appear to be kings and queens, though we know all the time that at the end of the play the actor will return to his humble, everyday self. In this case the magnificent appearance is meant to distract us from the falsehoods at the heart of the thing. As Plutarch uses the term of the 'politicus', it refers in part to his outward impressiveness; whether the inner man is magnificent in the good or bad sense has to be judged from the context. The word magnificence is not an ideal translation but it is useful to keep the same term for convenience; as usual, translators have various expressions in different places, which conceal from the reader the fact that the same subject is in hand.

To take some simpler cases first, magnificence is applied to high office and the symbols of power. Tarquinius (*Rom.* 16.8) is said to have introduced the custom of using a chariot in the Roman triumph, making the occasion much grander and thereby exposing the triumphator to the risk of feeling himself superior to everybody else. This is one of the explanations cautiously advanced for Camillus (*Cam.* 7.1) celebrating his triumph with a chariot drawn by four white horses, a sacred vehicle: 'because people congratulated him on his victory, he was himself exalted to a magnificence and pride more overbearing than is compatible with office held under laws and among citizens.' Here the outward magnificence of the spectacle, it is suggested, may have contributed to an inner magnificence, a sense of personal grandiosity produced by success. Thus a problem facing the 'politicus' is how to diminish the obtrusive magnificence of his power and, above all, to avoid its adverse influence on himself. Publicola (*Publ.* 10.7) succeeded admirably, as 'he separated the axes from the rods and, on entering the assembly, he lowered the rods before the people, making the outward aspect of the democracy look important'. In this way he was able to reconcile the people to consular power and to put his own *aretē* beyond criticism. Magnificence is also attached to noble family and to wealth; thus Nicias has it, partly because he is rich, partly too because he has a good reputation as a general (*Nic.* 15.2); but Lamachus (*Alc.* 21.9), a general who was poor and had to ask the state for a clothing allowance, was clearly not magnificent.

When we turn to consider quality of character, the situation becomes confusing, though usually what is meant is an undue grandeur and self-importance – undue, because the 'politicus', though a leader of the state, must still think of himself as a citizen among citizens. Pausanias (*Cim.* 6.2) committed many bad actions 'because of his power and foolish magnificence'. Pausanias, an incidental villain in the *Lives* (it would hardly have been possible for Plutarch to write *his* biography), was engaged in treasonable dealings with the Persians and it is doubtful whether in Plutarch's view he has *aretē* at all. Coriolanus, however, undoubtedly does have *aretē*, as a soldier, general and patriot; but (*Cor.* 13.4) 'because he was already full of magnificence and great in spirit . . . he openly opposed the demagogues'. Thus his magnificence puts a barrier between himself and the lowest citizens; at a later stage, when his aristocratic friends go on an embassy to plead with him, they too encounter the same attitude (30.5); Coriolanus stayed seated (a sign of discourtesy to his peers), in a state of magnificence and intolerable arrogance. Probably, there is not only a reference to moral aloofness here, but also to the pomp and majesty of Coriolanus as general of the forces now opposing Rome. Lysander's (*Lys.* 18.4) case is more complex. After defeating Athens he enjoyed more actual power than any Greek before him : 'even so his magnificence and pride seemed to exceed even his power.' Plutarch goes on to list some of the honours which were voted Lysander by various states. This leaves it doubtful whether magnificence here can justifiably be referred to the moral condition of Lysander, since the honours were awarded by others, not arrogated by the hero. But Plutarch probably does mean us to think of a swelling pride in the man, not just of an external show. For one thing Lysander accepted the honours; for another, in Plutarch's view, good will (*eunoia*), even without honours, is a sufficient recompense for *aretē*, as we shall see later.

On the basis of these examples it can be said that there is an outward magnificence of power to which there corresponds at times a grandiosity of soul. The 'politicus' then becomes stern and aloof, forgetting that his *aretē* is the means whereby he and the citizens together are drawn up towards the divine. Now so far we have examined instances where magnificence has bad effects and describes a harmful state of soul. But some men, it seems, have an authentic magnificence. The elder Cato (*Cato i* 16.8) is contrasted with flattering demagogues, and the Roman people of the day are praised for having had the good sense to prefer him. Thus magnificence can be a mark of the good 'politicus', though even Cato is

65

said at one point (14.2) to have attached magnificence to his exploits by boasting about his achievements, a form of self-praise which does not commend itself to Plutarch.[19] With Dion, however, it is a natural trait which, in the political circumstances he encountered, caused him great difficulty. It should be noticed that the effect of magnificence depends on the society of the time; Cato's Rome could stand and accept it, whereas Dion's Sicilians could not. The 'politicus' must always remember that his *modus operandi* will vary, that he must be many-sided. Dion's virtues, such as his dignity and plain speaking, were misrepresented by his enemies as arrogance and obstinacy; and his natural magnificence and ruggedness made him hard to approach. With Dion, then, this quality worked to his disadvantage because his remoteness lent plausibility to accusations of autocracy. The lesson is that, in replacing an absolute régime, one must be careful to make power and virtue unbend a little.

Authentic magnificence, as we have called it, will be opportune or not according to the moral receptivity of the times. But it is a positive good quality, quite unlike that magnificence in externals which went to the head of Pausanias. There is a contrast of this kind between Pericles and Nicias. Pericles is said to have acquired magnificence from his friendship with Anaxagoras, mentioned as the last and most influential of his teachers. It is usual in Plutarch to find that philosophy makes the individual better, and so it is here, since Pericles' own magnificence is more impressive than demagogic action. Just as Dion was misrepresented as arrogant, so too Pericles was accused by Ion[20] of being puffed up and boastful. Plutarch does not accept the charge or admit the justice of Ion's comparing Pericles unfavourably with Cimon, the remoteness of the former with the easy-going versatility of the other. He says that it is not essential for *aretē* to have playfulness as an ingredient in the way that a tragic festival is incomplete unless the tragedies are followed by a satyr-play. That is a poet's opinion of things, not the true view. Thus Pericles' magnificence refers to his moral distance from the people, a remoteness which gave his leadership an authority denied to demagogues. This elevation of mind and character was enhanced by Pericles' abstention from parties and dinners, so that he seemed and was magnificent. It is plain that Pericles thought that making himself scarce would add to his political authority; but this outward show, though undeniably present, is not to be confused with that genuine authority which Pericles got from Anaxagoras.

But with Nicias things are different, as is made explicit (*Nic.* 3.1). 'Pericles ruled the city through true *aretē* and his power as an orator; he did not need any cover or persuasive front to commend himself to the people.' Nicias was deficient in *aretē* and oratorical excellence; and so he used his wealth to commend himself to the people and to counter the demagogic flattery of his rival Cleon. Plutarch considers Nicias not to have had true virtue because of his fears of prosecution (*Nic.* 2.6), his reliance on wealth and his religiosity. He is of course regarded as superior to Cleon, the archetypal demagogue who aims to please rather than inform. But in his political and social habits Nicias resembled Pericles. He kept himself close at home while his friends explained that he was preoccupied by cares of state. 'The man who above all assisted in this act (Plutarch uses the word tragedy) and added magnificence and reputation to him was Hieron . . .' (*Nic.* 5.3) Hieron, a slave educated by Nicias, acted as his public relations man, telling the assembly about the hardships of Nicias' life, alleging that he was always preoccupied with public affairs. And in fact, Plutarch adds, his life was like that; Nicias himself quoted Euripides' Agamemnon: 'magnificent is the aspect of my way of life, but we are really the slaves of the mob.'[21] Nicias and Pericles both *seem* to have magnificence; but the majesty of Nicias is external only, contrived and stage-managed by Hieron. Plutarch does not mean that if we had got past Hieron and his friends we would have found Nicias not thinking of state policy, as he claimed, but idling away his time. The activity and devotion of Nicias are unquestioned; what does not measure up to the appearance of things is his purpose (*proairesis*) and stability.

Plutarch's approach to the public image and appearance of *aretē* seems to be twofold. In some cases he starts, as it were, with a conviction of the man's grandeur and is alarmed by the ways in which it has been slandered by others, as Ion traduced Pericles and the courtiers at Syracuse abused Dion. On the other hand, seeking to penetrate the outward show of things, he makes us ask what is behind the pomp of honours, or whether the character has not to some extent itself been duped by outward magnificence. He would probably agree with the view that *aretē is* magnificent but add that it is dangerous, both politically and morally, to wear one's *aretē* too ostentatiously. Thus the titles and crowns of the successors to Alexander are described as creating a 'magnificence and over-bearing behaviour in their daily lives and intercourse' (*Demetr.* 18.5).

It remains to see how *aretē* is made acceptable to the public without degrading it to the level of a demagogic entertainment. The man of *aretē* is not, as such, a man of the people; but Plutarch's view is that he will be more likely to succeed if he has the ability to seem 'popular' (*dēmotikos*).[22] In the *Lives* this word often has a class-reference; thus it is used, and naturally, to mark off the plebeians at Rome from the patricians. It is not in this sense that I speak of the ability to be popular, and the meaning will become clearer if we look at some instances. At the start of the Roman republic Publicola gave offence because of his house, which was imposing and overlooked the forum (*Publ.* 10). Realizing that it seemed an error to the many, Publicola got some workmen together and razed the house to the ground. By this act he won admiration for his great-mindedness (here his willingness to con-centrate on essentials, preserving the spirit of the new state, and do without externals). By this gesture, as well as by his legislation, he earned his name, as one who cares for the people. Again, when Agesilaus took over the command in Asia, he formed a striking contrast with his predecessor Lysander. He was, to look at, 'simple, ordinary and popular', a true Spartan, therefore; and at first he had some difficulty in getting himself accepted by people in Asia as the new leader, since they were used to the grandeur and display of Lysander (*Ages.* 7). Thus to be popular suggests the virtue of being able to live as the mass of the people do. The man of *aretē is* different but should not appear to be so. Even a fault can *look* popular; for instance Nicias was in fact lacking in confidence and in Athens was always afraid of being prosecuted. This seemed popular since it appeared to show a respect on the part of Nicias for those who, in this extreme democracy, might be regarded as the legal conscience of the state, the prosecutors (*Nic.* 2.6).

In all this Plutarch shows his dislike of display and ostentation. In much the same way he assesses the good will of the people towards the 'politicus' by other tokens than lavish honours. This

good will is expressly contrasted with honours, as that which makes
the honours real or authentic. Thus Titus (*Tit.* 17.1) received
'fitting honours from the Greeks and that which makes honours
real, an astonishing good will towards him because of his moderate
character'. The funeral of Timoleon, which was attended by vast
numbers of Sicilians, teaches the same lesson. The huge crowd
came, not because it was an official function decreed by the state,
but because they were witnessing to their just affection, 'paying
him the grace of true good will' (*Tim.* 39.4). Pompey, too, received
the good will of the Romans throughout his life, a tribute to his
numerous virtues both in war and in peace (*Pomp.* 1.2).

Although Plutarch does at times mention the good will of the
'politicus' towards the people he is more interested in the good
will of the people towards the 'politicus'. This is natural since his
subject is *aretē*; *aretē* as such is well-disposed towards others, but
it is not always so obvious that *aretē* will be acclaimed and receive
the thanks of the people. Though being popular has its importance
for *aretē* in the world of appearances, the idea has lost much of
the scope which, for instance, Aeschines[23] gave it. The fourth-
century orator needed, as Plutarch did not, to win the approval of
the popular assembly, to flatter its sense of superiority to any and
every politician. In his view the popular 'politicus' must have five
things to his credit; free parents on both sides, a family record of
service to the state, a moderate way of life, ability as a speaker,
and lastly, courage. Only the last three of these seem to matter to
Plutarch; and, among these, oratorical ability matters, not because
it is popular, but because it is a necessary means of action, something which the 'politicus' cannot do without. In short, *aretē* is
grand and magnificent, above the masses; but restraint and ordinari-
ness in one's style of life, which are themselves virtues, are able to
make the whole *aretē* of the 'politicus' persuasive and thus secure
the good will of the people.

## 2.4 ENVY

It is apparent that the 'politicus' needs a certain degree of luck for
his *aretē* to prosper. *Aretē* is indeed of such an order that political
failure cannot take it away from the man who has it (*Phoc.* 1); but
political *aretē* will only be fully itself when it imposes itself on a

state and is accepted. There are many obstacles in the way of this, among which perhaps the most important is envy (*phthonos*). Plutarch regards envy as one of the persistent factors in Greek and Roman politics, so much so that nearly every hero becomes exposed to it at some time in his career. One treatise in the *Moralia*, the *Envy and Hatred*, discusses the matter directly; another, the *Self-Praise without Offence*, touches on it at length, as the Latin title, though not the Greek, conveys; and there are numerous references elsewhere. We shall see how Plutarch sees it at work in politics, and what means he recommends to the 'politicus' in order to keep it within bounds.

The formal definition of envy, which was familiar to Plutarch, is a sense of pain occasioned by the success of another, even if this does no harm to the envious.[24] This definition is a rough and ready guide to Plutarch's treatment of the subject in the *Lives*, though two points should be made here. Firstly, envy is so widespread that it can be aroused by the eminence a hero has attained, his political success in the obvious sense, or by his *aretē* alone. To put it another way, envy can be directed at the honours (*timē*) a hero has received, which for Plutarch is merely a man's fame (*doxa*) until it has been further analysed, or at a particular virtue such as justice. Thus the Athenians felt envy of Aristeides, the just man par excellence; his virtue of justice was misrepresented by Themistocles and it was in any case something 'above the many'. In the second place, Plutarch deals with many instances of envy of great men, where the envious clearly have a sense of actual or imminent injury to their own interests; Coriolanus is an obvious case (*Cor.* 13.6). Envy is further defined as being an opposite of good will which, as we saw, represents the ideal relationship between the man with *aretē* and those for whose benefit it is exercised. The 'politicus' who encounters envy has only met that which was to be expected; to be welcomed and acclaimed (like a Timoleon) by the good will of the people is to attain a rare felicity.

Probably the commonest form of envy described in the *Lives* is the envy felt by an individual or group which feels that it is the social and political equal of the eminent man. In this case the latter's *aretē* or political success can be felt as a threat to the well-being of others. Thus some Romans from noble families felt envy when the elder Cato was about to become censor; they argued that

70

for a new man to receive such honour would bring discredit on this high office (*Cato i* 16.4). 'Group-envy' of this kind can always speak plausibly of being threatened by a tyranny, as Dion was charged by the courtiers of Dionysius and by his demagogic opponent Heracleides (*Dion* 11.7f. and 48f.). Plutarch's general theme in such cases is that the envy is produced by an excess of ambition (*philotimia*) within the group, leading to political contests instead of peaceful cooperation. Secondly, there is envy felt by that which is inferior (the people or the many) for that which is above them, as the Roman people objects to Coriolanus and to Publicola's house. Such envy does not have close links with ambition, it seems, but comes ultimately from the egalitarian impulse of the masses; it is particularly active in Plutarch's version of politics in fifth-century Athens. It is noticeable that quite often the envy felt by equals, so to say, makes political advantage out of the abiding sense of envy felt by inferiors. A 'politicus' can be more efficiently threatened if he is portrayed as objectionable to all men than if he is merely seen as a nuisance to one or two individuals. Thirdly, there are hints in some of the *Lives* that there may be some divine power, whether it is fortune or a special sort of *daimōn*, which feels envy at great eminence achieved by mere humans. It is not always clear, here, whether Plutarch is giving the views of his characters or his own ideas. He seems, in general, to suggest that some such view is needed to explain certain facts which cannot be argued away. It is a view which had been popular in earlier Greek thought; for Plutarch it ought to have raised some difficulties about the goodness of the divine order, and he does appear to have felt some awkwardness.

A simple illustration of peer-envy is given in *Fab.* 23.4, and 25.2. Both passages stress the association of envy with ambition, seen as destructive of cohesion. In the first passage Plutarch reports the envy felt and expressed by Marcus Livius, who resented the honour (the second triumph seems to be meant) paid to Fabius by the Romans after he had recaptured Tarentum. Livius had been in command of the town when it was captured by Hannibal and had saved the citadel during the Carthaginian occupation. Plutarch thinks that Livius' envy was regrettable. He tends to think of politics in an idealizing way as a form of activity in which the *aretai* of individuals should not be in conflict with one another but should act as supports and buttresses. This tendency does not make him register the importance of such Roman values as *gloria* and *dignitas*, which have a strong competitive side.[25] In the later passage Fabius himself speaks against Scipio's proposal to carry the war from Italy to Africa. At first his views were seen as the expression of his habitual caution; but he then emphasized them so much that it looked like ambition on his part, an attempt to cut Scipio down to size as a rival who might endanger Fabius' own fame. At any rate Fabius did not impress the people, who considered that he was acting out of envy. Plutarch's point here is that Fabius' opposition went to such extremes that it was doubtful whether his policy was still in accord with his own nature.

Plutarch's thought on envy is often controlled (in a loose way) by the overriding idea that political institutions – the law-giver's arrangements, as he sometimes thinks of them – should not be divisive of the state's unity. It is for this reason, probably, that he says (*Publ.* 9.9) that the Roman triumph was 'not a thing of envy (*epiphthonon*) nor did it give pain to the spectators. Otherwise it would not have aroused such emulation or ambition (*philotimia*) that has lasted for so many years'. Here ambition is obviously ambition to the right extent, not envious of others' achievements. But other passages in the *Lives* suggest that even in his own terms he might have seen the triumph as group-divisive. Marcellus was refused a third triumph because of his enemies' opposition (*Marc.* 22) and took the ovation instead. Aemilius' triumph was opposed by Servius Galba (*Aem.* 30.5) and the resistance was only overcome after some spectacular oratory by one of his friends. One would think, on the basis of these passages, that Plutarch might well have come to the conclusion that the triumph did as such provoke excess of ambition and envy. But perhaps his answer would be that envy is so endemic that it attaches itself to any custom or institution, whatever may have been the purpose of the law-giver.

Many of the struggles between politicians in fifth-century Athens are seen by Plutarch as begotten by envy. The point is made sharply in the *Pelopidas*, where, in a fine passage of Boeotian sympathizing, Pelopidas and Epameinondas are extolled by comparison with the Athenians of an earlier age. 'If one were to look at the political careers of Aristeides and Themistocles, Cimon and Pericles, Nicias and Alcibiades, and see how they are full to bursting with quarrels, envy and rivalry, and then look again at Pelopidas' kindness and honour of Epameinondas, one would rightly entitle these last as co-rulers and co-generals . . .' Thus the cooperation of the Boeotians is contrasted with the envy that beset the Athenians. The reason, for Plutarch, lies in the *aretē* of the Boeotian pair; they did not pursue fame or wealth but had a 'divine *erōs*' for each other which led them to unite in the service of their country. This is not to deny *aretē* to the Athenians, one must suppose, but to suggest wherein it was deficient. Even in the grand age of Thebes it becomes plain that envy was still at work, since the orator Menecleidas attacked both men. 'All the other Greeks were respectful to their *aretai* and admired their good fortune; but envy, which is native to those who are fellow-citizens, grew as their reputation grew and prepared a shameful and unfitting reception for them.' *(Pel.* 25.1)

What I have called the second type of envy, the hostility of the masses towards eminence, is seen in Athenian democracy of the fifth century. Themistocles incurred the envy of the Spartans, next of the allies and lastly of his own citizens. Aristeides was resented by the many as one whose reputation for justice might be held to anticipate the verdicts of the democratic courts. Cimon succumbed to envy because he was honest, and impolitic, enough to praise the Spartans at Athens. The masses became more and more confident because of their success and growing power. They were willing to listen to accusations against the friends of well-tried leaders like Pericles *(Per.* 32.3). It is in connexion with envy that Plutarch explains the Athenian custom of ostracism;[26] 'it was not a punishment but a way of abating and alleviating envy. Envy takes pleasure in humbling those who stand out and it expends its wrath in this form of disfranchisement.' *(Them.* 22.5) This explanation is a good example of how Plutarch seeks to expound what he looks upon as the timeless political factors. He is far from seeing any connexion between the institution of ostracism and the expulsion of the tyrants at the end of the sixth century. Perhaps this is understandable as he writes mostly of the Athenians of the fully-grown democracy, when fear of a tyranny or a Peisistratid's return would not be obvious to one who was not primarily a historian. He can with justice be accused of failing to see that ostracism became a device for solving differences of policy.

Lastly, as we have indicated already, there is the idea that human achievement may rise too high. This view is set forth in the *Dion* (2), in connexion with the story that Brutus and Dion were visited by apparitions shortly before their death. It is not likely that such men – stable, philosophical characters – actually saw nothing or were affected by superstition. They mentioned the incidents to others. 'Perhaps we may be compelled to admit the paradoxical theory of the ancients, that bad, malignant spirits (*daimonia*),[27] being envious of good men and opposed to their actions, introduce confusion and fear, as a way of shaking their *aretē* and causing it to fall, in order that they may not persist steadfast in their good course and so may not obtain a better lot than these *daimonia* after their death.' Here the envy of the spirits is felt to be an awkward theory, but less awkward than denying the historical facts of Brutus' and Dion's visions. Malignant spirits can be fitted into a demonological scheme deriving in part from Plato. A similar fear of daemonic envy is expressed in the *Aemilius* (34.7). 'Aemilius was an object of envy to none of the good, unless there is indeed some daemonic power (*daimonion*) which has allotted to it the task of taking away from great and magnificent success and mixing the life of man so that no one is entirely free of troubles . . .' Here the writer alludes to the fact that Aemilius lost two of his children, one of them five days before his triumph, the other three days later. The Romans of the time are said to have felt awe at this cruelty on the part of fortune; and Plutarch seems, on this occasion, to find authority in Homer[28] for the view that no man's life can be untouched by disaster. In this case the explanation of daemonic envy is moral rather than theological.

Connected with the idea of daemonic envy is the notion of *nemesis* which sometimes appears in conjunction with envy and at others stands on its own. Plutarch uses this idea to express his sense that there are forces at work in the world which tend to act against *aretē* and impede its continuance. It is rare to find instances of virtue achieving lasting success, though Timoleon is an exception. Thus Aemilius says that he is afraid of a *nemesis* which will be a kind of compensation (in the bad sense) for his victory and triumph over the Macedonians. Plutarch sees such events as Aemilius' losing two of his children in the hour of triumph as confirmation of what he calls the feebleness of man. Even men of *aretē* who have good

fortune and succeed are likely to meet with a compensating disadvantage; for example, Camillus succeeds at Veii but is then
exiled. While Plutarch feels pity for such happenings, he points out
that these men are admirable because they accepted their troubles
bravely. Camillus, for instance, does not sulk like Achilles[29] and
he reacts to his exile with proper *aretē*, unlike Coriolanus; he prays
that his country will soon change its mind and need him, if the
verdict against him is unjust.

It does not seem that men like Camillus and Aemilius have
deliberately challenged or provoked the forces of disadvantage. On
the other hand, there are cases of self-assertiveness, when the hero
acts or speaks in such a way that it is less surprising that disaster
follows. Cato the elder (*Cato i* 24.1) denigrates doctors and then
loses his wife and son. Pericles passed a law limiting citizenship to
those who were true-born on both sides of the family; later, when
his legitimate sons died, he asked the Athenians to modify the law
so that his illegitimate son might qualify (*Per.* 37.5). Now these are
not instances of badness but of *aretē* behaving or speaking presumptuously. Thus one should be restrained about proclaiming
one's *aretē* – it is asserted not for one's own sake but for the sake
of all – and one should also be restrained when disaster strikes from
a clear sky. It is almost impossible for the 'politicus' to act without
incurring envy of one kind or another. Even so, he can make things
much worse for himself by talking boastfully about his own exploits; perhaps the most obvious instance is Cicero (*Cic.* 24.1) who
would not let the Romans forget his consulship and, particularly,
his suppression of the Catilinarian conspiracy. Such gratuitous self-
reference resembles those presumptuous actions or sayings which
attract *nemesis*. On the other hand the *Self-Praise* makes it clear
that at certain times the 'politicus' is justified in self-praise; if he
is under wrongful attack he is entitled to talk grandiloquently
about his career and policies, as to do so will be necessary to his
defence. The whole theme of self-praise and its relevance to the
apologia of the 'politicus' was suggested to rhetoricians and
moralists by Demosthenes' speech *On the Crown*. Plutarch gives
Themistocles (541D) as an example of one who spoke out boldly
in his own praise when wronged by the citizens, since he said to
them: 'Why are you tired of receiving benefits from the same
people?' This passage in the *Moralia* seems to explain the account

of Themistocles in the *Life*, where Plutarch says that Themistocles incurred the envy of the Spartans, then of the allies and lastly the citizens (*Them.* 22.1–2). 'By now the citizens too were lending a willing ear to slanders against him because of envy; and he was *compelled* to be a nuisance by referring often to his own achievements before the people . . .' In such circumstances self-praise testifies to the free speech (*parrhesia*) of the 'politicus'; it is a legitimate device, but only when imposed by the need to explain oneself.

Just as Plutarch gives many case-histories of envy, so too he comments on how the 'politicus' may seek to lessen its effects. One recipe is suggested in *Nic.-Crass. comp.* 2.5. 'When the issues are great the "politicus" should not aim at that which is untouched by envy but at distinction, diminishing envy by greatness of power.' Nicias, it is said, was at fault because he was constantly afraid of political enemies and of becoming unpopular with the people. Although Crassus can be criticized for using violence, he had the right idea in that he tried to outshine great men like Caesar and Pompey. Politics, then, is essentially about the struggle for eminence to which envy cannot but attach itself. But, it seems, one can attain such greatness as a 'politicus' that one's rivals are eclipsed and so too is envy. The lesson is that one cannot avoid envy, but must try to overcome it. 'Really great success and distinction often quench envy.' (538A) Alexander the Great is here quoted as an example of one who was beyond envy, though he was hated and plots were formed against him. One cannot help thinking that this method of defeating envy is in conflict with Plutarch's other thoughts on the subject, as we shall see; clearly it would be most likely to be of use in a monarchy, and would hardly apply to an aristocracy or a good form of democracy.

For the most part, however, Plutarch considers that envy is best handled by the virtues of the 'politicus' as citizen rather than as leader. Marcellus' third triumph was resisted, as we saw earlier, because of envy; but Marcellus is commended for having accepted the lesser triumph, the ovation, and for answering the accusations brought by his enemies and the Sicilians as a private citizen; he did not rely on the majesty of consular office to defend himself (*Marc.* 22–23). To give proof that one is an ordinary citizen helps the 'politicus' to allay envy and so can lead to a restoration of good will. Pompey was applauded for continuing as a member of the

76

equites, after he had celebrated a triumph at an early age. He could easily have become a member of the senate had he so wished, but did not do so (*Pomp.* 14.9). The 'politicus' bows before the laws or submits to popular sentiment without demeaning himself. Agesilaus was leading a Greek army against the Persians when war broke out in Greece and the Spartan government recalled their king. The Greek war was an act of envy (*Ages.* 15.3) directed against the fine project of freeing the Greeks in Asia. Agesilaus, however, submitted to the needs of his country and showed his obedience and justice by his return.

So too the 'politicus' is admired for showing modesty and submissiveness in the face of daemonic envy. Timoleon attributed his success to good fortune (*Tim.* 36.5); this is not regarded as cynical manipulation of people's religious fears, but as a way of showing that one is an instrument of the gods in human affairs. Themistocles was less adept; he erected a shrine to Artemis Aristouboulē, as a compliment to the goddess for inspiring the Athenians against Xerxes. But this manoeuvre did not help Themistocles since the building was near his own home and housed a statue of himself; thus it only served to remind the Athenians of Themistocles the leader, object of envy, rather than Themistocles the citizen and instrument of the gods. Aemilius and Camillus (*Cam.* 5.8) do not, in the hour of victory, use the occasion to applaud and magnify themselves. Rather, they choose to utter the prayer that if there is any envy of Rome it should fall on themselves, not on the community as a whole. Camillus accepts exile (*Cam.* 12.4) but is not resentful like Coriolanus; he utters 'the curse of Achilles', but he does not sulk when Rome needs him; and Aemilius regards the loss of his two children as a sign that envy of Rome has vented itself on his family and left the state unharmed (*Aem.* 36).

There are, then, two ways of handling envy; to rise above all other citizens and eclipse envy by one's own grandeur; or to show, in various ways, that one is an ordinary, obedient citizen, like other men, lesser than the gods. They are not wholly compatible with each other; and the reason is that the activity of the 'politicus' embraces two ideas which are to some extent in conflict. In one way he pursues what is *kalon* and his *aretē* must inevitably make him outstanding, above the general run of people. In another way, though a man with *aretē*, he is a member of a community, a citizen like others. On the whole it is fair to say that Plutarch has placed most emphasis on the citizenliness of the 'politicus' when he has to allay envy of his achievement.

# 3

# The 'Politicus' (2)

In the last chapter we saw in outline how the 'politicus' differs from the demagogue and the tyrant, those who pretend to have the political art. His general aim is to create or restore harmony within the state, to make his *aretē* acceptable to others without humiliating himself, and to prevail over envy. We shall now examine certain limited areas of his political activity, especially his use of wealth (section 1) and attitude to religion (section 2); then we shall see how he has to conduct himself at that critical stage when he has won a military victory and makes the difficult transition from war to peace (section 3). I conclude with some remarks on the relevance of these political ideas to the circumstances of Plutarch's age (section 4).

## 3.1 WEALTH

It is proper to consider this subject because of Plutarch's view of political *aretē*; he says that according to many thinkers an important part of this excellence is the management of one's own household. The city, he means, can be thought of as a large complex of individual units called households (*oikoi*); the 'politicus', therefore, being a member or head of an *oikos*, will be measured by his skill in managing his own affairs as well as in governing the city. There may even be a conflict of interest since the cares of state may be such that they prevent the 'politicus' from looking after his own financial interests. This is a particular form of the general question, what value should the 'politicus' attach to wealth, be it the wealth of the state or of individuals. The topic is considered in several passages in the *Lives* and there are some hints in *The Love of Money* and the *Precepts on Public Life*.

A convenient text from which to start is *Per.* 16.3–7. After mentioning that Pericles was incorruptible, Plutarch goes on to speak of the pedantic way in which every item of expense in his household was kept under daily supervision; the family knew that there was money to spend but it was not easy to get Pericles to part with it. 'Now all this is not in tune with the wisdom of Anaxagoras. The latter, because he was inspired and great-minded, left his home and let his land lie fallow, a pasture for sheep. But, I am certain, the lives of the "politicus" and the contemplative philosopher are not the same. The latter uses his mind to study fine things, but he does not need instruments or external goods; the other, however, is mixing his *aretē* in with human needs and requirements, and there are times when wealth [for the "politicus"] is not merely in the class of things necessary but also of things fine (*kala*). This was true of Pericles who helped many poor people.' The language here, as is perhaps appropriate in a comparison with a philosopher, has a number of technical terms from moral philosophy. The main point, which is generally valid for Plutarch, is that for the 'politicus' wealth is an instrument (*organon*);[1] it is not therefore an end in itself but a means of political action, in which respect it resembles oratory. Oratorical excellence, too, is not to be pursued for its own sake but as a means of expounding policy and winning adherents.[2] We can illustrate Plutarch's thought here by remembering that for him political *aretē* is the highest good; man should be concerned with *aretē*, not with reputation (*doxa*), still less with pleasure; and the life of pleasure is most easily pursued if we have money to spend. Thus wealth could be regarded as a means to one of the lower ends. Yet, according to this passage, wealth does at times fall within the class of things that are *kala*. However, this seems to me loose writing on Plutarch's part; as the story about Pericles makes plain, it is the use which is made of wealth, not the acquisition of it, which deserves to be called fine.

The subject is treated from another point of view in *Cato i* 18. Here Plutarch writes of Cato's attempts[3] to curb Roman ostentation and lavish expenditure, and describes the unpopularity of his measures. The reason is that the many think that sumptuary curbs on the display of wealth are tantamount to taking their wealth away from them. Thus they have a false view of what wealth is for and are at variance with the 'politicus'. The many (those with wrong views) wish to spend on non-essentials, but the 'politicus' will aim at producing that degree of wealth which is useful and necessary. To have more than enough and spend it, is to be guilty of display; to have more than enough and live moderately (the case with Cato himself) is also to suggest that one has a wrong view about wealth. 'The man who accumulates a lot of money but uses only a small part of it is not self-sufficient. Either he does not need it, in which case he has wasted his time getting the wherewithal to spend on things which he does not desire; or he does have the desire but is wretched because he checks his enjoyment out of meanness.' (*Arist.-Cato i comp.* 4.3) Here Plutarch is concerned to criticize the acquisition of more wealth than is needed, since it is potentially a source of corruption; he has in mind that modest competence, as one might say, which will assist the 'politicus' to carry out his function. When he writes of 'the eagerness for wealth' he is criticizing the widespread human desire to have more than one needs. Such wealth, superfluous to requirement, 'is not associated with any natural feeling (*pathos*) but is imported into our minds because of vulgar (i.e. non-philosophical) opinion.' (*Cato i* 18.5) The natural desire is for a drink; nature does not prescribe a goblet.

Obviously, to spend one's time acquiring money would not be fine (*kalon*) since it would prevent one from exercising political *aretē*. There are other dangers, too, as becomes clear from *Solon* 3. 'People think that Solon's readiness to spend, his elegant way of living and his referring in his poems to the pleasures in a manner that is vulgar rather than philosophical, were caused by his life as a merchant; for this kind of life, they say, incurs many great dangers and demands in return pleasure and enjoyment.' It seems that Plutarch does not take the view that Solon was himself rich (*Sol.* 3.2), but he would probably agree with the idea that the full-time pursuit of riches does beget what is for him a false sense of values. He comments very rarely on the means by which some of the heroes acquired their money. Philopoemen is commended for 'attempting to increase his *oikos* by farming, the most just form of making money' (*Philop.* 4.5). Probably farming is said to be just because its prime function is to supply man with the basic needs by working on the land. Cato the elder (*Cato i* 21.6) receives a passing censure for investing some of his money in underwriting ships.[4] This form of lending is described as objectionable, perhaps because it involves a disproportionately high return and at the same time exposes other men to the risks of navigation. Plutarch's most severe reprimand is directed at Crassus, who became wealthy 'as a result of fire and war'. He bought some property when it was going cheap during the Sullan troubles and acquired more at a low price when the owners were afraid that their property would collapse because adjacent buildings were on fire. Thus he made money out of the misery of his fellow-citizens, clearly not the act of a good 'politicus'. Crassus, in fact, boasted of keeping an army of slaves; Plutarch says he was right to regard his slaves as the 'living instruments of management (*oikonomikē*)'; but wrong to say that no one is rich unless he can maintain an army. 'The wealth needed for war is limitless.' (*Crass.* 2) By contrast we can say that the wealth needed for life in peace is limited to that which is necessary for the satisfaction of the *natural* desires of the community.

Plutarch is far from thinking that one has to be rich in order to practise as a 'politicus' or that poverty is an impediment to the political life. It is not ignoble to admit to poverty: 'the poor have no less power than those who give banquets and furnish choruses, if they have the free speech and credibility which comes from *aretē*.' (822E–F) He has two heroes, both of whom were outstanding for *aretē*, Phocion and Aristeides, and were also poor men. Phocion, by contrast with Demades, who like him pursued a pro-Macedonian policy, 'showed forth his poverty as an *aretē*' (*Phoc.* 30.5). The opening chapter of the *Aristeides* has some of Plutarch's most passionate writing on the subject. Demetrius of Phalerum[5] had attacked the view that Aristeides was poor and left no dowry for his daughters. Plutarch gives a number of evidential arguments against Demetrius' view and concludes by saying that Demetrius is anxious to rescue Aristeides from the stigma of poverty because he thinks it a great evil (*Arist.* 1.9). For Plutarch this is not so, as wealth and poverty alike are both media through which one can show one's *aretē*. Similarly he makes much of the alleged poverty of Epameinondas and praises Pelopidas (said to be wealthy) for associating himself with his friend's poverty by wearing ordinary clothes and eating frugally (*Pel.* 3).

It is clear that the 'politicus' will not (ideally speaking) attempt to make money as this will take him away from his proper task. It is true that Aristeides is said to have brought justice into disrepute as a virtue which is useful to others only, not to oneself and one's *oikos*. As a result of his political career the family of this great man was left in poverty, without resource, and his descendants made their living in disreputable ways. 'They did not do anything grand or conceive of any design worthy of that hero.' (*Arist.-Cato i comp.* 3.5) This seems to detract from Aristeides' achievement; and the reason is that there are elements in Plutarch's thought which do not fit well together. On the one hand he accepts the idea that political *aretē* must include the management of one's *oikos*; and once he accepts that, he finds that it is an imperfection to have been a successful leader of the state and at the same time to have (apparently) mismanaged one's *oikos*. On the other hand he believes that there is a difference between what is necessary and what is fine. Hence Pelopidas says (*Pel.* 3.8), when his friends rebuke him for neglecting his affairs on the grounds that making money is 'a necessary thing', 'Yes, it is for Nicodemus', a man who was lame and blind. Pelopidas meant that Nicodemus was not capable of fine actions; for those who are, there are better things to do than making money.

It is in the right use of wealth that the 'politicus' shows whether he has *aretē* or not. Cimon,[6] for example, (*Cim.* 10) made money out of his campaigns against the Persians. In itself this counts as something fine (to become richer by defeating the enemies of the Greeks) but his use of these resources was finer still. He unfenced his land, so that people could help themselves, and provided simple meals for the poor. Plutarch is impressed by the generosity of Cimon and by the absence of ostentation, for he did not give expensive banquets. He says that Cimon brought back to Athens the legendary partnership attributed to Cronos. Thus his wealth is used with discretion in order to foster unity within the state. In all this Plutarch shows that he is politically innocent in the narrow sense. He refuses to accept the accusation, made by Cimon's contemporaries, that Cimon's spending was 'flattery of the people and a sort of demagogy'. He rejects this view because his picture of Cimon is based on his fixed notion of Cimon's political style, his *proairesis*, according to which Cimon was 'aristocratic and Spartan'. He favoured an understanding with Sparta and said at his trial that he imitated Spartan economy and restraint (*Cim.* 14.4).

Plutarch is blind to the political significance of Cimon's generosity since, if he accepted the idea, he would have to call him a demagogue. In the fifth and fourth centuries this term need have meant no more than a prominent politician whose sympathies were democratic. But for Plutarch, as we have seen, demagogue tends to mean one who corrupts the people by flattery or aims to make the lower orders politically superior. And in this respect Cimon was clearly not a demagogue, though it remains true that he built up a following by his generosity.

In such ways as this the 'politicus' shows his great-mindedness – he sees wealth as a means to an end – and his liberality. It is important to notice that the right use of wealth is not to encourage luxury or extravagance. Nicias, for instance, is said to have used his wealth 'more politically' than Crassus did. Nicias spent money on dedications in temples, presiding as gymnasiarch and on equipping choruses; Crassus, however, gave a huge feast to the people of Rome during his first consulship with Pompey and in addition supplied them with corn for three months (*Crass.* 12.3). The reader may well wonder where Plutarch sees a difference between the two, since, after all, both men were spending on public entertainment. The answer is, in part, that Nicias' expenditure does not depart from the customary framework of Athenian institutions, in which the better-off citizens were called upon to finance projects like those mentioned. Nicias' spending, therefore, was neither more nor less than other rich citizens would do. In part, too, the objection is to the scale of Crassus' banquet, which seems to have been too ostentatious for Plutarch's taste; it makes a contrast with the other meals referred to in *Crass.* 3.2, which were characterized by 'plainness, providing a simplicity and friendliness that were more pleasant than an expensive dinner'. Thus he finally refers to Crassus as one who is uneven, having an inconsistency within himself; he makes money in discreditable ways and then pours it out uselessly (*Nic.-Crass. comp.* 1.4). Crassus is uneven since he shifts from avarice and meanness to indulgence in a gargantuan bounty. Lucullus also is criticized for his extravagance, though not the same stigma attaches to the way in which he acquired his wealth; after several stories about his expensive way of life Plutarch says, 'He abused his wealth by spending it in that way, as though it were a prisoner and a barbarian' (*Luc.* 41.7).

Since the Lives contain many exploits of Greeks and Romans against other peoples, it is natural for Plutarch to emphasize the right use of spoils captured from the enemy. A typical theme is the hero's great-mindedness, his heroic rejection of money as a triviality. Thus Coriolanus refuses the special booty offered him after the capture of Corioli – he describes it as pay, not honour – and asks for one gift only, the freedom of his friend among the Volsci. By showing his contempt for money he earns more admiration than by his valour in battle.[7] 'To make a good use of money is finer than to use arms well; and not to need it is more dignified than using it well.' (*Cor.* 10.8) The most striking instance of this kind of grandeur is Aemilius, who is portrayed as the antithesis of his adversary Perseus. Whereas the latter shows an improper parsimony – he tries to cheat his allies of their promised pay – Aemilius does not even deign to look upon the booty captured from the Macedonians, but hands it over to the quaestors to keep for the public benefit (*Aem.* 28.10–13). The refusal to benefit financially from military exploits is grander and more positive than abstaining from misappropriation of public monies. But this too is a virtue in the 'politicus' and probably is in part the virtue of justice, as abstaining from what is not one's own. It is true that financial probity in high office was probably the exception rather than the rule in Greece and Rome, and Plutarch praises men like Aristeides, Pericles and Cato the younger for their rectitude. He cannot deny that Demosthenes was fond of enriching himself in ways that are wrong for the 'politicus', though he points out that others were bad too (*Dem.* 25.2; 31 and *Dem.-Cic. comp.* 3.5–7). But, in general, abstention from financial misconduct is a lesser virtue than rejecting the wealth which has been earned by right of war.

So far we have looked at examples of individual *aretē* with regard to wealth. Individuals are admired if they freely display those virtues which are needed by poverty, such as frugality and moderation, together with a generosity that shares out a surplus to the social benefit of the community. This leads us to ask about the function of wealth in the community as a whole. On this subject Plutarch has the attitudes of a philosophical moralist rather than a political economist. A state does not have to be wealthy in order to live the good life, any more than it needs to have a great empire. In fact he thinks of great wealth, both for states and for individuals, as bringing with it luxury and extravagance. The acquisition of great wealth by private individuals like Crassus is morally disastrous for the man himself; and bad for the state in that it leads to civil dissension between the economic classes. This is why Plutarch has a high regard for the Lycurgan reforms in Sparta and for Cleomenes' attempt in the third century to restore the old régime. Lycurgus, according to Plutarch, tried to prevent economic inequalities among the citizens by granting them equal lots of land. The accumulation of private wealth was hampered by an inconvenient coinage; the common messes were no occasion for self-indulgence, but united those who were relatively rich and poor at a frugal meal. Thus the lawgiver sets out to avoid the social divisiveness of unequal wealth within the state. In Sparta, he says, meaning the Sparta of Lycurgus, wealth really was blind[8] (*Lyc.* 10). As an ordinary Greek saying this meant that wealth tended to bestow its favours haphazardly on the wrong people. Plutarch has given the proverb a twist; in Sparta wealth is blind and prostrate, since it visits no one at all; wealth is like a picture, a thing inanimate and devoid of motion. Thus, in states, as in individuals, what Plutarch praises is the virtue of self-sufficiency; the state should be a partnership of individuals who should not be economically disparate.

## 3.2 RELIGION AND SUPERSTITION (*deisidaimonia*)[9]

There are various reasons why religion was of vital importance to Plutarch. He was a priest at Delphi, which meant that the religious practices of the past were not for him a dead thing, unconnected with the present. Passages in his works that seem at first to stem from mere antiquarian interest are often seen, on closer examination, to be concerned with his own views and beliefs. His view of *aretē* as that which is most admirable in human beings implicates the divine as well, for it is by *aretē* that man can overcome the imperfections of mortality and ascend towards the divine. Thus religion is important for individuals and states; and it is not surprising that Plutarch has many comments in the *Lives* on the conduct of the 'politicus' with respect to religion. The main objective of the 'politicus' is to 'save' his city, by which is meant preserving its integrity as well as ensuring its survival; that the rulers should admire the divine contributes more to fulfilling this purpose than defeating the enemy (*Marc.* 4.7). This is perhaps an extreme statement, arising from the observation that victory over the enemy must be preceded by correct ritual. But it shows clearly that Plutarch does not set out to recommend the survival of the state at any price but only so far as it is capable of the good life in his sense of the word.

It follows that all citizens in the state should have correct views about the relationship between god and man. There is one false view, in particular, to which societies are especially prone, the belief that the gods are malevolent and are the cause of such disasters as plagues, famines and suffering in war. This is false, according to Plutarch, because for him, as for Plato, god is the source of order and harmony and cannot be the cause of evil for mankind. To think that the gods do cause pain and injury is false judgment of the worst kind, since like the false idea that wealth is good, it leads to bad conduct. Some false judgments are accompanied by passion (*pathos*), others are not; for example, to deny that there are gods is to have a false belief, but it is a false belief without passion. For passion is a kind of motion and the atheist is in general one who is 'unmoved in respect to the divine'. Thus the atheist is somewhat better off than the superstitious man, the *deisidaimōn*;[10] the latter does have a movement towards the divine, but it is of the wrong kind (*On Superstition* 164E–165C).

Plutarch's comments on *deisidaimonia* in this work are on the whole in accord with what he has to say in the *Lives*. The virtue, which indicates that man has right beliefs about the gods and pays his respects to them in the proper way, is piety (*eusebeia*); defined, following Plato, as 'a knowledge of how to attend to the gods' (*Aem.* 3.3). On the whole, when Plutarch refers to *deisidaimonia* he is speaking of wrong belief leading to wrong practice. Thus his theoretical presuppositions are precise and he puts a lower value on superstition than Polybius does. Polybius[11] considers that a state composed of wise men would have no need of what he calls superstition; but, in the real world, statesmen are the leaders of ignorant and credulous masses, and will find it useful to introduce certain beliefs about the gods and the underworld as a means of controlling public behaviour. In effect Polybius draws near to the position that the statesman deliberately uses what he knows to be false simply as a device in order to ensure public order. There has, he says, been much criticism directed at what he calls superstition; but in his view it has acted as a cohesive agent and helped to create unity and order in the Roman state. Plutarch, on the other hand, does not expect his 'politicus' to manipulate ideas in this way; in general his 'politicus' sets out to curb superstition and see that the citizens are pious in their beliefs and practices. He does not think that scrupulosity in carrying out a ritual is an act of superstition; one should respect such traditions because they in general reflect society's sense of the way in which the universe is ordered. There is, however, one exception among Plutarch's 'politici', Numa, who does in part resemble the manipulating statesman of Polybius. It is not so much his alleged association with the nymph Egeria; here Plutarch argues that if we can accept the view that divine powers have consorted with poets, it is surely credible that they may have helped lawgivers in this way. The main difficulty comes in his account of Numa's use of religion; after saying that Numa invoked the assistance of the gods (in order to make his uncouth people more civilized), he adds, 'On occasions . . . by reporting unusual daemonic apparitions and unpropitious utterances he humbled the attitudes of the people by means of superstition' (*Numa* 8). There is no denying that Numa, by Plutarch's usual standards at any rate, practises religious deception upon the people. But this encouragement of superstition is an isolated case; it is in part explicable and to be justified because of the particular needs of the Romans at that time. A state founded by an 'act of daring and boldness', with citizens of a hard and warlike disposition, needed a touch of the other extreme – over-sensitivity about the divine – in order to strike the mean. Besides, though Numa resembles the Polybian statesman in his use of deception, he differs in that otherwise he clearly does have a right judgment about man's relationship with the divine.

Other Roman statesmen are praised for taking steps to see that their people were not afflicted by this irrational fear. Fabius, after the defeat at Trasimene, persuaded the Romans to propitiate the gods and to attribute the disaster to their general's contempt for the divine. 'He did not implant superstition in them but encouraged their *aretē* by piety, attempting to take away their fears of the enemy by their hopes in the gods.' (*Fab.* 4.4) The concealed doctrine is that the gods approve of *aretē* and, in general, reward it; it is by showing *aretē* that one wins divine favour. He does not think of the Romans' meticulous attention to detail in certain rituals as an instance of superstition. Minucius' appointment of Flaminius as master of the horse was nullified because the procedure was interrupted by a mouse squeaking. 'They were precise in such small details and did not come close to superstition, because they did not depart from their traditional rites.' (*Marc.* 5.7) Here there is an assumption that inherited practices do contain the wisdom of our ancestors about the divine and that this wisdom should not be transgressed. To reject them is to go against custom and appear arrogant; it is better to go along with ancient opinion on such matters. Nicias can be criticized for succumbing to superstition when he followed the advice of his seer about the eclipse. But, it seems, this is better than the contempt shown by Crassus for the curses imprecated by Ateius[12] (*Nic.-Crass. comp.* 5.3). The 'politicus' who goes against tradition is doing violence to the views of his fellow-citizens, presuming to change the habits of generations.

The foregoing suggests that it is better to err in the company of tradition than to flout it deliberately. But what if tradition is based on scientific or philosophical ignorance? This raises a theme which is of great importance for Plutarch. According to him, one prime source of superstition is ignorance of causes; the way to remove it is by the study of nature which releases us from 'the inflamed and fearful state of superstition and implants in us unerring piety with hopes of good' (*Per.* 6.1). The 'politicus' will benefit from a knowledge of causes in the way that Pericles learned from Anaxagoras. But knowledge of the causes of those events which seem 'divine' is not incompatible with seeing a religious significance in them. This is made plain by the story of Pericles, Anaxagoras and the seer Lampon. The latter was asked to say why a ram had only one horn; he replied that it was a sign of coming events, when the leaders of the two parties in Athens, Pericles and Thucydides, would be reduced to one (presumably an ex post facto version of the ostracism of Thucydides). Anaxagoras, however, had the skull opened and showed that the contents of the brain had not filled their natural cavity. At the time Anaxagoras[13] was greatly admired; but later on, when Thucydides was ostracized,

Lampon too seemed to have been right. Plutarch adds that there is nothing to prevent our supposing that both were right. The philosopher has given the material cause correctly, while the seer has spoken of the final cause. It is wrong to suppose that the 'discovery of the cause is the destruction of the sign'. He draws a curious analogy with man-made objects. We may know how a noise or light is produced but it still signifies something. Similarly, he argues, the theory of Anaxagoras shows how the divine portent of the ram's horn came about, but this does not mean that the oddity is no longer a pointer towards the future.

Plutarch's theory here makes an interesting contrast with a doctrine such as Epicureanism. For Epicurus a knowledge of causes is *as such* sufficient to release man from superstition; for instance the doctrine that the soul is made of atoms entails that there is no personal survival after death, and, consequently, that there is no reason to fear punishment or expect reward in an after-life. In this case scientific or philosophical knowledge does cure the disease. But Plutarch's science does not deny god; and his theory, ambitious though it appears, does not solve the problem as it purports to do. It is clear from his example that knowledge of the cause does not *as such* do anything to help us to understand the significance of a 'divine' event. We have to turn from the philosopher and apply to the professional religious man. For Plutarch, in fact, the proper way to remove superstition is by having a correct idea of the relationship between the gods and mankind. Science and 'natural' philosophy give knowledge, but not knowledge of the order made by providence.

Perhaps it is fairer to Plutarch to suppose that he is talking about a possible ambiguity in the notion of 'divine' events. When we use this expression we may be saying in a loose way that the event is causally inexplicable or even that it runs counter to events as they usually occur; or we may mean that it portends the future. He means, then, that we should not speak of events as 'divine' in the first sense, when a cause can be ascertained, or merely because the event seems improbable or contrary to scientific fact. There is still scope for events to be 'divine' in the sense that they form part of the scheme of providence.

If this is his view, it is inadequate as a theory. We could still believe that earthquakes are a punishment sent by god while at the same time knowing how earthquakes are caused. But Plutarch thinks that as a matter of historical fact the scientific knowledge of causes has helped men to avoid the superstitious belief that god's purpose is to harm them. Nicias (*Nic.* 23) would have been helped had he known the explanation of lunar eclipses. At the date when the Sicilian eclipse occurred (413 BC) there was some public knowledge of how solar eclipses are caused, but lunar eclipses were more mysterious – they had been explained by Anaxagoras, but his views were not very well known. There was still public intolerance of natural philosophers, because they seemed to 'reduce the divine to irrational causes and powers without providence' (*Nic.* 23.4). Plato was the first to remove the stigma attaching to this kind of explanation. He subordinated 'natural necessity' to the higher causes; and his own reputation as a good man helped people to see that there was nothing irreligious in the scientific explanation of eclipses. Even so, Plutarch says, Nicias could still have interpreted the event correctly, if he had had an experienced seer. He would have been told that it was a good sign, as the course of action he was contemplating (retreat) needed concealment and 'light is inimical to such actions'. Here again Plutarch sets out to maintain that scientific knowledge liberates man from the particular form of superstition which he abhors; but it remains true that the foundation of correct belief must be found within theology rather than science.

Some of the events in the earlier periods of history taxed Plutarch's ingenuity. A good case in point is the story of the statue of Fortuna Muliebris, which was paid for by the generosity of the Roman ladies, and spoke the words, 'Ladies, your offering of me is pleasing to the gods'.[14] It is credible (Plutarch says) that statues should sweat or exude moisture, but not that they should speak; for this, a body is needed as the instrument of utterance (*Cor.* 38.3). Are we then to reject this story as incredible? History, however, provides some persuasive witness that such things have actually happened. Plutarch here takes refuge in the idea that a god's powers are marvellous and may be able to do things which we could not imagine anyone's doing without a body. Thus he is loth to abandon his principle of scientific credibility; but he does not, in his own terms, lapse into superstition, the belief that gods intend harm to man, since he writes enthusiastically of the divine power's care for mankind. Thus some historical facts seem incredible but we have to accept them, because they are well attested and require an explanation. A similar problem arises with Dion and Brutus who were visited by hostile apparitions before their death. If we argue that such things have no objective reality but are figments in the minds of those who are deficient in reason, we shall have to say that Dion and Brutus were mad, or ill, or deficient in reason, when they saw what they reported. This theory would have the advantage that it explains the bad spirit as nothing other than our own state of disturbance; but it would present us with a new fact that is inconsistent with the character of Dion and Brutus, men who were 'stable, philosophers, not easily the victims of a passion'. We must therefore accept that they were sound and sane; hence Plutarch prefers the theory that there are bad spirits which deliberately try to cause harm and inconvenience to men with *aretē*.

Plutarch's attitude to scientific theory seems liberal, but this is a false impression. Scientific explanation, for Plutarch, is not free and independent of his theological beliefs. The question he asks is not 'Is this theory a true account of the facts?' but 'Is it true and also compatible with the supremacy of god and good in the universe?' Democritus' theory asserts that our perception is at the mercy of images sent from the environment and requires us to pray for 'good images'. This is unacceptable to Plutarch, probably because our conduct will then depend upon the accident of our perceptions and we may excuse any misconduct on the ground of bad images. Plutarch says that the theory is 'untrue and leads to limitless superstition'. He does not therefore reject the theory on the sole ground that it is untrue but cocks his eye at the moral consequences as he sees them (*Aem.* 1).

To summarize the above account, the 'politicus' will not himself be superstitious and will seek to allay this condition among his people. He is not, in general, a manipulator of religious feelings for the sake of narrow political advantage. Most of the religious ceremonies of Greek and Roman states are not, for Plutarch, evidence of superstition, but sure proof that man acknowledges his subordinate position to superiors who intend him no harm. Human sacrifice is obviously repugnant but this 'un-Hellenic' practice has been rare.[15] The 'politicus' is helped in some cases by scientific knowledge, which can remove fear about the immediate causes of 'divine events' though it must be compatible with a right view of god's relation to man. Aemilius is perhaps typical of the attitude Plutarch admires. When the moon was eclipsed before the battle of Pydna, Aemilius made generous sacrifices to the moon and Heracles (*Aem.* 17.10). He is clearly not regarded as superstitious; he knows about the theory of eclipses but offers sacrifice as the customary gesture of piety. Although Plutarch's essay on the subject maintains that atheism is less dangerous than superstition, it is impossible to imagine that an atheist 'politicus' would be acceptable to him. The right 'politicus' occupies the middle between these two extremes, and is characterized by piety.

### 3.3 THE USE OF VICTORY: THE GENERAL AND THE STATESMAN

A modern reader will probably find little difficulty in familiarizing himself with the view that political *aretē* includes the right use of wealth and religion. He may well find it more surprising that the art of the 'politicus' also comprises the art of leadership as commander of the armed forces. Many of the 'politici' admired by Plutarch in the *Lives* established themselves as soldiers and generals before they became political leaders in the narrower sense; and it is easy to point to examples (like Pericles and Nicias) of men whose time of eminence shows them in this dual role. In this section we shall study the relationship between the two roles, with particular reference to the theme of how the successful general should adapt himself after victory to the political circumstances within his own state.

Plutarch recognizes that for his own time it would be false to make a sentimental appeal to the past military glories of Greece; and he states, in his instructions to Menemachus on political life, that because of Roman rule the would-be Greek 'politicus' does not now have to concern himself with the control of the military.[16] Nevertheless there are historical and theoretical reasons why he treats the heroes in the *Lives* both as generals in charge of armies and as statesmen at the head of senates or assemblies. It is a historical fact, which Plutarch could not escape, that most of the city-state offices held by his heroes required them to command in war as well as in peace. The consulship at Rome and the strategia at Athens were both military and civilian in scope. Plutarch, in fact, notices with regret the tendency in fourth-century Athens to separate political authority from military command. Thus he praises Phocion for seeking to fulfil in his own person the two functions, as had been the usual practice in the fifth century. Theoretically, too, the general cannot be divorced from the statesman, since political *aretē*, seen from one angle, is the art of command. It is the function of the general to effect a state of obedience in his troops by winning the good will (*eunoia*) of his men (*Cim.-Luc. comp.* 2.3). We have already seen the importance for the 'politicus' of conducting policy on the basis of *eunoia*, not by flattery or force. Again, the *Lives* are in general a study of *aretē* as it is active in the world; it is not just talk or theory (*logos*) but action (*ergon*),[17] to put it in terms which Plutarch is fond of using. The particular virtues can be exemplified in the spheres of peace or war; thus one can be just as a general or just in times of peace. Plutarch would add, probably, that there are local differences in the two 'acts of justice', but both can be considered under the same head.

Anyone who glances at the comparisons will be struck by the fact that Plutarch's assessment is often based on a division between actions in war and 'political' actions. This is a formal distinction which expresses his view that the hero's *aretē* is knowable through both. To some extent the hero's function is the same, whether he is acting as a commander or as a 'politicus'. The 'politicus' must preserve his office and the state; while the general is praised above all not for taking risks but for showing prudence and forethought for the safety of his troops. Also, a general's courage differs from that of a common soldier; a general is to be criticized for throwing away his life impetuously, as Pelopidas, Marcellus and Lysander did. Chabrias, a minor figure, compares unfavourably in this respect with Phocion. On the other hand, the general's art can never be more than a part of political *aretē*, which aims at the good of the whole state. The end-product of the general's activity is victory, which is no more than one of the preconditions in which the state can pursue the good life. A state may be founded through an act of war, like Rome, but its raison d'être is not the conduct of war or the acquisition of empire. It is therefore not the simple fact of winning a victory that makes Plutarch acclaim the general.

He wishes to be satisfied about the purpose for which the war was fought, and to examine closely the use which is made of victory, for the answer to this shows whether an individual 'politicus' or a whole state is just. This means that 'actions of war' are often opposed to 'political actions' as the lower to the higher form. Thus Plutarch (*Pomp.* 13.10) praises the early Romans because they applied honorific names not merely to those who were outstanding in war, but as a reward for 'political actions and virtues'.[18]

In several *Lives* Plutarch makes the point that success as a general has certain dangers which can disable one for life as a 'politicus' in peace. One obvious reason is that in war the general has no one to challenge his command; whereas in peace he has many competitors who may detract from his achievements and certainly try to deny him the first place. In the *Pompey*, Plutarch shows first how Pompey earned his reputation as a general by assisting Sulla in the wars against the Marians and then by his campaigns against Sertorius in Spain. Although his military exploits were outstanding, he did not act presumptuously. Sulla did not mention Pompey in his will, but Pompey took the omission 'moderately and "politikōs" ';[19] he did not join Lepidus and the others who tried to prevent the state burial of Sulla, but cooperated with those who made the funeral a dignified occasion. Here, then, the general in his rise to eminence is praised for taking certain rebuffs as a citizen should, for showing that he is one among many rather than one who expects special treatment. The critical time for Pompey comes later, after he has defeated Spartacus and has held office as consul with Crassus (70 BC). This is the time when the man who has followed a military career is likely to experience difficulty, for it is now that he is tested as a leader of citizens. According to Plutarch, Pompey changed his style of life after this consulship; 'he gradually deserted the forum and appeared rarely in public.' It was difficult to meet him apart from a crowd of followers, who formed Pompey's protective bulwark of 'dignity and magnificence'; he thought it right to keep his prestige untouched by too close an acquaintance with the many. 'Life in the *toga* is full of risks which can lead to loss of reputation for those whose greatness is military and who are not well-suited to popular equality. They claim that they should be first in peace as in war; whereas those who are less successful in war find it intolerable that they should not have superiority in peace. And so people tend to subdue and pull down the man whose armies and triumphs have made him glorious, when they get him in the forum. But if he abdicates and withdraws they go on cherishing his military honour, which is unsullied by envy. Events soon showed that this is so.' (*Pomp.* 23)

The precise reference of this general statement is puzzling. Does Plutarch here mean that certain later events show that Pompey, by his withdrawal from the public gaze, yielded political primacy to others while keeping intact and free from envy his prestige as general? This does not seem to be borne out by the narrative which immediately follows; for Plutarch goes on to describe the proposals of Gabinius and Manilius, which empowered Pompey to command first against the pirates and then take over the Mithridatic war from Lucullus. Both measures were popular with the people but met with criticism from senators, who are described as envious opponents of both schemes. But this is the very group of Romans which should have been satisfied with political eminence in the smaller world of Rome without grudging Pompey the opportunity to continue his career as a great general. Secondly, it is unlikely that Plutarch is here referring to the commands against the pirates and Mithridates as purely military: they are represented as making him sole ruler, an expression which covers political as well as military power.

I think that the important general truth here is contained in the statement that those who are less successful in war try to surpass the general when peace has come. Plutarch has in mind at this stage those events in Rome which followed after Pompey's return from the east in 61 BC. The senate opposed his request that he might enter Rome before his triumph, and Lucullus, assisted by Cato, attacked his Eastern settlement. Thus Pompey was obliged to ask for the help of the tribune Clodius, who is to be counted as one of Plutarch's more objectionable demagogue-figures.[20] Clodius used Pompey to support his proposals which are described as typically demagogic in that they were designed to curry favour with the people. Pompey, then, is one whose success as a general made it difficult for him to succeed as a 'politicus'. His rivals out-manoeuvred him and drove him to take refuge with a demagogue; then came his entente with Caesar, which looked 'politikon' on the surface – an amicable, citizenly arrangement – but was really a plot designed by Caesar to overthrow the Roman constitution. The story of Pompey describes a general who succumbs to peer-envy on his return to civilian life, and then fails to succeed as a 'politicus'. Plutarch thinks of him as having shown much political *aretē* on his way to fame (cf. *Pomp.* 15), and has sympathy for his inability to impose himself in political life.

The *Marius* examines the same question, though it shows the general reacting in a different way to the challenge of politics, partly because of his different character. Marius, for Plutarch, is a soldier and general rather than a 'politicus', a man unmellowed by the graces and made harsh by anger. This is in part responsible for Plutarch's unfavourable portrait of him, a fact which has been emphasized by historians who have boldly set out to understand the historical Marius and rescue him from the slanders of the ancient sources. The opinion is often held that Plutarch's account of Marius is adverse because his sources were unfavourable; the argument is that he read works like Sulla's memoirs and repeated the accusations against Marius because he was uncritical. It is of course obvious that he did not employ the critical methods of a modern historian, who judges information by ascertaining or, more often, guessing at, its provenance. But he does employ, in broad outline, his own theory of what a 'politicus' should attempt to do in particular circumstances. He accepts what the sources have to tell him and expresses the facts in his own terms, having especially in mind the figures of 'politicus', demagogue and tyrant. It is true that historians who disparage Plutarch's *Marius* as a historical source on the grounds that it regurgitates such hostile versions as Sulla's memoirs, are justified over particular details.[21] But it should be remembered that Plutarch does not take a favourable view of either Marius or Sulla. Both are seen as tyrants; Marius because he used force on fellow-citizens (*Mar.* 43), Sulla because of his attitude to pleasure (*Lys.-Sulla comp.* 3.1). If it were true that Plutarch's *Marius* is uncritically dependent on Sulla's memoirs, it would follow that the *Sulla* would be less critical of its subject. That this is not the case shows that Plutarch does apply judgment of his own kind to his material, but it is not always analytic of sources. He has instead a rough sense of hostile motivation on the part of a witness, as can be seen by his reference to malice (*kakoētheia*); and he is always ready to approve or blame actions if they obviously seem to him to describe a particular type of political purpose (*proairesis*), or, rather, the absence of it.

Marius, according to Plutarch, faced the same problem as Pompey on his return to Rome after defeating the Teutones and the Cimbri. In Roman terms, the nobiles were hostile to Marius as a novus homo, resented his prestige as a general and opposed the legislation in his sixth consulship. Plutarch, however, examines the events of this year for the light they throw on Marius' character, in order to see how this general has managed the return to politics in peace. Unlike Pompey, according to Plutarch, he wanted to be first in peace as he had been preeminent in war. Pompey, we saw, did not so much choose the support of the demagogue Clodius but was driven to depend on him; not because he wanted political power in Rome for its own sake but to protect the arrangements he had made as conqueror of Mithridates. Marius, on the other hand, is portrayed as seeking his sixth consulship simply from love of power and fame. Naturally there was opposition to him (*Mar.* 28), and Marius took cover with the demagogue Saturninus. Thus both generals are instances of the recourse to popularity-mongering. The difference is that Marius, at Plutarch puts it, deliberately abandons the best course in order to be the greatest man in Rome. He acts 'against his own nature', putting on a popular façade which is foreign to his true self as Plutarch conceives it. He acts in an unprincipled way for the sake of his own advantage; and Plutarch contrasts him with Metellus,[22] not as a novus homo with a nobilis, but as one who practises deception in a way that is clearly unworthy of the 'politicus', whereas Metellus strikes Plutarch as self-consistent. Marius' attempt to be popular (*dēmotikos*) was at variance with Plutarch's overall picture of a fierce, ambitious and uncompromising soldier-general who did not care what others thought; and Plutarch therefore does not accept that Marius genuinely had this asset, which, as we saw, is so important for the 'politicus'. Both Marius and Pompey seem, at a first glance, to decline into the arms of demagogy; a close reading shows that Marius deliberately chose this course in order to retain power. Pompey, by contrast, can be said to have shown more gentleness.

Coriolanus is a third case of that military eminence which finds difficulty in succeeding in politics. The difference here is that

Coriolanus is not envied by his peers or would-be equals; instead he is highly regarded by his own class, as a man of great *aretē* in war, and this class takes the rejection of Coriolanus by the people as an affront to itself. Thus some circumstances are different, though once again Plutarch is interested in the reasons for the failure of the soldier-general. Coriolanus does not act a popular part, in the way that Marius does. Though, like Marius, he is without gentleness in politics, he differs in that he acts in politics as he proceeds in war. He shows courage by contempt for the enemy, and emulates in peace his martial valour by expressing his scorn for the mob. This consistency with his military virtues is inappropriate to the times of peace, when it is still possible to show courage – a 'politicus' needs this quality as much as a general – but courage now is attested by one's ability to persevere in a course of action that aims at the best. Coriolanus' way of life is self-assertive since his virtues divide and do not unite the state. Thus the soldierly courage of a Coriolanus is as disastrous for him politically as Marius' unnatural switch from courage in war to timidity before the people in their assemblies.[23]

In these *Lives* the theme is that military eminence meets with various obstacles when it turns to a purely political career. Success in war, for instance, tends to beget a love of one's personal reputation as the main objective, which is at variance with the life of the 'politicus', as Plutarch conceives of him, whose aim is *aretē* and the creation of harmony within the state. The 'politicus' must be able to act as a general, since war too is a sphere in which *aretē* is displayed; but his main purpose is the good life of all citizens, among whom he is only one, outstanding though he may be and often is. The figures admired by Plutarch are those who have achieved greatness as generals but have not abandoned their original policy. Aemilius remains the moral leader of the Romans after victory, as he was before; when elected to the command against Perseus he gives a warning against indiscipline, and after victory he sermonizes on the mutability of fortune. He stays loyal to his aristocratic style even though his success was such that he might have been tempted to flatter the people and act like a demagogue. Generalship and the art of the 'politicus' have in common the function of commanding; the ability to lead a disciplined army is another form of the ability that composes and unites the different groups within the state. But the end-product of generalship, victory, is subordinate to the goal of the 'politicus'. The latter, therefore, is valued not for achieving victory, but for the use which he makes of it.

## 3.4  THE RELEVANCE OF THE 'LIVES' TO PLUTARCH'S TIMES

Modern scholars and historians of the Roman Empire should not forget that Plutarch's concern with the past was not academic. He had read widely but did not have the pedant's obligation to be thorough. As long as he could render a character as a whole, he did not mind omitting details; he did not always record different opinions and when he did, he was often imprecise about attributing such views to named writers. Secondly, as we saw in Chapter one, he wrote the *Lives* because he supposed that moral knowledge of the past was directly useful to life in the present. He would justify a subject by that criterion, not on the grounds that it is deemed to lie within the scope of an academic approach to a particular area of knowledge.

Once we have understood this much about Plutarch, we are entitled to ask whether the *Lives* were morally relevant to the conditions[24] in which Plutarch lived. I am speaking here of morals in relation to the public life of politicians, since that is the main subject of the *Lives*. And it seems, at first, as though we must reckon these biographies as a form of escapist literature, which would not be of much help to Greek and Roman politicians at the end of the first century AD. In the intellectual world of the *Lives* we are presented with a model, the 'politicus', who is both good leader and good citizen. He is differentiated from two types of wrong political action, tyranny and demagogy. Most of the heroes, villains and nonentities exist in small independent city-states, in which the masses are a political force to be reckoned with. The 'politicus' must know how to deal with the assembly at Athens or Rome, to persuade these bodies of what he knows to be the best course. But in the real world of Plutarch's time the primary assemblies of the city-state had lost much of their power and status.[25] The tyrants and demagogues, against whom Plutarch warns us, had no counterpart in the Roman empire at this time. If anyone were a tyrant it would be the Roman emperor himself. Demagogue-flatterers had no scope in a world where the primary assemblies had declined in importance; the place of flattery was in the secret world of intrigue at Rome, as Tacitus shows us. Consequently, we might suppose, the 'politicus', tyrant and demagogue were out of date as political models. The 'politicus' and demagogue, especially, do not seem to have much bearing on contemporary needs. If we compare these figures with some of Tacitus' characters – his steadfast generals, like Corbulo and Agricola, and his sycophantic freedmen – they seem to come from a world of fiction like the pirates and adulterers of Roman declamation.

We can express our feeling of the contemporary remoteness of the *Lives* in another way. Other writers of this period display an obvious concern with contemporary issues that is not apparent in the *Lives*. Tacitus gives us the traditions and attitudes of an aristocracy that felt it had been persecuted. The major works of Dio Chrysostom[26] are on the subject of kingship and the proper course for one who holds supreme power. Seneca's letters to Lucilius are the work of a mind which has taken refuge in philosophy against the arbitrary ups and downs of political success and failure; this sort of philosophy is not a means of improving the world, like the philosophy imbibed by the ideal 'politicus' of Plutarch, but of defending oneself against fortune.[27] It is relatively easy for us to see at a glance the relationship between these works and the political conditions under which they were written. But the *Lives* seem to be about a past world, in which the city-state and such institutions as the assembly had been vigorous; it is in this sense that the *Lives* are open to the charge of escapism.

Plutarch himself was well aware that political conditions had changed, but for his views on this subject we have to go not to the *Lives* but to the *Precepts on Public Life*. This treatise should be regarded as complementary and gives explicit advice about political life in the present. We are warned that one should not, in addressing the multitude, refer indiscriminately to the great achievements of our ancestors: Marathon, Eurymedon and Plataea – the battle-triumphs of the Greeks – merely produce an empty swelling pride among the many. These subjects should therefore be left to the schools of the sophists, where (presumably) they can be appropriate as an exercise in oratory (814A–C). Clearly Plutarch means that his budding Greek politician cannot now derive any advantage, whether for himself or his flock, by commemorating the military exploits of independent Greece. The Romans are the overall masters, as he reminds us at 813D–E; the Greek politician now must say to himself: 'You are a ruler ruled, the ruler of a city which is governed by proconsuls, who are the representatives of Caesar.' But the fact that Greece does not enjoy autonomy as a military power should not be a cause of despondency about a political career. It is true that leading a state in war, setting out to destroy a tyrant or establish an alliance can no longer form part of one's initial objectives in politics (805A); as we have seen, Plutarch insists that one's political purpose (*proairesis*) must be soundly based, not an arbitrary whim. But his readers are still able to undertake important works like lawsuits that affect the whole community and serve on delegations to the imperial power. Indeed many Greeks of Plutarch's standing did make a name for themselves by representing their cities on the kind of embassy to which he refers here.[28]

These passages help us to realize that Plutarch did not see the changed position of Greek cities, their dependence on Roman rule, as an impediment to the political life. He compares himself with Epameinondas when he wishes to illustrate the principle that the dignity of the man can bestow worth and dignity on an unimportant office. Epameinondas did not object to a post which entailed supervision of the roads and markets, and Plutarch, at Chaeronea, looked after the weights and measures – 'not for myself, but for my country' (811B–C). The comparison may seem ludicrous to us, but it did not appear so to Plutarch; and one reason for this, which is probably not to his credit, is his habit of thinking of past events as facts isolated from the whole career, which can be made to yield principles of conduct. He does not use the example or paradigm just to show off his allusive knowledge or to score a point for its own sake. His purpose therefore is different from that of the epideictic or the forensic orator. But though his objectives are serious, his habit of taking facts in isolation, as I have called it, and then treating them as examples, stamps his mind as closely related to the orator's. Another reason why Plutarch can compare

himself with Epameinondas in the example given, is, I think, more
to his credit. He thought that the city-state way of life had survived and wished to do all he could to ensure that it would
continue. But he thought, too, that many of the political 'goods'
for which his heroes had struggled had been achieved. He gives a
list of five such 'goods', peace, freedom, prosperity, a sound popu-
lation and concord (*homonoia*) (824C–D). It seems that only the
last of these remains as an objective for the contemporary 'politicus';
but it is considered to be important and worthwhile. His ideal
statesman will teach his fellow-citizens to associate amicably with
one another and to see the advantages of gratitude for Roman
rule.

These are the explicit comments in the *Precepts*, which make it
plain that the *Lives* (for many of the examples given in the *Lives*
are repeated in this handbook) are, in the author's mind, closely
related to the real world. The *Lives* tend to emphasize certain
qualities which might have surprised the heroes to whom they are
ascribed but which, nonetheless, are well suited to the purpose of
achieving concord (*homonoia*). Plutarch values highly virtues like
justice and leniency (*epieikeia*); he praises the statesman who can
accept office when he is needed but does not seek it over-ambitiously
or feel resentment when it is denied him. As we have seen, though
he describes and characterizes the warrior-statesman, he is more
interested in the question whether the successful general has
managed to become a good 'politicus'. This theme in the *Lives*
could well have been of use to one who was prepared to accept
Plutarch's view that leadership in war was no longer a feasible
starting-point for a political career.

It seems to me that the *Epameinondas* was probably the cardinal
*Life*. Although it has not survived, we can see from numerous
references in the extant *Lives* how greatly Epameinondas was
admired by Plutarch. He is praised for his interest in philosophy
and, above all, for his cooperation with Pelopidas (*Pel.* 4). It is this
aspect of political activity which Plutarch wishes to recommend in
the strongest terms. Though Epameinondas was 'imitated' by
others, such as Timoleon, Philopoemen and Philip II of Macedonia,
they did not all recapture the complete virtue (*aretē*) of the model.
Philip, for instance, had his courage; but he lacked the qualities
which made Epameinondas truly great, such as his self-control,

his justice and gentleness.[29] These are the virtues which are said to be most important for Menemachus and others who are to make use of the *Precepts*.

It is clear that the *Lives* were not intended to be a text-book of revolution against Rome.[30] Plutarch preached the doctrine that political life was not only possible but good under the protection of the Roman empire. His readers are expected to learn from the *Lives* and from the *Precepts* the virtue of political cooperation, which will enable them to live with Greeks and Romans. But since this particular message is less explicit in the *Lives*, it is not perhaps surprising that they have at times been held to encourage a cult of greatness. It is relatively easy, when reading the *Lives*, to lose sight of the emphasis on cooperation and think mainly of the individual eminence which Plutarch commemorates. But I doubt whether this formed part of Plutarch's intention. He hoped that his fellow-Greeks would be inspired by the *Lives* to enter into public life. His Roman friends did not need any advice on this point for themselves but would have welcomed the attempt to persuade Greeks to be local politicians within their own cities. The Roman Empire would only prosper if the subordinate towns and municipalities could produce a sufficient number of public-spirited men, content to serve the interests of their own area. Plutarch's own way of life, I mean above all his residence in Chaeronea, is a confirmation of his purpose in the *Lives*. Yet, after all, there is an element of make-believe about this aspect of the *Lives*; surely few Greeks of this time could have read them without being irritated by the present condition of Greece. And the tendency of the age shows that Plutarch's hopes were wide of the mark. The Greeks who became politically important in the second century were not on the whole men who were content to lend dignity to their birthplace by residing there; they sought fame and fortune in the larger towns or at the imperial court.

# 4

# *The Analysis and Description of Character*

The main constituents of character, as a writer sees them, are not chosen *in vacuo* but are in part determined by his purpose in composing biographies. In this context we must remember that Plutarch's whole approach to character is affected by his insistence on man's role as a 'politicus'; he wants to know how an individual has acquitted himself while holding office or submitting to the rule of others, since the ability to rule and accept rule are the obverse and reverse of the same activity. But it is not enough to enumerate fine actions and deduce from them that the character has virtue, whether in whole or in part. Plutarch wishes to be certain that fine actions are the expression of a persisting quality that can be shown to have governed the whole tenor of a life. His admiration goes out to those heroes who have performed fine actions of set purpose or choice (*proairesis*); the function of choice in his account of character is described in section 1.

The heroes, taken as a group, are to be reckoned as examples of the active or 'practical' life, which, traditionally, has honour as its objective. To see the *Lives* in this way is to place them midway in the familiar, threefold,[1] division of lives; the life of 'contemplation' (*theōria*), which studies truth, the life of action, concerned with honour and glory, and the life of acquisition, which accumulates wealth as a means to pleasure. If we test the *Lives* by this threefold, traditional scheme, they will appear to be about a second-best activity; but this conclusion would make nonsense of Plutarch's very obvious conviction that an active, political life is one of the highest forms of activity available to man. He was able to put the political life on a higher plane for two reasons; firstly, his 'politicus' is (ideally at least) nurtured on philosophy and is therefore to be regarded as living a variant form of the first life, at work in different material; and, secondly, Plutarch insists that the goal of his 'politicus' is virtue, not honour or glory which are mere counterfeits of virtue. But he admits that honour appeals to the young and that it has an educative function at the start of political life. To enter on public life, in the first place, needs a certain raw energy or impulse which Plutarch usually discusses in terms of ambition (*philotimia*); his views on this topic are outlined in section 2.

But though ambition is a *sine qua non* of public life and an important clue to character, it is not a quality which stands for the best of which man is capable. Even when ambition is ordered, it is not a major virtue. Yet to describe and comment on the virtues proper would require a book on its own; I have therefore chosen to discuss Plutarch's remarks on the virtue of justice, since he is more explicit about this particular virtue and it is, besides, central to his view of human action in politics (section 3).

Choice, ambition and justice (or the absence of them) are three leading ideas by which Plutarch measures the value of a character. His emphasis on these qualities presupposes that there is such a thing as a stable, lasting basis of character that can be discovered by the biographer. But if character is in part given by nature (*phusis*) and developed by education, it will be knowable because it is consistent with itself. A character will be expected to act in much the same way throughout life and it will be disconcerting to biographer and reader alike if some evidence indicates a virtue while other facts point towards a vice. Plutarch, at times, finds that he has to suppose that there has been a change (*metabolē*) of character, an idea which gives him some difficulty; this is discussed in section 4.

For much of his judgment about characters Plutarch relied on the time-honoured method of inferring the moral attitude from the actions of a hero. But he also believed that the mind could at times be discovered in the face; he had seen many statues which at least purported to be the likenesses of his subjects, and he did make a broad use of portrait-evidence for this purpose (section 5).

The first five sections discuss some of Plutarch's more important ideas in his analysis and evaluation of character. They are not the only clues to his approach but they do combine to give his biographies their own cast of thought. As a way of drawing attention to his particular qualities I conclude (section 6) by comparing his character-methods with those of Suetonius, the contemporary exponent of a very different kind of biography.

## 4.1 CHOICE (*Proairesis*)

One purpose of biography is to record the interesting facts about a person and to explain why he acted as he did. What is considered to be interesting will depend on the biographer's point of view; in the case of Plutarch we have already indicated that many of the facts are selected because they have a bearing on the importance of the hero as a 'politicus'. Secondly, the search for motive does not necessarily demand that a biographer should have a precise acquaintance with theories of the mind or human conduct. Biographers now, who are specially versed in psychology or ethics, are not necessarily more successful as biographers, since most such theories when applied to particular cases are likely to arouse scepticism. A reader will often feel that the facts of the life are being accommodated to the theory, unless the writer is a skilful artist. Plutarch, for his part, was confident that behaviour should be explained in terms that would be acceptable to a student of ethical theory. The language in which he describes parts of the soul and human character, and his vocabulary for analysing motive, were drawn from a long philosophical tradition which went back to Plato and Socrates. This means that his language has behind it a history of precise analysis which is sometimes relevant to his own usage, though at times he uses terms in a less exact, more common-sensical way.

Plutarch's general conception of man, though it may seem idiosyncratic to us, would have been accepted in most of the philosophical schools of his day. He supposes that it is man's nature to act rationally, in accordance with reasoned choice, for reason is the part of man which is most truly characteristic of his proximity to the divine nature. The latter is reason unalloyed; but man is a mixture of reason and the passions, which are the concomitant of reason when in a body. Thus we can distinguish, as a first step

towards discovering a character, between actions which are thought
to exhibit reasoned choice and actions which are motivated by the
passions, such as anger, jealousy and certain forms of pity. Action
based upon reason is the mode at which man should aim and is
the theme of this section; but before we examine Plutarch's remarks
on the subject, we should first look briefly at his view of the
passions.

His general position is not that the passions should be entirely
eliminated, but that they should be moderated. He commends
'apathy'² (*apatheia*), a favourite preoccupation with the Stoics, but
he does not use it in the same sense. He seems, rather, to refer to
the ability to carry on with one's public role even though one is
affected by grief. He means, then, not the total absence of emotion,
but the control of it. Demosthenes, for instance, spoke on matters
of public policy only a few days after the death of his daughter
(*Dem.* 22.3); and Plutarch, in speaking of his *apatheia*, is not denying that the statesman's grief was real. He commends therefore
where Aeschines had denigrated. Similarly, Aemilius addressed the
Romans on the mutability of fortune, even though he had recently
been bereaved (*Aem.* 36.4). Plutarch does not deny the right to
feel grief but he insists that a sense of family loss may have to be
subordinated to the needs of the state. But, in some circumstances,
the suppression of emotion may seem overdone. Thus the reaction
of the elder Brutus, who gave orders for the execution of his sons
without showing any personal emotion, seems to Plutarch difficult
to interpret. Either the virtue (*aretē*) of Brutus was superhuman
and therefore he acted from *apatheia*; or his feelings of grief were
so great that he was numbed into a state of not perceiving the grim
personal consequence of his action. Neither case would be characteristically human; if the former explanation is held to be true, the
action is to be regarded as, literally, divine, since the gods do not
have passions; if the latter, the action is below the level of mankind,
characteristic, therefore, of a non-rational animal (*Publ.* 6.4–6).
Brutus' apparent lack of emotion presents a difficulty because he
is responsible for his own bereavement, whereas Demosthenes and
Aemilius suffer at the hands of fortune, over which they have no
control.

It is the function of virtue to perform fine actions (*kala*). Now
this does not mean that a biographer need merely record these fine

actions and so assert that his hero does therefore have virtue. That procedure would be admissible in panegyric but would not pass muster in Plutarchan biography, which teaches by analysis as well as by commemoration. Plutarch asked the question whether the hero has acted from considered choice (*proairesis*) or whether an action which on the face of it seems fine does not rather, on examination, show the influence of a passion. The death of Marcellus seems, at first, a courageous act; but when we consider the circumstances we may decide that it was prompted not by virtue but by impulsive rashness. A general must act in accordance with the *proairesis* of a general, not like a common soldier, and he should not take the same risks. A Plutarchan character is composed, so to say, of his individual virtues and passions; the examination of the character turns on the search for his *proairesis*, and the facts of the life are tested to see whether the hero has been consistent with himself. To see how this works in literary practice I shall take some examples to show how Plutarch discusses whether a man has acted from *proairesis*[3] or not.

The early part of the *Timoleon* relates how the hero's brother, Timophanes, 'showed contempt for what is fine and just', and made himself tyrant at Corinth. Timoleon tried to persuade his brother to abdicate but his appeals were rejected. After persuasion had failed, Timoleon and some sympathizers used force. While Timoleon stood on one side weeping, two of his friends killed the newly created tyrant. It is clear that the episode is related as an action performed by Timoleon, even though he did not join actively in the assassination. However, some Corinthians accused Timoleon of impious conduct (for killing a brother or consenting to his murder) and he was cursed by his mother. He was dissuaded (with some difficulty) from committing suicide; but although he decided to go on living, he retired from political life and remained a private individual for some twenty years.

In his analysis of this event Plutarch draws our attention to two elements of the story. To kill a tyrant (i.e. a self-gratifying usurper) is 'fine and just'; but to behave as Timoleon did subsequently argues a change of mind which in turn indicates that the original purpose was not soundly based. His passion or emotion, whether it was pity for the dead brother or a feeling of shame before his mother, throws discredit on what seemed to be a fine action. 'It

seems that not only must the act be fine and just, but also the
opinion which is the basis of the action must be stable and firm,
in order that we may only act after approving our scheme . . . The
choice (*proairesis*) that is founded on knowledge and reason does
not change even if the course of action is a failure.' (*Tim.* 6.2–4)
Our judgments – such is the moral – acquire this stability from
reason and philosophy. Thus Plutarch is far from praising the act
of tyrannicide and then uttering a few phrases of conventional
sympathy for what might well be regarded as natural grief for one
who was after all a brother. The attempted suicide and the retirement from politics are perhaps evidence of giving way to a passion
(*Aem.-Tim. comp.* 2.11); and this weakness suggests to Plutarch
that there was a degree of infirmity in the original plan.

Clearly, to judge actions and to impute motives in this way is
very different from modern practice, which can more readily
accommodate the idea that the hero can change his mind without
losing the credit for a great exploit. Plutarch argues back from
later events in a way that does not seem to do justice to our sense
of the individual's ability to react to changes. In short, Plutarch's
notion of what constitutes a valid choice (*proairesis*) expects a
higher degree of rationality than most of us can hope to achieve.
But the idea is important in his analysis of a character's actions.
One test of a sound *proairesis* (assuming that the objective is fine)
is whether an individual has stayed loyal to it over a period of time.
People like Demades,[4] who are always switching their words and
actions, cannot have started from any such principle. Plutarch's
standard of rational choice may seem impossibly high, but failure
to take his theoretical presuppositions into account can result in
considerable misconceptions. Thus, after referring to Plutarch's
exculpation of Timoleon for the death of some mercenaries, Finley[5]
writes: 'The tale is as transparent as the habit with which Plutarch
regularly restricts Timoleon to passive participation in tortures and
executions, as in the assassination of his brother many years before.'
Now it is certainly the case that in Plutarch's version Timoleon is
not active in the killing of his brother, whereas in Diodorus Siculus
(xvi.65) he strikes one of the blows. But an attentive reading will
show that this is not the main point; for Plutarch, Timoleon's tears,
both at the time of killing and later, suggest a defect in the hero's
*proairesis.* He does not tell the story as it stands in order to make

the hero's responsibility less, while giving him credit for conceiving the enterprise in the first place. He uses the tale to criticize Timoleon (though not unkindly); and Finley, I suggest, misrepresents Plutarch here because he has not paid sufficient attention to the context and to the fundamental importance of *proairesis* in Plutarch's schemes of writing. There is no need here to investigate whether modern writers are justified in seeing Timoleon as a tyrant;[6] what must be accepted is that Plutarch does not write as a panegyrist about the assassination, but as an analyst of choice as he conceives it.

In the *Demosthenes* Plutarch discusses the consistency of the orator's policy, his prolonged opposition to the expansion of Macedonia. It was fine (*kalon*) to stand up against Philip on behalf of the Greeks and to persist in this attitude when the policy was defeated at Chaeronea. We are justified here in speaking of policy; as long as we remember that for Plutarch the orator's policy (in our sense) is also an expression of his character; it is proof of a choice since he did not change his mind. Plutarch disagrees with the views of Theopompus,[7] who had included Demosthenes in his digression on demagogues and had criticized him in terms that Plutarch rejects because he is convinced of the man's solid *proairesis*. 'I cannot see how Theopompus came to say that Demosthenes was unstable in character and was incapable of loyalty to the same ideas or men for any length of time. It appears that right to the end he kept the position which he adopted at the very beginning of his political career.' (*Dem.* 13.1–2) Plutarch goes on to contrast Demosthenes with other politicians, who acted out of sheer expediency, regardless of what was *kalon*; and he quotes Poseidonius, who maintained that Demosthenes' speeches are the work of a mind which knows that the *kalon* is to be chosen for its own sake. The policy, as we might call it, reveals the *proairesis*; and persistence in the same cause, even though it was lost, shows that the choice was reasoned. Plutarch does not deny that Demosthenes had faults, for he admits his lack of courage and criticizes him for his susceptibility to bribes; but he puts a higher value on him than Theopompus did, because he thinks that there is enough evidence to demonstrate that there was a sound and admirable *proairesis*.

Plutarch thought that enquiry into a hero's *proairesis* was of fundamental importance because he was eliciting from the facts known to him the man's standing as a politician and citizen. The significance of right choice is also made plain in the *Precepts on Public Life* where the principle is affirmed at the beginning of the handbook (798C). 'First of all there must underlie one's political activity, like a firm and solid foundation, the *proairesis*, which should have as its basis judgment and reason, not a state of excitement caused by empty reputation or ambition or a lack of something else to do.' Similarly a later passage from the same book (799A) distinguishes between those who rush into politics by chance and without thought and those who enter politics only after preparation. The latter have as the goal of their actions that which is fine; Plutarch means that such 'politici', though they may be flexible or many-sided, will not chop and change, as their actions are not governed by a sense of expediency disjoined from an idea of what is fine. Perhaps this passage is no more than a rough and ready guide to the *Lives*; for here Plutarch is assuming that rational choice will be choice of what is fine and the means that lead towards that objective. But actions based on choice do not necessarily aim at what is fine; choice, as Aristotle points out, is qualified by the *aretē* of the man who makes the choice. Antony (*Demetr.- Ant. comp.* 2), it seems, acted from choice; but his purpose was to impose on the Roman people an absolutist form of government, to which they were not used; and what made matters worse was that they had only just got rid of the autocracy imposed by Caesar. Demetrius had a similar purpose in a way, since he aimed at sole rule over the Macedonians; but this is regarded as less objectionable than in the case of Antony, since the Macedonians were used to the kind of government which he tried to impose. With Julius Caesar, Plutarch has a difficulty.[8] He considers that Caesar acted as he did in virtue of a long-term purpose, to overthrow the republican government and rule on his own (*Caes.* 28.3). The objective cannot really be considered fine, since it was alien to the political customs of the Romans; and the methods employed by Caesar were based on deception and lies, on making things seem other than they were. Caesar, therefore, although he acts from a choice in which he persists, is not to be regarded as an example of a true 'politicus'; but nor is he a demagogue, since his search for popularity is not founded on fear of the people but is simply a

112

means to further his end. Is he then a tyrant? He is clearly not motivated by self-indulgence like Dionysius II. It has to be admitted that the form of government was in externals tyrannical; but for Plutarch the absolutism is modified by the leniency (*epieikeia*) of the ruler, and the biographer also takes into account the needs of the Roman people, whose troubles now demanded rule by one man. Although Caesar had a purpose, which at other times and places would have met with Plutarch's disapproval, he seems to regard it as justified by the virtue of leniency and by his thought of what the age needed.

It will be useful at this stage to give a general outline of Plutarch's view of *proairesis* as it affects his study of action in the *Lives*. Actions based on choice are thought to be more characteristic of what is best in man, his rationality, than actions based on the passions. Because the *Lives* are mostly concerned with those who have virtue, the choices he describes are usually good and aim at what is fine. I consider that Plutarch would have found it offensive to write the biography of a man whose purpose would have to be established as bad, such as the life of one who was a traitor by design rather than accident.[9] While choice is higher than passion, those who do bad actions because of passion are, so to say, better than if they did the same action out of choice. Coriolanus, for example, acts against Rome out of uncontrolled resentment or disappointed ambition. Obviously, this is not what action should be, ideally; but given that human nature is weak and that complete virtue is difficult to attain, it is understandable that a Coriolanus can behave as he does. He is then less blameworthy than if he had coolly set out to destroy Rome; his conduct (and Alcibiades is in some ways similar) is a mismanagement of himself, but it would be worse if he appeared as a citizen who turned enemy out of policy rather than passion.

Plutarch deepens his understanding of *proairesis* by considering whether an action has been performed freely or under compulsion. Men who do fine actions from choice, when it is possible for them not to act, are superior to those whose actions of virtue are imposed on them by circumstances. This distinction is explicit in the comparison of Theseus and Romulus. Theseus *could* have stayed at Troezen and ruled there as king by the law of inheritance; instead he chose to leave and perform great actions. Romulus, on the other hand, was under stress when he decided to resist and over-throw the tyrannical rule of Amulius, since he was an exile threatened with punishment. It might be possible to say that a man like Romulus was brave on this occasion simply through fear; in which case the action, though it seems to denote bravery, does not stem from having the habit of courage, but is (possibly) less rational, an impulsive reaction to the force of circumstances. In this way Plutarch is adapting an observation made by Plato (*Phaedo* 68a); that many men who behave bravely in face of death do so because they are afraid. For Plato and Plutarch, such actions, caused as they are by a passion, do not denote bravery proper, which is a form of knowledge. Thus choices freely made are a surer test of whether a man has virtue than choices which are made under necessity. A similar point arises in the evaluation of the hostility shown to autocrats by Dion and Brutus. Brutus' actions against Caesar clearly show *proairesis* in a purer form as he had no cause for private resentment; whereas Dion only acted to destroy the tyranny of Dionysius after he was expelled from his country. Like Romulus, then, Dion can be said to have acted because of necessity, not because he chose freely.

The kind of analysis practised by Plutarch suggests a somewhat simple-minded biographical method. First of all, he seems to assume, one comes to record and know the actions of a life. These are the bare facts to which the confident biographer puts his questions, asking whether they denote a rational choice or the influence of a passion. A difficulty which he does not acknowledge is that the facts are never bare or neutral, but (whatever the source) are nearly always described in such a way as almost to impose an answer. Secondly, Plutarch's reliance on the idea that choice is stable and long-lasting leads to the view that men have always purposed what they finally achieve. For instance, Plutarch's approach to Caesar's biography assumes that Caesar always in-tended what he accomplished at the end, sole rule over Rome. The actions and sayings of the younger Caesar are used as a means of showing the purpose behind the achievement. The danger of this method (on a modern view) is that it reads back from the end to the beginning, imposing on the earlier events a purpose which may apply to the last actions, but may well be irrelevant to the first or middle period of a life.

The record of the actions is a clue to the choice which is one of the important individual characteristics. But actions are not simply an account of choice made effective; they represent a combination of choice and chance, since the hero's attempt to carry out his purpose involves other factors which he cannot control, such as other men's purposes or luck sent by the gods. Hence we sometimes find a distinction between choice and chance, as at *Dion* 2.1 and *Aemilius* 1.6. Men can resemble each other both in their *proairesis* and in their accidents; thus both Dion and Brutus died before they achieved their objectives, and both were visited by apparitions shortly before their death. The distinction is apt to seem trivial to a modern reader. However, as we shall see later, Plutarch thought that luck[10] played a large part in human affairs; he is anxious to point out instances of good or bad luck, since they may confuse us about the man's *proairesis* unless they are clearly identified and put on one side. Plutarch is not just concerned with success or failure, but with uncovering the choice behind the actions, whether these are, broadly, successful or not. In part this is decided by luck, which is not as such a clue to the real man in the same way as choice.

## 4.2 AMBITION (*Philotimia*)

In the previous section we have seen how important it is, in Plutarch's view, to establish that a hero has acted from choice (*proairesis*). But though one's choice may be soundly based and lead to consistent behaviour, that is not by itself sufficient to make the hero act in the first place. He cannot act, being a creature compounded of reason and the passions, unless he has a certain impulse (*hormē*). The most important factor in the human make-up, in this respect, is the passion *philotimia*. There is no adequate way of translating this term; the conventional practice is to use 'ambition' and related words and although we can raise objections to this, there seems to me no better short-hand way of referring to Plutarch's usage. At least it has the advantage that we can see at a glance that Plutarch is discussing a range of ideas that is somewhat similar. These ideas are important in the *Lives* as many of the heroes are evaluated by their *philotimia* or compared with lesser figures who have this characteristic.

To put *philotimia* among the passions without further qualification is misleading. The word does at times stand for a passion; but it also stands for the right as well as the wrong attitude towards the passion. Thus when we read that a man is *philotimos* the meaning may be primarily that he is dominated by love of fame; or, on the other hand, we may have to take it in the sense that he is *philotimos* to the right or wrong degree, as we can speak of a man being ambitious in a good or bad sense.[11] Before examining some of these complexities we should bear in mind that from the fourth century BC onwards *philotimia* was used naturally in Greek to describe a benefaction to a community, made usually by a prominent citizen.[12] It was used to refer, for instance, to a public amenity paid for by a citizen who would then be rewarded by a decree in his honour. In such cases the literal meaning, love of honour, was probably less prominent than the tangible service which the benefactor performed or paid for. This usage occurs in Plutarch but contributes very little to our understanding of *philotimia* as a passion. It is like other passions in that it needs to be moderated or controlled by reason, not eradicated entirely. To be entirely without it would make one politically inactive. Thus Crassus (*Fab.* 25.4) in the Hannibalic war was a political nonentity because he suffered from a deficiency of ambition. On the other hand, the *Lives* are full of cautionary tales about those who have suffered from an excess of *philotimia*. Plutarch's views can be most readily grasped if we first consider his theory of *philotimia* in relation to virtue and then study some particular case-histories from the *Lives*.

Plutarch's main objective, as we have noticed, is to set forth examples of *aretē*; men who have done fine things (*kala*), of whose lives we can say that they were controlled by choice (*proairesis*) and that their actions exhibit such and such virtues. Our aim is to achieve this virtue ourselves and to do fine actions. The underlying thought is that such lives or actions, ideally speaking, need no further advertisement; one needs no other inducement than that provided by virtue. However, Plutarch admits that in the world as it is the function of honour and reputation is effective and necessary. 'The man who is absolutely and perfectly good would not need reputation at all, except to the extent that it allows him entry on to the stage of action and make others trust him. But we

must allow those who are still young and ambitious to pride themselves somewhat on the reputation that attaches to their fine
actions. At that age the virtues are still developing and are tender;
praise helps them to do right actions, and they grow because they
are exalted by a just pride.' (*Agis* 2.1–2). Honour and reputation,
then, are studied by Plutarch as clues to the psychology of the hero;
he is less interested (if he is interested at all) in the social and
historical significance of such concepts as honour (*timē*) and
reputation (*doxa*). He goes on in the same passage to admit a
danger. Excess of this ambition can lead to great harm, since, if we
are ambitious and also have great power, we may think 'not that
the good is of good repute but that having a good reputation is the
supreme good' (*ibid.* 2.3). Ambition seems to be a raw energy
directed towards achieving personal renown; this energy can be
controlled and harnessed so that it then assists in the doing of fine
actions. Or, as Plutarch puts it elsewhere (92D), one must be both
*philotimos* and *philokalos*, attached to the good as well as to a
good name.

The idea of excess indicates that Plutarch is to some extent under
the influence of the Aristotelian discussion of the virtues, according
to which a virtue is a mean between two extremes. Now it is doubtful whether we should ascribe to Plutarch the notion that ambition
is itself a virtue, since he tends to regard it as harmful for the
individual and the state except when he speaks of 'ambition for
what is fine' (*kalon*). Yet he is aware of the need to distinguish
cases of excess and deficiency and once or twice marks off
*philotimia* from the allied word *philonikia*.[13] Greeks did not always
make a sharp distinction here; but at *Philop.-Titus comp.* 1.4 we
read: 'Their mistakes came in the one case (Titus) from *philotimia*,
in the other (Philopoemen) from *philonikia*. Titus was quick to feel
anger, while the other was hard to beg off.' Here *philotimia* is
obviously a less extreme form of the condition, though it should be
emphasized that both conditions are the source of mistakes. But
Plutarch does not keep up this refinement elsewhere, and sometimes
uses *philonikos* where one might equally well have found the other
term. At *Fab.* 25.3 they are even combined, not disjoined, so
perhaps the usage in the comparison of Titus and Philopoemen is
an ad hoc refinement.

Ambition, then, is a source of energy, but unless it is well directed it leads to the cult of reputation instead of virtue. Plutarch's thought here is illuminated by the use to which he puts the myth of Ixion. Ixion was in love with Hera and pursued her but was fobbed off with a cloud shaped like the goddess. The product of their intercourse was a family of Centaurs, an apt symbol of the hybrid. Similarly those who associate with reputation instead of *aretē* (*Agis* 1.2) do not perform pure actions.[14] (Reputation, like wealth, is a thing on which no limit can be put [*Cic.* 6.4] and is therefore not rational.) Their achievement is a bastard one and their course of action is unstable, as they are guided by the passions. Thus ambition is seen to be closely connected with the pursuit of one's own fame, which is not in itself a right objective. It is to be contrasted with the virtue of gentleness (*praotēs*); ambition, for its part, is prone to make men choose erratically, whereas gentleness is a cause of stability, and of adherence to one's purpose.

There is a hint in the *Agis* (2.1) that ambition is likely to be dominant in the young. Plutarch asserts that there is a connexion between ambition and the age-factor, though he does so vaguely, as he writes of 'young' and 'old' without precise reference to age in years. Since the passions decline as man grows older and nears his end, Plutarch thinks it is in a way natural for man to be ambitious in youth and expects this passion to diminish in later life. When it does not do so, he notices this as a perversity. Fabius, for instance, is characterized as 'gentle by nature'; his opposition to Scipio in later life strikes Plutarch as a deviation from his nature and he seems to detect an ambition which was not present before. By the time one has reached old age one's appetite for reputation should normally have declined; men who still have this desire in later life, or start to betray its influence then, like Fabius, are felt to be acting unnaturally. Marius' ambition found a laudable outlet, in the period of his youth and maturity, in the campaign against Jugurtha and the northern invaders. Yet when he was older he was still eager for military glory and hoped to be given the command against Mithridates. 'Every day he went to take exercise in the campus, attempting to slough off the feebleness of age in an ambitious and youthful way.' (*Mar.* 34.5) The best citizens felt pity for his love of glory; the hero who had saved Rome from the Cimbri was still behaving like one who had nothing. Plutarch adds that one version of Marius' last days maintained that his ambition was then completely shown up; during his last sickness he went mad, thought he was in charge of the Mithridatic war and gave orders like a general. 'Because of his love of office and jealous rivalry (modes of ambition) he was dominated by a violent desire to lead in the Mithridatic war.' (*Mar.* 45.11) There are similarities in the case of Titus, though he is a much less barbarous figure than Marius, and is celebrated for his justice. Titus was 'by nature ambitious'; in early manhood and maturity he earned glory by defeating Macedon in Rome's second war against her. 'His ambition had a good name as long as it had sufficient matter and Titus was engaged in the wars mentioned . . . When he was older and no longer in office, he was convicted of not being able to control his passion for glory, a youthful exuberance of that passion, at a time when his remaining years were short of great actions.' (*Titus* 20.1–2) Titus is portrayed as hurrying Hannibal to his death by diplomatic pressure; and this action is, for Plutarch, evidence of diseased and untimely ambition in old age. He refers to the view that there may be a right time for retirement from public life as there is for the athlete (*Luc.* 38.4), though this idea is not wholly in line with the precepts of the *Old Men in Politics*.[15]

Plutarch, in fact, speaks with several voices on the topic of ambition and its effect on the individual. In one way, as we have seen, ambition can assist the growth and development of the virtues. If the hero's nature is not light but stable (*Cor.* 1.4), ambition takes a firm hold of him and drives him to attempt more fine actions. Honour, the object of ambition, is not a reward but a pledge of the greatness still to come. The hero can become his own model, like Coriolanus and Caesar, trying to surpass his own achievements. On the other hand, honour as such is no more than a counterfeit image of virtue; the pursuit of honour is higher than the pursuit of wealth but it is still below the highest activity of political man. And in one respect both honour and wealth share something in common, for both are 'things without limit'. The devotee of either can never in principle be satisfied. Virtue, however, does have this mark of limit, a control imposed by reason on the passions.

We should next consider the effect of ambition on the whole political society in which the individual hero lives. In general

Plutarch sees ambition as a disruptive force; not that it immediately does harm to the state as a whole, but it produces strife instead of cooperation within the ruling class. In several passages he observes that ambition produces envy, by which he means (as a rule) the animosity of peers towards one of their number who becomes too great. 'Absence of ambition is no small step on the way to political gentleness (*praotēs*); and, on the other hand, ambition is a harsh thing, productive of envy. Aristeides was entirely free of it, whereas Cato had a lot.' (*Arist.-Cato i comp.* 5.4) The next few lines describe the cooperation of Aristeides with Themistocles, which Plutarch contrasts with Cato's opposition to Scipio. The cooperation of the Greeks brought success to Athens whereas Cato, urged on by his ambition, very nearly frustrated Scipio's campaign against Carthage. There could be no clearer evidence that Plutarch's own values, here his ideas about ambition, were such that he could not have appreciated the part played in Roman history by such values as *gloria*. He is frequently haunted by a favourite idea that the political activities of the best men should be cooperative. In the same way the power-struggle between Lysander and Agesilaus is, for Plutarch, evidence of excessive ambition on the part of both men, which prevents their working together as he thinks they should.

Ambition, then, is objectionable because it creates envy. We cannot isolate the effect of the individual's ambition on the state from Plutarch's view of the state as a harmony, as can be seen from a passage in the *Agesilaus*. The ephors imposed a fine on Agesilaus because they considered that by his political tactics he was building up a personal following among the Spartans, 'making those who were citizens of the state his own men'. Plutarch then refers to an elaborate theory which might seem to justify the reaction of the ephorate. 'Those who study nature (*phusis*) think that the heavens would be halted if strife (*neikos*) were removed from the universe, that generation and motion would cease because all things would be in harmony; similarly, it is held, the Spartan lawgiver introduced ambition (*to philotimon kai philoneikon*) into the state as a way of kindling virtue. He wanted the best men to be at variance and in dispute with one another . . .' There are two points of interest here. Firstly, Plutarch is playing on the various spellings of *philonikos* (love of victory); it appears in this passage as *philoneikos* (love of strife). Secondly, he does not himself agree with this theory that the legislator's purpose at Sparta is to be so justified. 'This could not be allowed without qualification; for excessive *philoneikiai* are a burden to states and bring great dangers.' (*Ages.* 5.5f.) This represents his view of ambition. He does not think that political life should be based on strife and the struggle for preeminence at the expense of others and he praises the Athenians under Pericles for recalling Cimon from ostracism. 'At that time their differences were "political";[16] their anger was moderate and could be reined in if the common advantage required; and ambition, that domin- ates all the passions, gave way to the country's needs.' (*Cim.* 17.9) Probably the worst effects of ambition, in Plutarch's view, were seen in the struggle between Marius and Sulla (*Sulla* 4.5); on this subject Plutarch quotes approvingly the fine passage from Euripides' *Phoenissae* where Jocasta criticizes *philotimia* as the worst of goddesses.[17] The rivalry between two of Rome's great generals led to tyranny.

In the interpretation of individual *Lives* ambition is a key concept in a good third of the whole number. But even those heroes whose ambition is specifically mentioned are not to be judged by their degree of ambition alone. The ambition of a hero has to be assessed by taking into account his other virtues and failings. Plutarch is interested above all in the question whether ambition is compatible with the highest functions of the 'politicus'. He cites Epameinondas as a man of action (presumably, here, he refers to his abilities as soldier and general) who did not show anger or contentious ambition in disputes within his own state; he had the virtue of gentleness (*praotēs*). Epameinondas was the model for Philopoemen, who was his equal as a general but was found want- ing in that important political virtue (*Philop.* 3.1–2). In fact ambition seems to be most noticeable in the soldier-generals, though Cicero is an important addition.

The *Titus* is the story of an ambitious man, whose energy is expressed in beneficial ways, except for one or two incidents at the end of his life. 'He was very ambitious and a lover of personal reputation; and he wanted to perform good and great actions on his own. He was better pleased with those who needed his service than with those who could help him; he looked on the former as the matter of his virtue, while the latter were his rivals in reputation.' (*Tit.* 1.3) Titus, though a soldier-general, is celebrated by Plutarch for justice (*Tit.* 1.5). He earns high praise because he is regarded as the conqueror of Macedonia and the liberator of Greece. His ambition did not cause conflict at Rome; and in Greece it led to just results such as the removal of contentious disputes among Greeks and the restoration of liberty. Although Titus' justice is mentioned several times, it is not precisely defined. One suspects here that Plutarch's picture of Titus is coloured by his regard for him as a liberator of Greece;[18] he seems to accept Titus' restoration of Greek freedom as something genuine, whereas, in terms of the power-politics in the early second century BC, it meant little more than a qualified dependence on Rome. Titus was quick to take offence and feel anger but did not stay resentful for long. Also he was ready to do a kindness and was always well disposed to those whom he had benefited.

The ambitious man is likely to be prone to anger and resentment, because he is spirited (*thumoeidēs*), and derives his ambition from that part of the soul (*thumos*) which is also the source of anger. Titus' ambition was not marred by excess of anger; with him we should contrast Plutarch's Coriolanus. Ambitious and soldierly, he has the particular virtue of early Rome, courage.[19] He does not seem (in Plutarch's account) to have the justice of a Titus. He is a man whose ambition has not been tamed by the Muses,[20] Plutarch's way of stating that he has not received philosophical direction. His ambition does not have an adverse effect on his own social group but helps to perpetuate a division between the people and the upper classes. It turns to resentment and anger when he is refused the consulship and is then prosecuted and sentenced to exile. Plutarch explains his subsequent behaviour as proof that he suffered from a sense of rejection and was troubled by an unsociable disposition which is the enemy of political mastery. 'When this quality is present in one who is ambitious it becomes utterly savage and implacable. Such characters do not pay their respects to the people, as not standing in need of office (honour); then they are angry when they are not appointed.' (*Cor.-Alc. comp.* 4.8) To go by Coriolanus' lack of respect for the people, you might think that he disdained the office which it was in the people's power to bestow. But true disdain, according to Plutarch, is shown by those who can take their rejection in the right spirit and come or return to office when their country needs them. The point is that those who pay no respect to the many should not punish them; to show excessive anger, when we do not get office, is a proof that we vehemently desire that which we apparently disdain. Plutarch links the ambition of Coriolanus with his anger and lack of education. The whole passage in the *Comparison* is a good example of how he tried to get behind appearances at what he considered to be the inner moral truth. Coriolanus' disdain of the many is not genuine aristocratic disdain, but is seen, in the end, to be evidence of excessive ambition. His thwarted *philotimia* begets a state of anger in him which is so powerful that it governs his subsequent conduct. He leaves the political framework, within which alone *philotimia* can have some moral value, and attempts to satiate his rage by leading the armies of the Volsci against his own country. Here there appears to be a similarity between him and Alcibiades, but the likeness is only on the surface. Plutarch means (*Cor.-Alc. comp.* 2.4) that one might at first suppose that Alcibiades'[21] manoeuvres, which deceived the Spartan ambassadors and led to the rupture between Athens and Sparta, are comparable to the act of deception whereby Coriolanus provoked war between Rome and the Volsci. But to isolate deception as the element common to both cases is to miss the important difference. Alcibiades was motivated by feelings of rivalry with Nicias and his competitiveness was therefore directed against one individual with a view to obtaining an advantage for Athens as a whole as well as for himself. Coriolanus' policies, after his failure to become consul, were no longer prompted by this kind of *philotimia* but by anger; and *philotimia*, though it can be destructive, is preferable, since acts motivated by anger do not win any return.

It is obvious from the above sketch that Plutarch frequently discusses cases of ambition in the *Lives* and that he uses the idea to explain character in a flexible way. The character of the ambitious man had been a subject attempted by several other writers. Plato gives a brief sketch of him in the eighth book of the *Republic*,[22] where he is studied as the type representative of the timocratic state, which is next in rank to the ideal state. This general idea, rather than the details of the portrait, would probably have been accepable to Plutarch, who states that the ambitious man aims at honour, the image of virtue. Aristotle's discussion of the idea in the *Ethics* is another influence (*EN* 1125ᵇ). Where Plutarch expresses the view that excess of ambition is a bad thing, he is probably indebted to the Peripatetic notion of the mean. He is more tolerant in his attitude towards ambition than Dio Chrysostom, whose discourse (*or.* iv.116f.) on the subject shows some differences from Plutarch's approach. For Dio the life of ambition is concerned with a false end and resembles therefore the lives that are devoted to pleasure and to acquisition. All three are spurious compared with the life of *aretē*, and all three are lives often chosen (or followed) by the many. If anything, ambition is worse than the other two, as it betrays a more extreme confusion of soul. The ambitious man deceives himself, supposing that he is a lover of something fine (*kalon*). Plutarch would argue that ambition need not be directed at honour only, and would clearly rate the life of ambition above that of the hedonist. Both writers use the myth of Ixion and Hera in a similar way, but Dio also connects Ixion's wheel with ambition in a way that Plutarch does not. In Dio, Ixion, carried round on his wheel, is a symbol of the ambitious man moved by forces he does not control, compelled to put on a greater variety of expressions than the figures on the potter's wheel. The ambitious man resembles the painting of a Boread; he is always 'light and in the air'. Plutarch, we have seen, rates ambition more highly; it is not *per se* insubstantial, but can work to good effect if the hero's nature is stable. Nor does he suppose, as Dio does, that ambition must necessarily stoop to flatter the many; that depends on other qualities of the hero and the political context of the age. We have, I think, no evidence that Plutarch knew of Dio's sketch; the fact that both used the story of Ixion and Hera is to be explained as the common property of sophistic image-making; but he puts a higher value on ambition than his contemporary does and studies it more closely, since he sees it has a connexion with the functions of the 'politicus'.


4.3   THE VIRTUE OF JUSTICE

*Philotimia*, as we see, is a difficult idea to read in the right way, since it modulates between being a passion, a vice and a virtue. Yet even when it appears as a virtue it is not one of the cardinal glories of the Plutarchan hero. It is a necessary spring to action rather than a merit characteristic of what Plutarch regards as the best of which man is capable. The qualities we should seek to emulate are virtues like justice (*dikaiosunē*), restraint (*sophrosunē*), leniency (*epieikeia*) and gentleness (*praotēs*), which are always positive. This list of positive virtues is not closed at this point, for one must also include great-mindedness (*megalophrosunē*) – the readiness, given the ability, to measure up to what is *kalon* – and that sense of legitimate pride (*phronēma*), which is rather similar. To discuss the virtues at length, as Plutarch sees them, would need at least one book; and so, in order to give an indication of his approach to the virtues as a way of delineating character, I have confined this part to a study of justice. The reasons for so doing are that justice is the essential virtue for man as a creature living in states and is therefore particularly relevant to Plutarch's emphasis on the hero as a 'politicus'; and, besides, justice is the subject of explicit general comment in more than one passage of the *Lives*. I shall give first an account of Plutarch's general views and then go on to examine what is the content of justice in the careers of particular heroes, and discuss why Plutarch felt able to ascribe justice to them.

In *Arist.* 6.2 the term 'just' is described as the most royal and divine of titles; it is a matter of some satisfaction to Plutarch that it was applied as a nickname to Aristeides, whom he believed to be poor and of humble origin. He goes on to explain why justice is the attribute of kings and gods. There are three respects in which the divine is superior to that which is merely human; incorruptibility, power and virtue (*aretē*). Other things in the universe, such as void, are incorruptible; power is evidenced by such things as earthquakes; but only that which is divine because it is rational can participate in law and justice (which seems to be taken here as the typical virtue). Now it is obvious that incorruptibility and power on the scale mentioned are beyond human scope: human nature does not admit immortality nor can one man shake the globe. But man is in a sense divine because, like the gods, he is endowed with reason, and it follows that he can draw nearer to the gods by imitating them in the specific virtue of justice. How the gods are just or in what human justice consists is not clarified.

Just as there are three respects in which the divine is superior, so too there are three attitudes to the gods, each of which corresponds to a particular superiority. Men envy the gods because of their incorruptibility; we fear their power; but we love and honour the gods for their justice. This is the sole attribute of the divine which is within man's power to attain. It follows that the many are mistaken when they vainly yearn, as they do, for incorruptibility and power. In much the same way some of the kings of history are rebuked for giving expression to a wrong sense of values. Those who call themselves Besiegers and Conquerors[23] are talking as though power were the brightest jewel in their royalty, forgetting that justice is the royal art. To flaunt one's power is to deviate towards tyranny, which is worse than demagogy. 'It is discreditable to flatter the common people in order to gain power, but to be strong through being an object of fear, by doing harm and crushing others, is unjust as well as discreditable.' (*Cor.-Alc. comp.* 1.4) The strictures on the titles of the Hellenistic kings recur in *Demetr.* 42.5–9 where it is stated that justice is the most becoming function a king has to carry out. Homer[24] is cited as witness, for he uses the words 'associate and pupil of the gods' about Minos, who was famous for his justice. Demetrius, however, delighted in a title which is the exact opposite of that applied to the monarch of the gods. Plutarch then draws the general moral : 'when the man with power is uneducated (i.e. in the right values) dishonour usurps the place of what is fine and fastens injustice to his reputation.'

In these passages Plutarch does little more than remind us of the primacy of *aretē*; the particular virtue of justice stands for *aretē* as a whole. The content of justice emerges only dimly as a concern for the maintenance of law as against the arbitrary whims of tyranny. But though justice is the virtue essential to the 'politicus', it is evidently rare, less common than other virtues (*Titus* 11.4–5). The reasons for this pessimistic utterance begin to appear in a discussion of the younger Cato's virtues. A virtue such as justice wins the confidence of the many but provokes the envy of one's peers; thus Cato was accused of arrogating to himself the functions of the courts (*Cato ii* 44.11–14). Here there is a contrast with courage and political intelligence (*phronēsis*). Ordinary people respect courage but feel timid in the presence of the courageous; they admire political intelligence but distrust it; but they like the just man and have confidence in him. These different attitudes are founded in people's opinions about the different virtues. They suppose that courage and intelligence are natural gifts; whereas to be just implies that one has deliberately chosen this as one's goal. The just man will be remarkable because he will have achieved something that is within the reach of all and is more difficult than courage, since some courageous men have a start or advantage supplied by the generosity of nature. On the other hand, the unjust man cannot extenuate his actions in the same way as the coward when the latter offers the plea of physical weakness. Here Plutarch insists on the effect of justice upon those who see it at work, the fact that it evokes a liking for the just man, at least among those who are themselves politically weak. The reader of this *Life* will have noticed that the point is emphatically made about Cato himself, where Plutarch describes the effect of his virtue on the men with whom he served in Macedonia (*Cato ii* 9.5–10). This effect of justice is of great importance since it thereby creates a willingness on the part of others to emulate this virtue.

These general discussions illustrate the importance of justice in Plutarch's scale of values and show that the just man, perhaps more than others, is likely to stimulate his associates to *aretē*. Besides the above, there is another passage which raises a general question about justice, the same question which is debated at length at an early stage in the *Republic*; is the just man useful only to others, not to himself? The question arises in the comparison of Cato and Aristeides (*Comp.* 3–4), because, as we saw in the account of the 'politicus' and wealth, the poverty of Aristeides might seem to imply that justice benefits others and disadvantages oneself. Plutarch does not answer the important question, whether justice is worth pursuing for its own sake, even if it involves financial loss for oneself. He points out that justice is not incompatible with the successful (in a worldly sense) management of one's own affairs; and given that this is so, we must fault Aristeides here. But Plutarch thinks that it is more important to pass on to another point and asserts that poverty *per se* is not a fault. When it is the condition of one 'who is deploying all his virtues in the public domain' it is a sign that one has greatness of mind. In effect, Plutarch has it both ways. In the first place he maintains that there is nothing to prevent the just man from also benefiting his family or *oikos*; in the second place he asserts that if one becomes or remains poor as a consequence of being just in politics, this does not detract from the high quality of one's actions. The question of the *Republic* – is justice only of advantage to others? – has become entangled with the moralist's desire to warn his readers against confusing poverty and wealth with bad and good. His usual tendency is to contrast justice with the desire for personal gain, whether it be the desire for money or power. In this way he makes an effective opposition between Brutus, renowned for justice, and Cassius, who was suspected of seeking power for himself (*Brut.* 29.2–5).

What, then, makes it possible for Plutarch to be sure that he has found the virtue of justice in a particular life? It seems that he did not take his judgments ready-made from the traditions, though of course he was only too glad to inherit and confirm a tradition like that of Aristeides the Just. Also, he was prone to see the better and prefer it, since neither straight malice nor the simple form of irony was congenial to him. Clearly he thinks of himself as extracting the virtues from the *res gestae* of the career. It is relevant here to point out that he acknowledges a difficulty: according to him, the virtues do not make themselves uniformly apparent in different *Lives*. 'There is a difference between one man's courage and another's, as with Alcibiades compared with Epameinondas . . . and a difference between one man's justice and another's, as with Numa and Agesilaus.' (*Phoc.* 3.7) This is not to say that Plutarch is a historian of the ways in which moral and political values had changed in the course of Greek history. He means that the scope of action changes but assumes that a virtue, once recognized in an action, is in an important sense identical with other examples taken from different parts of history. The standard is always the same though the particular historical matter may vary. The example of Numa and Agesilaus is probably meant to strike paradoxically. Numa, along with Lycurgus and Solon, is one of the great legislators of the *Lives*; as an eminent 'politicus' he is bound to be a case of justice. But Agesilaus was primarily a general, of whom it is said that his political conduct was marked by generosity towards those who had helped Sparta, even if they acted illegally. In this way he excused Phoebidas for his attack on Thebes (*Ages.* 23.7). Why then does Plutarch mention him in the same breath as Numa? Agesilaus[25] did at least emphasize the primacy of justice over courage and he showed justice in his respect for treaties when dealing with the satrap Tissaphernes (*Ages.* 9.2–4). The soldier, then, is just in a different way from the politician-legislator, but the justice of both is deemed to come under the same head.

It seems to follow from the remarks in *Phoc.* 3.7 that Plutarch can ascribe the same virtue to men who have led very different lives. The remark that justice is the rarest of the virtues occurs in the *Life* of the Roman Titus Quinctius Flamininus (*Titus* 11.4–5), a surprising choice for the reader who will remember Titus as the Roman general who defeated Philip V at Cynoscephalae. The context, however, shows why he is held to be just. Plutarch has already mentioned Titus' famous proclamation at the Isthmian games in 196 BC, when the Greek states were officially declared free by the liberating Roman general. He then contrasts the wars of Greek generals with the war fought by Titus; the Greeks (he mentions Agesilaus, Nicias, Lysander and Alcibiades) had fought for their cities in order to subjugate other Greek states, whereas Titus the Roman had made use of his victory over Philip to declare the independence and freedom of the Greeks. One must admit that this view of the events in 196 BC shows a naïve and uncritical acceptance of the fine-sounding terms of the declaration. Yet to do so is to find fault with Plutarch for his failure in historical insight rather than to explain and understand his biographical practice. The reason for his relatively adverse comment on Agesilaus and the others is that they did not use their victories for any purpose one could call fine (*kalon*). They succeeded as generals but failed as 'politici' in Plutarch's view. (Of course he is here taking the somewhat unusual step of judging these eminent Greeks as 'politici' within a pan-Hellenic framework, not assessing them solely as Spartans or as Athenians.) As we saw above, the right use of victory has precedence over the winning of wars and is a better guide to a man's political *aretē*. Titus, then, seems to be called just because he showed great political *aretē* by liberating the Greeks, and justice is regarded as the most valuable of the virtues belonging to the 'politicus'. He freed Greeks from what Plutarch considers the tyrannical interference exercised by Macedonia. Thus the reason for calling Titus just can only be understood if we take into account Plutarch's general views about the function of the 'politicus' and his assumption that Greek states should be free.

Those who do not allow for his assumptions will be surprised at his enthusiasm for Titus. Yet this was genuine, as he shows in the *Comparison* (3.5), where he gives Titus the prize for justice and generosity. His method is, of course, still open to the objections that can be made against his evaluation of choice (*proairesis*), that he has confused *post hoc* and *propter hoc*. His judgment of Titus implies that he sees a purposive connexion between the victory and the peace.

Plutarch's attitude to Marcellus is based on similar considerations. Until the time of Marcellus the Romans had impressed other peoples as great warriors but had not given any proof of political *aretē* : 'Marcellus seems to have been the first to show the Greeks that the Romans were very just.' (*Marc.* 20.1) The reader who is used to a stereotype of Marcellus as the warlike Roman inspiring the Romans against Hannibal, will be surprised by this verdict, which is not repeated in the *Comparison* though it stands out in the narrative. Plutarch's view of Marcellus is conditioned by his treatment of the Greek cities in Sicily; those that suffered, like Enna, had only themselves to blame, whereas numerous places were benefited by Marcellus. Thus Roman atrocities in Sicily are underplayed or omitted; even Livy said that the massacre at Enna was 'either a bad or a necessary action', whereas Plutarch describes at length how one place, Engyion, was mercifully treated by Marcellus at the request of the pro-Roman leader. One might have expected Plutarch to say that this illustrates the leniency (*epieikeia*) of Marcellus rather than his justice. The fact is, however, that the virtues overlap; they are not always carefully distinguished and one incident can therefore be evidence for more than one virtue. Plutarch might say that it is on the whole unjust to destroy a captured city (a sign, therefore, of injustice in the destroyer) because it represents a misuse of victory; he is not interested in the legalistic question which, in Livy's account, centres on the phrase 'the right of war'. Clearly, too, the incident might have been used to ascribe mercy to Marcellus. In later chapters the attribution of justice to the great Roman commander is confirmed. I include under this heading Plutarch's account of the Roman triumph (*Marc.* 22); Marcellus was disappointed in his hope of a third triumph and celebrated instead an ovation, which Plutarch regards as the reward for generals who succeed 'by persuasion'. A later chapter (23) describes Marcellus' scrupulous refusal to take advantage of his position as consul when some Syracusans came to Rome to prefer charges against his conduct in Sicily.[26]

The cases of Marcellus and Titus are of interest because they show how the search for a virtue is based not merely on a simple reading of the factual record, but involves Plutarch's general attitude towards the 'politicus' and political virtue. There is perhaps less difficulty in understanding the justice of Aristeides or the younger Cato; for what is clear in the case of these men is their respect for the law. Cato, for instance, insists that the penalties and rewards of the law should be applied to all without favour. But even with Cato we should not isolate Plutarch from his preconceptions; the *Cato ii* contains several remarks about the hero's emphasis on the need to 'persuade and instruct' (*Cato ii* 9.6) and I do not think that Cato's justice can, for Plutarch, be understood without reference to the persuasive function of the 'politicus'. The latter operates through oratory, whereas the tyrant rules by force.

With heroes like these, one can see why Plutarch has been led to ascribe justice to them. His treatment of the evidence before him often involves other considerations, particularly his view of the ideal 'politicus'. But it should not be supposed that we are always in a position to see why particular virtues have been chosen; although Pericles and Fabius are both said to be just and gentle (*praoi*), the narrative seems to bring out the latter quality alone, the ability of both men to cope with the irrational hostility of others to their reasoned policies (*Per.* 2.5).

In this discussion of justice I have proceeded on the assumption that virtue (*aretē*) as a whole is no more than the sum of the particular virtues; that a hero's standing in relation to *aretē* is to be determined by the degree to which he shows the virtues rather than by whether he is successful. Dion, for example, has many particular virtues which are described in detail in his *Life*. His main defect is a certain obstinacy or personal ungraciousness, which is not so much the opposite of a virtue as a failure to make his virtues plausible. This accounts for his historical failure but is not a serious deficiency in his *aretē*.

We can take it that this assumption about virtue is in general reasonable because Plutarch sees man in history as, for the most part, a case of *aretē* pitted against fortune; the *aretē* persists, whether the man concerned fails or succeeds in his objectives. Indeed, Plutarch is eager to rescue *aretē* from the oblivion to which failure seems to consign it (*Phoc.* 1.4–6). On the other hand it is obvious that the heroes have been chosen in the first place because they were outstanding men in their own day; even though some of them failed, they were not abject. The most noticeable failures, Demetrius and Antony, have the least *aretē*; and two who had great *aretē*, Aemilius and Timoleon, succeeded in a manner that is more common in panegyric. Consequently there is a suspicion that Plutarch may at times think of *aretē* as the peculiar attribute of the eminent *qua* eminent. Men must have performed fine actions in the first place, in order to qualify for an examination of their *aretē*; and although Plutarch studies the choice behind the actions, the actions he selected were those which stood out from the pages of history as he read it.

## 4.4 CHANGE OF CHARACTER

It is often said that the Greeks and Romans did not conceive of changes of character as the moderns do. We can see how this notion seems at first sight to apply to the *Lives*, because some of Plutarch's ideas about character and human nature are not compatible with the idea that characters can and do change. If one takes for granted, as Plutarch does, that character is to a large extent pre-formed by the nature one is born with, it is easy to think that the record of a man's actions merely unfolds or discloses what is already there. One's natural tendencies are trained through the social framework or by means of philosophical education; nature then becomes good or bad habit, which makes itself known through the actions of a life. For the most part the heroes 'act in accordance with their nature'; and it is this assumption of consistency that gives Plutarch the confidence, as a biographer, to be so certain that character is knowable. Nevertheless, this way of looking at character gives rise to certain difficulties; for instance, what are we to make of an action which seems out of character with what is otherwise known about the hero? Are we to assert that there has been a change? Or argue that it is a pretend-action? Or, finally, just leave it weakly, unexplained, as an action 'against nature'? This is one set of questions which faced Plutarch; and we should add that he does at times explicitly discuss the question whether character has changed.[27] In this section we shall examine some of the texts which are relevant to the topic.

Some passages suggest that Plutarch expressly rejects the idea of change. His verdict on Philip V[28] of Macedon is as follows: 'Philip seems to have undergone a very great and extraordinary change, turning into a licentious man and cruel tyrant after having been a mild king and moderate young man. Yet this was not really a change of nature, but a disclosure, when he was no longer afraid, of a badness that for a long time had not been acknowledged through fear.' (*Arat.* 51.4) Here the badness of the nature finally emerges, and, because it is on a monstrous scale, we are invited to dismiss Philip's early goodness as not being a true expression of his character or nature. Hence it is not surprising to find that in a later passage Philip is described as 'wicked by nature' (54.2). Evidently the true man was only revealed by tenure of power. But though Philip is explained in this way, as having a bad character which took a long time to appear, in another place the idea of change is not dismissed so easily. In a brief survey of the characters of Marius and Sulla, Plutarch says that Marius was not worsened by power, but merely intensified his natural harshness of character. Sulla, however, at first behaved moderately (as a 'politicus' should) when he was successful; later he became cruel and used his power to proscribe numerous citizens. 'Understandably, then, his career has attached to great power the charge that it does not allow character to stay put in its original ways but makes it violent, tumid and inhuman. Whether this is a motion or change of nature caused by fortune, or whether it is a disclosure, at a time of great power, of a badness that was already there, can be decided by another form of enquiry.' (*Sulla* 30.5) Thus Plutarch disappoints us here of his thoughts on the subject of change, probably because he feels that the digression has already lasted long enough. The biographer, like a historian, leaves us with a pair of alternatives, with no means of knowing which view he would support. I shall attempt to supply the other form of enquiry.

In both cases so far we have to do with a change from apparent goodness to real badness. It is clear that Plutarch is rather shocked by this supposition, as he makes plain by referring to Philip's change as most extraordinary. A change from good to bad would be unacceptable for Plutarch, because he thinks of virtue as stable and permanent. If we have virtue, we have a form of knowing what are the right ends of human action, and this knowledge tends to be regarded as something unshakeable. This point emerges from the *Sertorius* (10.5); Sertorius blotted his character towards the end of his career by cruelty to some hostages, which might suggest that 'his nature was not really mild but veiled, as a calculated move because of political necessity. I cannot think that any external accident could ever make virtue, when it is pure and in accordance with reason, move to its opposite. But it is not impossible that when good choices (*proairesis*) and natures have suffered contrary to their deserts, the character should change along with the man's fortune.' We have discovered another factor, apart from Plutarch's ideas about nature (*phusis*), which would make it difficult for him to say that a good man has changed and become bad. A man who has virtue in the fullest sense cannot become bad, as he could only do so by losing his *aretē*, which is by definition one of the most permanent things he has. Plutarch's solution is not unsympathetic to Sertorius; clearly he thinks that the evidence for Sertorius' virtue from his early career is not wholly undone by the act of inhumanity towards the end. It is a kind, common-sensical judgment, but lacks the rigour of the tenet that a man with virtue cannot become bad; the upshot is that Sertorius, even if he does not have virtue pure, does have it to an extent, and we are left with no adequate explanations of the bad action. There are other instances where a change from good to bad is mentioned with some disquiet; Lucullus' retirement into semi-hedonism seems inconsistent with his undeniable virtue as a general and is the subject of adverse comment in the comparison with Cimon (*Comp.* 1.4).

Plutarch, then, adopts several procedures when he is considering biographical cases where we might without embarrassment speak of a change from good to bad. If the alleged change is to wickedness on the grand scale, he can say, as with Philip V, that the underlying nature was bad all the time; the apparent virtue was a mask, discarded when the villain behind it felt safe and secure from outside threats. In the case of Sertorius he does talk, rather half-heartedly, of a change; but one is made to feel that the blame rests with the world and circumstance rather than with the hero's virtue, though this is clearly not perfect. In other cases the word change is not mentioned; it is said that a certain course of action was 'against the man's nature' and it stands as an oddity in the man's career, not as an indictment of the whole. This is perhaps the explanation offered for Fabius' opposition to Scipio; but it should be noticed that another theory appears here, that the virtue of caution was enfeebled and turned to inaction through the onset of old age (*Fab.* 26.3). This kind of explanation sounds familiar and is broadly accepted by a modern without qualms; but it is not compatible, as we have seen, with the philosophical moralist in Plutarch, who insists on the permanence of virtue.

If a change for the worse makes Plutarch cast around for explanations, he is less troubled about speaking of change when men improve. This is much the attitude we would expect from one who practised philosophy as a school of self-improvement and wrote a treatise on how to be aware of one's progress towards virtue. He thinks that man is meant by nature to be a civilized creature, living in amicable concord in states under law and justice. The pirates who were resettled by Pompey had been acting 'against nature' in the course of their lawless marauding at the expense of civilized communities. The *Lives* are intended to make us better and themselves contain examples of men who did improve. Alexander struck and wounded Lycurgus, who took the insult with admirable composure; his retaliation was to make Alexander his servant and teach him the moral lessons to be derived from his company. The best thing for the unjust man, as the Platonist will remember, is that he should stand trial immediately and be cured of his trouble.[29] Alexander was fortunate enough to have a painless cure and he became a good man after having been a violent and obstinate youth (*Lyc.* 11.6). Dion justifies his treatment of Heracleides by saying that no man's badness is so savage that it cannot change after being prevailed upon by those who continue to confer benefits, the benefits of justice and mercy. The application to Heracleides proves to be a failure, but the principle remains as authentic Plutarch (*Dion.* 47.7–9).

The feasibility of change from bad to good is discussed at some length in the *God's Slowness to Punish* (551E). The speaker is giving reasons for the delay in divine punishment and explains that one such reason is that it gives man time to improve. 'Consider how many instances of change there have been in men's characters and lives. That which is the subject of change has therefore been named the bent (*tropos*) and character (*ēthos*), since training (*ethos*) sinks in deep and exercises great influence.' The etymological play shows that the change envisaged is not so radical after all; it is a turning of the nature towards what is good, away from what is not. The nature is therefore not so much changed as deflected into a right course. The speaker then goes on to describe men who came to absolute power by bad means and improved once they held office. The reason why they have been given time is that god is a good judge of character; he sees the goodness and nobility that are in men and waits for time and maturity, the adjutants 'of reason and virtue'. We see that change for the better is not after all so very different from change for the worse. Plutarch only conceives of change in a very weak sense; in both there is already present an underlying, already existing quality, which has not yet shown itself in its true colours. It is, of course, the nature of man to improve and ascend towards the divine; so this is another reason why Plutarch is not troubled about speaking of change when it is a case of improvement.

Another topic, allied to the concept of change of character, is the question whether a man retains his identity throughout life or whether he is one man today, another man tomorrow. Plutarch reports this theory as a sophistic argument, giving as an example the saying that 'the man who was yesterday invited to dinner comes today uninvited, because he is now older than he was' (559B). The point was discussed in the philosophical schools but as a theory of character it obviously had no appeal for Plutarch. Such a theory would make man politically irresponsible for his previous actions. Secondly, it implies a lower value to be put on memory than is compatible with Plutarch's idea of the life 'according to virtue'. The unity of the good life is in part a function of the memory, which is happy to dwell on past blessings and satisfactions, and is not distracted by hopes for the future. Thus a good memory bestows unity and a kind of changelessness on the man who has virtue (473D–E). In the *Lives* the heedful contentment of Plato is contrasted with the restless aspiration of Marius, who was still covetous of power and new honours at the end of his days (*Mar.* 46). Complete virtue is in a way not mutable, though it may be buffeted by fortune and has to take account of various political situations. To suppose that identity could alter daily would be in conflict with the view that virtue has the characteristic of unity. It would also have been impossible for Plutarch to write this kind of fragmenting biography, since there was not that amount of detailed information.

This question of identity was not the only topic to do with change that philosophers discussed in the schools. Theophrastus had asked whether character is changed by circumstances; and whether it is affected (Plutarch uses the word 'moved', with which we should compare the wording of *Sulla* 30.5) by the sufferings of the body and so comes to lose *aretē*. In connexion with this he told a story about Pericles, who wore an amulet round his neck when he lay dying of the plague. To Theophrastus this suggested a change of character since he plainly regarded Pericles as a man with virtue who only put up with this piece of nonsense because he was unbalanced by sickness. Plutarch does not here commit himself on the general question whether virtue is adversely affected by the sufferings of the body. Instead, he relates another anecdote about Pericles, which suggested to him that this hero still retained true *aretē* : Pericles' friends were discussing his achievements, not realizing that he was able to hear, and talking in praise of his military victories. The sick man showed them that they had a misconception about *aretē*; his greatest achievement (in his view) was that no Athenian had put on black because of him. He meant that he had never used his position to destroy his political enemies within Athens; thus he had been just to his enemies, clear proof of that political *aretē* which Plutarch also discusses in the *Precepts on Public Life*. Here Plutarch does not answer the general question, whether virtue can ever be affected by the bodily condition, but denies that this was true of Pericles. Elsewhere he asserts or assumes that the bodily disposition does have an effect upon the character. Lysander is melancholy[30] and Alexander is fiery[31] and spirited in constitution. But these are lasting qualities of the bodily make-up, not new qualities accompanying a violent illness. The make-up of Lysander and Alexander begets and intensifies certain qualities. Plutarch would probably have been reluctant to accept that *aretē* can be adversely affected by the sufferings of the body, as Theophrastus seems to have argued; but we cannot do more than guess.

Because his interest is primarily in political virtue, Plutarch assumes that the character is to be inferred from political acts or publicly declared policies. A policy that aims at distributing more power or benefits to the people suggests a demagogic character; whereas one who seeks power for himself will be tyrannical, unless, like Caesar, he comes to use his power for the good of the whole state. When an individual is shown to have pursued different policies at different times, there is an apparent contradiction of characters, which gives rise to some difficulty. The *Pericles* is a striking case. Plutarch considered that Pericles[32] was an 'aristocratic nature', remote from the people in his way of life even though he was politically on the side of the people against Cimon and the aristocrats. So the first difficulty is that Pericles' early policies suggest the character of a demagogue in the bad sense, though other evidence indicates a different character. Secondly, Plutarch discovered a conflict of opinion in his sources which, in his honest way, he tried to resolve. Thucydides described Pericles' political activity as in theory a democracy, but in fact rule by the first man; whereas other writers (including Plato, though he is not named here) had accused Pericles of corrupting the people by jury-pay. Both Thucydides and Plato are authorities whose opinions must be respected, unlike the writer of comedy whose malice is obvious and can be discounted. To reconcile these views Plutarch posits that there was a change (*metabolē*) in the policies of Pericles; and he argues that the two opinions refer to two different phases of Pericles' life. But as his explanation develops, we begin to see that the change in policy is not interpreted as a fundamental change of character. The early Pericles, known to have an aristocratic nature, acts 'against nature' by taking the democratic side; later on, when his power is established, he can now act out and express his genuine qualities of leadership, by not indulging the people but by persuading and cajoling them to do what is best for Athens. The result is that Plutarch sees the earlier Pericles as a feigner, not having the character implied by his policies at that time; but the true character is indicated by his final period of unchallenged power after the ostracism of his rival Thucydides. It seems to me idle to ask whether this judgment is historically true; it is a judgment passed by Plutarch because of his assumptions, his methods and a kind of honesty in attempting to reconcile authorities whom he respects.

It follows that the biographer can always avoid having to face the difficulties of genuine change by stating instead that certain actions are 'against nature' and do not therefore reveal the true character. In order to accept this we have to put more trust in Plutarch's judgment and mode of working than the slender information of the *Lives* seems always to warrant. One might argue a particular case either way, depending on one's general attitude to the person, quite apart from any sense of fairness to the known biographical facts. The story of Dionysius II[33] illustrates this point. After his expulsion from the tyranny at Syracuse he retired into private life in Greece; the tyrannical character, the man of power, lived indolently among the harlots at Corinth. Some argued that he thereby showed his true nature as a licentious person; others maintained that these were actions 'against his nature', an attempt therefore to render himself less suspicious to the Corinthians. These are views reported by Plutarch, and they show the kind of difficulty which he sometimes experienced in detecting a man's nature. It is fair to add, however, that acting 'against nature' or feigning, as I have called it, is not a resource of which he really approves. The ideal 'politicus' will, if possible, express his own nature in his policies, though he has to take account of local circumstances. He will not assume the natures of other men, like Alcibiades, who tried to be all things in all societies. Acting 'against nature' is imposed on the 'politicus' as a temporary expedient; for the would-be tyrant it is the only way whereby he can deceive his people into granting him the power he seeks, not for their good but for his own.

Plutarch, then, though he does at times discuss change of character, finds it more acceptable to reduce two sets of discrepant actions to one. The one set then becomes the evidence for the true nature of the man; the other is explained as 'against nature', a piece of policy, sometimes in the pejorative sense. We have seen that he would be shocked by any argument that man can change from good to bad, because he thinks that it is man's nature (teleologically) to aim at virtue and that virtue is permanent. A change in the other direction would seem to him to be in accord with what he expects of the divine rationality in man. But even here he finds it difficult to think in terms of a complete change; the man who becomes better has not changed – he has, rather, undergone a retraining of his natural aptitudes. The emphasis on

139

a discoverable nature makes this the important objective for the biographer; the nature is modifiable, but cannot undergo a radical change of a kind which might seem to us, for instance, to explain certain cases of conversion.

## 4.5 CHARACTER AND COUNTENANCE[34]

Most of Plutarch's conclusions about a hero's character are drawn from the written evidence of his actions. However, he does not confine himself to this kind of material but also refers to the personal aspect of a hero as portrayed in statues. Before we consider his treatment of this evidence, it is as well to be reminded that Plutarch attributes a lower educational value to art than to biography. The artist and the biographer resemble each other only in the limited sense that they *select* their facts in order to bring out character (*Alex.* 1.3). But biography is the higher art, as Plutarch would say, since it either represents what is fine (*kalon*) for us to imitate, or expressly portrays what is not fine as an example of what to avoid. Besides, even though the comment in *Alex.* 1. suggests that the artist does portray character, another passage (*Cim.* 2.2–5) draws a distinction between art and biography which probably reflects Plutarch's views more accurately. There we read that the image, as shown in biography which represents character, is a finer thing than the image which merely exhibits the body and the face. Biography, that is, goes to the inner man; we shall therefore expect to find that Plutarch does not always assume that the character is accurately indicated by the countenance, even when the latter is known.

Before a writer can make use of iconographic evidence, whether to confirm or to deny the character that is known from a man's actions, he must make certain assumptions. He must have confidence that a given statue (to take the example with which we are concerned) is correctly attributed. The practice of the Greeks and Romans of Plutarch's day might well have made him cautious, for it was not uncommon to deprive a statue of its name and allocate it to someone else.[35] In this way a city could indulge in flattery of a benefactor without much expense to itself. Dio Chrysostom and others complained about the practice but the need for economy probably made it not uncommon. Plutarch knew that wrong attributions could be made for other reasons as well. The treasury of the Acanthians at Delphi was marked with the legend 'Brasidas and the Acanthians from their victory over the Athenians', which misled many people into thinking that the statue by the doors was a likeness of Brasidas himself. Plutarch goes on to say that it was in fact a likeness of Lysander, though he gives no evidence for this and describes the statue in such a way that it might have been any Spartan, conventionally idealized with long hair and a flowing beard (*Lys.* 1).

Another difficulty, once the question of attribution has been solved or begged, turns on the purpose of the artist, who may have intended to represent an individual or merely use him as a type. One might, for instance, make a statue of Milo in which the athlete would be subordinated to the man, or use the commission in order to glorify one's ideal of the athlete. Plutarch does not give us a general discussion of this problem and probably he did not think of it. His comments on the artistic glories of fifth-century Athens (*Per.* 13) betray little more than an enthusiasm for art that looks established and permanent even when it is new; and I doubt whether he would have had much interest in the evolution of the portrait-statue. He often uses the word likeness (*eikōn*) when speaking of statues that in his view are correctly attributed; and this term itself tends to suggest that the face as rendered by art is thought of as a copy of the living person.

Plutarch appears to use the evidence of portrait-statues in two distinct ways. He sometimes asserts that the character seen in the statue corresponds to the character known from the record of the life. He describes a statue of Marius[36] as follows: 'I have seen a stone *eikōn* of him at Ravenna in Gaul which was very appropriate to the grim and bitter character of which we hear in the tradition.' (*Mar.* 2.1) Although the remark, like many others about the personal appearance of the heroes, occurs near the beginning of the *Marius*, it is obvious that the writer has already made up his mind about the character; the evidence of the statue corroborates his judgment on the written record. We can go further and say that Plutarch would not have called this statue a fine thing; but he might have said that the statue was finely done, since the expression was appropriate to the repellent features of the character. But neither the expression nor the character is fine (*kalon*) as Plutarch understands the term.

The case of Aratus is rather similar. Here the record informs us that Aratus, when a young man, competed in the pentathlon and received a crown for a victory. The tradition, according to Plutarch, is confirmed by his statue, though perhaps we should here use the plural as he was commemorated in several Greek cities. 'The form of the athlete is apparent on his statues; his intelligent face and royal aspect do not entirely belie a huge appetite and the use of the hoe for exercise.' (*Arat.* 3.2) Athletic training is not an integral part of the education required by statesmen,[37] which accounts for the writer's embarrassment over Aratus' corpulence which he would almost rather wish away. Sulla's appearance, too, is the subject of comment; the main point here is the strange colour of Sulla's eyes, which is described in detail (*Sulla* 2.1). For his other features the reader is referred to the statues, which are evidently considered to be accessible enough to save the writer the task of delineating them. In this case the fact which has caught Plutarch's eye is known from the literary tradition rather than from the statues; but, again, there seems to be a correlation between the violence of the expression and the violence of Sulla's career.

On the other hand, Plutarch sometimes adopts the view that the facial expression (whether it is known from a statue or not) does not help to authenticate the character transmitted by the sources. In one case, that of Phocion, he has to take refuge in the idea that the character which appears in the expression completely belies the true character of the man. He refers to Phocion as having a gentle character but adds that he was grim and forbidding to meet. People who used Phocion's expression as an index of his attitude would therefore make a serious error about him. The point here is that virtue does not always put on a winsome or attractive appearance; the censorious 'eyebrows of Phocion' made a bad impression on contemporaries who preferred the more amusing ways of Chares. But virtue does not need the comic mask;[38] and, besides, the biographer uses an anecdote to show that the severe expression of Phocion had not done the Athenians any harm (*Phoc.* 5.2).

Plutarch refers to a statue in *Phoc.* 38.1 but we cannot say that he made use of it when he came to write about the hero's appearance and character. About Philopoemen, however, he is explicit; he mentions a statue of him at Delphi in order to refute the idea that this hero was 'ugly' in appearance (*Philop.* 2.1). Thus the statue is consulted, so to say, in order to correct the wrong judgment transmitted by the literary sources. One reason why Philopoemen was supposed to be ugly was that he did not bother about his clothes and personal appearance; it was therefore not surprising when a woman mistook him for an attendant and told him to help with preparing a meal. Plutarch regards this tale as evidence that people are all too ready to take the appearance for the reality; for him, however, Philopoemen's negligence of himself is a positive quality and stands for the virtue of simplicity. The impression made by the statue is here used to correct the common-sensical reading of the hero's unkempt appearance; the anecdote is purified of its coarseness and the reader is reminded that 'ugliness' is a quality of mind, not to be confused with poor clothes or lack of fashion.

It is undeniable that Plutarch did at times make use of evidence based on portrait-statues even though his treatment of the subject is sketchy and based on presuppositions which are not clearly thought out. He is ready to accept not only that the statues are attributed to the right man but also that they offer an accurate representation. Yet he treats this material in an eclectic manner, to suit his own purpose, whether it be to emphasize that there is a correspondence between the outer and the inner man or to note that there is no such connexion. He is not in any sense under the spell of physiognomical theory[39] which supposed that there was an art enabling one to read the moral construction in the face. He refers to the lore of a Chaldaean physiognomist in *Sulla* 5 but does not betray any knowledge of this arcane subject in his writings.

The references to personal appearance, from whatever source the details have come, are seldom, if ever, precise and detailed. It might be argued that in a way this testifies to good sense and discretion on Plutarch's part, at any rate as far as concerns the evidence taken from portrait-statues. That is a possible view; but it is more likely that he was not interested in details of personal appearance for their own sake, but only if they helped him to give the general cast of a hero, just as he avowedly sets out to give the *form* of a life (*Alex.* 1). He is interested, that is, in ascertaining the presence of virtue rather than in showing that a snub-nosed man has virtue. In this respect he differs noticeably from his Roman contemporary Suetonius, whose interest in this kind of information about personal features is apparently self-sustaining. The portraits in Suetonius are far more detailed and seem to be given for their own sake, just because the facts are known to the author (though not, it seems, through the medium of statues). The consequence is that the pictures of the Caesars are realistic and individual; but they are not related to the interpretation of character and the search for virtue which, for Plutarch, are the main reasons for writing biography.

## 4.6 SUMMARY AND COMPARISON WITH SUETONIUS

In the above account I have isolated and tried to analyse some of the leading ideas and assumptions which lie behind Plutarch's interest in character. The reference and scope of *proairesis* and *philotimia* can only be grasped if we remember that they are to be placed in a tradition of ethical philosophy; and one reason for transliterating these terms, instead of accepting some more or less hallowed English equivalent, is that the context of ethical theory can easily be forgotten if we use nothing but translations. I propose now to attempt a general assessment of the way in which Plutarch reads character by means of these ideas. The peculiarity of his procedure will be the more apparent if we compare his studies of character with the methods employed by Suetonius. The two contemporaries composed different forms of biography; and a brief comparison of the two will bring out their individual strengths and weaknesses.

Yet before we examine the different ways in which they construct character, we must remember that their biographical interests are qualified by their purpose as writers. We know from Plutarch's own words what his objectives are; to improve himself and his readers and to impress upon us the importance of political *aretē*. But Suetonius does not give us any such policy-statement; we do not know his own version of his programme, though we can be certain that his aim is not to improve in the same good-hearted way envisaged by Plutarch. He is horrified by vice and admires virtue, but enthusiasm for virtue does not seem to enjoy the same pride of place as in Plutarch. Any reader of Suetonius comes to feel that the dry, accurate description of vices and faults called forth the best energies and talents of the writer. The method of dry cataloguing, that is, achieves different effects according to the nature of the subject-matter; it will make virtue, if the subject has virtue, seem less warm and near to those whom it should assist; whereas, by recording the details of vice, it inspires a curiosity about vice that is only in part offset by the cool, clinical manner. It is as though Suetonius were a writer of pornography whose deficiencies of imagination were helped out by an encyclopaedic knowledge of the exact medical terms.

I am not saying that the description of bad emperors was intended by Suetonius to lead his readers on to emulate their excesses. Although there is no formal policy-statement, I am sure that Suetonius would have rejected any programme save that of helping towards moral improvement. What must be emphasized is that Suetonius' attitude – his readiness to be on equal terms with vice or virtue, as the case demands – is not itself so positive a recommendation of virtue as Plutarch's concentration on the good. If Suetonius' purpose was to improve future emperors, he would have helped it by giving even more space than he does to the slim virtues of the wicked; for when vice is described in Suetonian detail it becomes attractive to the reader, who can easily be beguiled by the principle that one must have chapter and verse for what to avoid as well as for what to imitate.

I have indicated that Suetonius' purpose, which is not, admittedly, the subject of a formal statement, comes through to us with different colours from that of Plutarch. In the second place, we must make some allowance for the fact that the two authors stand in a different relationship to their subjects. Once Suetonius had decided to write about the Caesars and had made his initial choice, there was, in a sense, no further room to manoeuvre; after he had finished one *Life* he simply went on to its chronological successor. Plutarch, on the other hand, because he was committed to depicting men with *aretē*, felt that he was able to choose from the whole range of ancient history as he knew it. The nature of his subject and the manner of his approach gave him some freedom to accept or reject a particular topic. If he had chosen a different line and confined himself, let us say, to the biographies of exceptional men in the fifth century BC, he might have found some personal repugnance in writing the life of a Pausanias. But because he was able to choose and pair off as he thought fit, he could, for the most part, take models of virtue rather than of vice; and when he does write about inferior men, as with Antony and Demetrius, he can point clearly to his theory as a justification for that kind of subject. In short, we can say that Suetonius' subjects are chosen for him by the framework of imperial history; whereas Plutarch, though some of his choices may seem obvious to us, enjoys considerable freedom in relation to the moral theme that he has selected.

I turn now to the depiction of character. There are numerous differences between the two writers' general method of bringing the character out or making their judgment clear. Two of these seem to be especially important. Firstly, we have noticed that a Plutarchan *Life* uses the chronological sequence; the hero's early years, maturity and old age are described in that order, and the character emerges or is understood with reference to this natural time-scheme. Suetonius, however, though he does not abandon this type of chronological background entirely, is notorious for his use of another method. In the *Augustus* (9) he proposes to outline the 'parts' of Augustus' life not chronologically but according to their kinds, so that these can stand out the more sharply and be better known. The implication is that the character will be presented through certain divisions of the material made by the author; for example his civil wars, foreign wars and offices or appointments. The break with an obvious time-sequence is complete; the civil wars of Augustus, in fact, do all occur in his relatively early career, but the account of the offices and appointments refers to the whole of his very long life. A similar principle[40] is to be observed in the *Lives* of Caligula and Nero; the virtues of Caligula, such as they are, have been illustrated by the end of *Cal.* 21, when Suetonius says: 'So far we have had the story of him as *princeps*; the rest is the story of a ghastly prodigy.' This is not a time-division, as one might expect from the adverb 'so far'; it is instead an overdrawn, almost melodramatic, contrast between the good and the villainous ruler. What makes Caligula good or villainous may be an incident or anecdote taken from any period in his relatively short reign.

This procedure may have the advantage of clarity in that it marks off the laudable acts of Caligula from the disreputable; but it cannot begin to answer the question which must occur to anyone with the least flair for biography; how can Caligula be both good and bad at the same time? Suetonius, probably, would say that in fact Caligula was more of a 'ghastly prodigy' than a good ruler (*princeps*), for he seems to regard this reign as a grim time, thanks to the character of the emperor. But the method of depicting the character, through the categories of good and bad, does not have the advantages (or raise the interesting questions) that are associated with a time-scheme, even when it is fairly rudimentary as with Plutarch.

The second difference is not unconnected with Suetonius' rejection of the time-scheme. He brings out character by listing an emperor's virtues or vices and by substantiating these with anecdotes. The method here is derived from rhetoric and is known as *divisio*,[41] the habit of formal enumeration. Now this device can also operate by relating incidents and stories without explicitly stating what quality they illustrate; the experienced reader (the rhetorically adept, so to say) will not be bothered or confused by the absence of a heading. This method of describing a character, derived from a technique of rhetoric, leads to a piece-meal effect and resembles one of the modes employed in panegyric; it is a description by qualities, not by phases of a life, and has therefore some affinity with part of Xenophon's *Agesilaus*. The method of Plutarch is quite different. He often, it is true, indicates the prime or dominant qualities near the beginning of a *Life*, as, for example, with the justice of Titus or the gentleness of Fabius and Pericles. But the narrative is not confined to documenting the quality which introduces a *Life*; the begining of a *Life* is a convenient place for Plutarch to indicate what he has noticed as one of the chief characteristics, for one of his aims (*Alex.* 1) is to seize upon the kind of life, that is, to render its general sense. Yet Plutarch's narrative does have a certain life that is independent of the character-notation, but this is much rarer with Suetonius. It is in a way easier to remember a Plutarchan character, to state broadly his virtue and to have a fairly clear picture of his choice (*proairesis*). But a Suetonian character does not fix itself upon our attention in the same way; it is the sum of all its parts and details which are already, in Suetonius, expressed in summary fashion. Yet even so the character of a Suetonian biography seems to come out as a mechanical mixture rather than a true blend of qualities.

The actual rendering of character in Suetonius is often developed through the same type of anecdote and incident as in Plutarch. Only in two cases, however, those of Caesar and Galba, are we in a position to make a detailed comparison. The reader of Plutarch's *Caesar*, who then turns to the account by Suetonius, should not attach too much importance to the agreements and differences over individual items of fact. The important fact about a *Life* by Plutarch is that the author's terminology, as I have shown above, implies a model of human behaviour whose component parts are taken from philosophical and moral theory. Both in Suetonius and in Plutarch there are numerous incidents which suggest to both writers the view that Caesar always aimed at supreme power, and they interpret the events of the early career with the later successes in mind. Yet the experienced reader of Plutarch knows that Caesar's choice (*proairesis*) is to be judged by the standards expected of the 'politicus'. Deception, for instance, is a mode of activity more characteristic of the tyrant and demagogue. But Plutarch does not condemn Caesar for seeking to impose on the Romans an alien form of government. He argues that the condition of the age demanded an absolutist form, which in fact proved to be less objectionable because of the gentle character of the ruler. These presuppositions are not present in Suetonius' version, who has no background idea like that of the good 'politicus' and his choice, by which he can measure the incidents known to him. Nor does Suetonius use an idea like the force of ambition (*philotimia*) which is adduced in many places to account for the energy shown by Plutarch's Caesar.[42] The virtues and vices reported by Suetonius do not have their place in an overall theory of man. They are not interconnected by a philosophical theory which puts greater value on certain actions (except in the obvious sense that virtue is preferred to vice). Similarly, too, Plutarch's *Galba* begins with general reflexions on spirit (*thumos*) which have no parallel in Suetonius.

Suetonius does have values of a kind but they are inherited Roman ones. An emperor's management of wealth is not treated, as with Plutarch, in the light of a theory about the function of virtue with regard to wealth. Instead, emperors are admired or praised if they have celebrated games on the grand scale, because this was a service traditionally expected of Roman aristocrats and the emperor is the heir of this tradition. Meanness about money (*parsimonia*) is not studied in the light of economic need but seen as a failure to live up to aristocratic munificence. Thus Suetonius does have a view about the place of wealth in the scheme of things, but it is a given, Roman scheme, not theoretically explicable like Plutarch's. We may add another example, the virtue of clemency (*clementia*). The emphasis on this virtue or on its absence was determined in the first place by the historical propaganda of Caesar's war against Pompey and by the claims of succeeding emperors. No reader of Suetonius can say that *clementia* is (in the *Caesars*) related to a theory of kingship or power except in the general sense that it is a good thing; but the reader of Plutarch does know that the similar virtue of leniency (*epieikeia*) is of use to the ruler as well as to the ruled.

The fact is that the virtues of an emperor, according to Suetonius, are not the virtues of a 'politicus' according to Plutarch. Suetonius, for example, does not grant the same primacy to justice; he does not have an anecdotal section illustrating this virtue, in the way that he does at times begin with *clementia, moderatio* or *pietas* and substantiate them. He mentions the justice of Galba, but only in passing. This is perhaps the clearest proof of all that his political values are different from those of Plutarch. I do not mean that he therefore thinks of justice as an unimportant virtue. But, clearly, it is not a display-virtue of which an aristocrat can be proud; as the virtue which is accessible to all men it is likely to have a subordinate position compared with other virtues which exhibit the superiority of the man who displays them, as the man who shows *clementia* must be (by definition) superior in power or justice. The just man has a virtue that is within the reach of all, which does not exactly become a Roman emperor. It is true that Suetonius devotes considerable space to some emperors' interest in seeing that the courts were conducted properly. But he does not seem to use this as evidence for an emperor having the quality of justice; Claudius' enthusiasm for taking part in the legal process becomes evidence for numerous qualities – his foresight, his folly, even his forbearance (*patientia*), but his justice is not explicitly named, even though one story in particular indicates that Claudius prided himself on his fairness. The emperor, in brief, when he is good, commends himself to his subjects by virtues which mitigate by grace the rigour and severity of absolute rule; the justice applauded by Plutarch comes near to being a virtue for equals in a society of equals. Suetonius, here, is probably more realistic.

I have suggested that the emphasis in Suetonius falls elsewhere than in Plutarch because he has no over-riding concern with man as 'politicus'. Yet one Suetonian virtue *is* expressed in language which seems to approximate to some of Plutarch's ideas under this heading. I refer here to the term *civilis*,[43] by which Suetonius refers to a variety of modes of behaviour which he commends. Used of Germanicus it compliments him on the fact that he entered free and federate cities without the *fasces*, thereby concealing from the inhabitants the visible signs of Roman magistracy. With Claudius it denotes his restraint in accepting honorific titles; and in the cases of Julius and Vespasian it commends the right way in which the man of power should deal with insults. It is *civile* to return an insult, though one should not initiate a slanging-match; and, similarly, it is *civile* not to attach too much weight to written insults. To be *civilis*, then, is to conduct oneself in certain areas as though one were on a par with the rest of the citizens. But since emperors are in fact exalted above their subjects, this is a virtue of make-believe and is a long way removed from what it means to be a good 'politicus' in Plutarch, even though the words suggest that they are about the same thing, a kind of citizenliness. The Plutarchan 'politicus', whatever his official position, always remains a citizen and is (or should be) concerned to promote the inter-dependence of all citizens. When he acts like a 'politicus', as we have seen, he is often out to remove serious discords from the body politic. The better emperors in Suetonius do add to the amenity of life, when they act in a way that is *civile*; but it must be said that the insistence on this quality can only occur in a society where one man is raised by law and custom above all others.

There is, apparently, rather more in common between the two writers in their attitude towards the question whether man has a persisting, more or less uniform nature, that constitutes his charac-ter. Just as Plutarch speaks of *phusis*, so does Suetonius write of *natura*. Like Plutarch, too, Suetonius at times finds himself in difficulties of a kind when the later stages of a career seem to indicate a different character from that which is suggested by the earlier. He solves these difficulties without indicating that he has any awareness that it is possible for character to change. The allegations about Augustus' early sexual misconduct are said to be refuted by the chastity of his later life. In other cases the contrast is so glaring that it calls for special comment, as with Tiberius[44] and Domitian. Because Suetonius regards both emperors as bad at the end, he feels called upon to explain away their apparent, early virtues. Thus he says of the early Domitian that 'he put on a marvellous pretence of moderation', which was belied by later events when the true Domitian came through and showed that his blushing was feigned. Suetonius, then, has here adopted one of the solutions to be found in Plutarch, that a contrast is to be explained in terms of an initial pretence. The assumption is that the nature can only be forced against the grain for so long; in the end the real nature will prevail and arraign the earlier behaviour as a piece of acting. Both writers, then, seem to share the view that there is a knowable nature; and we have seen that both at times make use of the pretence-solution as a way of avoiding any discussion of change. Apart from these points, it is fair to say that there are in Plutarch several indications that he did acknowledge the difficulties of interpreting the diverse actions of the same character. Suetonius, I would suggest, is not to be blamed for not raising such questions; it is simply that his level of theoretical interest is lower than Plutarch's. I should emphasize that this is not to say that he is for that reason inferior as a biographer – it is not the purpose of this comparison to allot marks.

As we have already glanced at the different ways in which they infer the character from the face, I will conclude this account by pointing to the special virtues of both. Plutarch's strengths are numerous; his purpose is to describe and recommend *aretē* and he works within a tradition that has a language enriched by ethical discussion. He has, besides, a capacity for noticing questions of theoretical interest that bear on character. If one were to look for such qualities in Suetonius, one would be disappointed. It is not obvious that his aim is to raise the standards of the Roman emperors, even though he expresses his aversion for vice. He is even less of a composer than Plutarch, and the technique of *divisio* strikes the reader as simple and laborious. Yet his merits are considerable; he was, after all, much nearer in time to most of his subjects than Plutarch was and he had an eye for recording details for their own sake, which is missing in the Greek. The result is that in a few words he can convey to us something authentic or recognizable about a character; at his best he writes with a terse realism that has great appeal precisely because it seems to be reporting the character as it really was. The absence of didacticism should not be over-emphasized, but it has, very probably, contributed to one's sense that Suetonius is concerned with the real man rather than with a paradigm of vice or virtue.

# 5

# *History: Some Problems of Method*

I have already argued in Chapter 1 that the *Lives* are to be regarded as a form of historical writing. Not only did Plutarch take many of his facts from historians; he was also indebted to them for some of the methods and principles used in the evaluation of his material, though it must be remembered that his reading of character from the actions was mainly based on his own scheme of values. In this chapter I shall discuss some questions of method and composition in order to indicate how Plutarch resembles and differs from historians.

The remarks about biographical method in the *Alexander* (1.2), famous though they are, are not the only pronouncement of a theoretical kind. In section 1 I examine some passages from other *Lives* which are relevant to the biographer's conception of his task and which, above all, illuminate his use of the emphases already created by historians. It was sometimes difficult for Plutarch to decide what to omit or include because the sources, particularly those relating to early times, contained much that seemed incredible. He therefore uses the historian's criterion of probability to help him accept or reject particular traditions; but his idea of what is probable tells us a good deal about his own beliefs (section 2).

Greek and Roman historians were expected to give a true and impartial account that would be found readable. To a large extent the demand that history should be good literature did the subject a disservice, for the energies of writers were diverted to the task of getting their presentation right instead of reflecting on their methods. One way of enhancing a tale was to introduce dramatic scenes of pity and emotion. Section 3 is a discussion of Plutarch's views on 'tragic history' and of whether this feature is present in the *Lives*. Yet another way of making history more lively, of turning it into a near-drama, was to see the historical process as a scene of conflict or cooperation between virtue and fortune. In section 4 I examine those *Lives* in which there are traces of this view.

Finally, there is the important question of the writer's attitude to his subject. Plutarch's own tendency was to put the kindliest interpretation on others' conduct, and his own work is characterized by a freedom from malice in which he takes special pride. At the same time he was perhaps over-sensitive to what he regarded as the malice (*kakoētheia*) in some of his sources (section 5).

## 5.1 THE BIOGRAPHER'S DEBT TO HISTORIANS

In Chapter 1 I drew attention to a passage in the *Alexander* (1.2) where Plutarch apparently differentiates between the methods of the biographer and the historian. I was there concerned to argue that historians had not neglected the study and presentation of character; and that Plutarch's use of 'minor events, sayings and jests' is sometimes a way of producing a compendious history rather than biography for its own sake. The biographer therefore is not so far removed from the historian as his theoretical statement would make it seem. Indeed, these remarks about biographical method were probably stimulated by the particular matter in hand, the problem of writing the *Lives* of Alexander and Caesar. Plutarch felt that the Alexander story offered more material than he required or was used to putting into the shape of a biography; yet even so the resulting *Life* is longer than a good many in the extant corpus. But the *Alexander* was not the only subject that prompted Plutarch to reflect on or explain his methods. In what follows I give an account of other passages which are relevant to a study of biographical methods, though they have not usually been examined in this context.[1]

In two other *Lives* with Greek sources, the *Nicias* and the *Artaxerxes*, there are comments on method which were occasioned by the fact that in both cases the subjects had been authoritatively treated already. The feeling of awe in the presence of a classic is especially pronounced in the *Nicias*; Plutarch introduces this *Life* by saying that it is not out of the way to make a comparison between Crassus and the Parthian disaster on the one hand and Nicias and the Sicilian disaster on the other. The mention of Sicily (1.1) reminds Plutarch that this episode (the Sicilian expedition with Nicias as the leading general) occupies a large part of the *Life*. He will seem, therefore, to be treading on ground that has already been mapped by the great Thucydides. Clearly, Plutarch is thinking of the sixth and seventh books of which he speaks with great admiration; the historian is here said to be at his most moving and to have composed an account that is unrivalled for its vividness and complexity. This suggestion of indebtedness to Thucydides is borne out by a brief examination of the *Life*, for a good two-thirds are devoted to the Athenian invasion of Sicily and the part played by Nicias. Thus most of the *Life* is about three years in the lifetime of the hero (415–413 BC), though his generalship during the Archidamian war had been distinguished and he had made a name for himself as a politician between 421 and 415 BC. It seems, then, that Plutarch's emphasis in this *Life* is affected by his impression of part of the historian's narrative. He might have distributed his account differently and given more space to the earlier and middle phases of Nicias' career; a modern study of Nicias and his times would surely attempt to do that. Plutarch's justification could well be that, after all, the sixth and seventh books of Thucydides contain the most consecutive writing about this hero.

It is important to make clear this dependence on Thucydides and the ensuing concentration on the last years of Nicias, because Plutarch himself does not raise the matter for us but directs our attention to the historian's style. He does not want his readers to suppose that he intends to set up his work as a piece of fine writing in competition with a masterpiece. He maintains that stylistic emulation is always a trivial exercise; and when the model is so especially outstanding, the idea of surpassing it is even more ludicrous.

In fact Plutarch refers to two accounts as outstanding, those of Thucydides and Philistus. To set up one's style against them would be to commit the error of Timaeus,[2] who sought to liven up existing histories by introducing factitious bits of drama. For instance, he suggested that the mutilation of the Hermae was a divine sign, a warning to Athens that she would be defeated by the Syracusan general Hermocrates. In Plutarch's view this feeble attempt at creating drama out of name-play is a poor substitute for the authentic emotional qualities to be found in Thucydides. But the style of a Thucydides is beyond the biographer's reach; indeed, as we saw earlier, fine writing does not form part of the objectives of biography.

Thus the emphasis of the *Nicias* is determined by an emphasis already created by Thucydides; and probably this unacknowledged borrowing is even more of a compliment to the historian than the explicit admiration for his style. Plutarch next refers to the subject-matter which is here common ground for the historian and the biographer. 'Since it is not possible to omit the actions related by Thucydides and Philistus – for these actions above all comprehend the character and disposition of the man which were unfolded through many great incidents – I shall run through these briefly, taking the essential points, so that I shall not appear to be wholly negligent and idle. I have also tried to assemble items that are unknown to most people, such as remarks made here or there by others or facts connected with ancient dedications or decrees. My purpose is not to gather useless information but to hand on facts that are relevant to the understanding of character.' (*Nic.* 1.5) We might now suppose that there is at least as much information about character to be gleaned from the non-Thucydidean items as from the summary version of historical events. But the impression made by the *Nicias* does not exactly correspond to the ideas suggested in this passage. No one can avoid noticing that Thucydides is used in a condensed way; but it is not possible to agree that the supplementary material contributes much to the understanding of character. The main features or traits are drawn from an account of the major historical events. Thus Plutarch makes much of the caution[3] of Nicias, which is presented as a virtue in the earlier part of the Peloponnesian War; but this quality was inopportune during the Sicilian expedition, when Nicias should have been more aggressive. The judgment is perfectly allowable but is derived from reflexion on the historian's events rather than the biographer's trivia. The same can be said of Nicias' courage, which is attested by his perseverance when suffering from kidney disease (17.3–18.1). Perhaps the most important factor of all is his superstition (*deisidaimonia*), which becomes prominent when the Athenian plan to retreat is impeded by the lunar eclipse (23). These are qualities of character which were elicited by putting biographical questions to Thucydides' narrative. Other material is less significant than the introduction would have us believe. There is, for instance, a good deal of this supplementary matter in (13), where Plutarch describes the incidents and omens that preceded the departure of the expedition. The chapter tells us hardly anything about Nicias' character (or anyone else's), though a modern reader would, rightly or wrongly, read it as a crude dramatic pointer to the rest of the tale. Another example, on a smaller scale still, is the epigram attributed to Euripides (17.4), commemorating the eight victories of the Athenians in Sicily. If this is meant to show the courage of Nicias and the Athenians, the reader is asked to draw a large conclusion from minor evidence. It seems, then, that non-Thucydidean evidence has not contributed as much to the creation of Nicias' character as we might expect on the basis of the prefatory remarks, which look somewhat defensive on a second or third reading. I do not therefore mean to suggest that Plutarch was dishonest; but he could not escape from the Nicias mediated by Thucydides and his consciousness of this debt made him claim more for his supplementary material than it deserves.

In some ways the *Artaxerxes* presents us with a similar problem. Here too Plutarch acknowledges the presence of a revered classic which cannot be improved upon. 'The battle [of Cunaxa][4] has been described by many writers and Xenophon almost brings it before our very eyes. He makes the reader deeply affected as though the events were taking place now, not in the past, and the reader comes to participate in the danger because of the writer's vividness (*enargeia*). It is then foolish to tell the story over again, except for those worthwhile points which Xenophon has omitted.' (*Art.* 8.1) There is here no explicit reference to the character-value of Xenophon's narrative; but the passage resembles the beginning of the *Nicias* in that here too Plutarch is conscious of a stylistic master-piece, an achievement which was beyond his talents and outside his biographical purpose. Yet, as we read on, we become aware that he has done little if anything to supply Xenophon's omissions. The rest of the chapter describes how the Greek mercenary com-mander, Clearchus, refused to budge from his position but kept his forces close to the river in order to avoid being encircled by the Persians. It is this fact, which is also in Xenophon, that provides material for something of a character-contrast between Cyrus and Clearchus. For the latter is criticized by Plutarch on the grounds that if he was going to make safety his prime objective he would have done best to stay at home. The caution of the Greek (which would normally be a virtue) is more culpable than the over-confidence of Cyrus. Xenophon himself has no such comment, though he reports the motives which made Clearchus act as he did; in fact his obituary of Clearchus gives him high praise as a general and man of action.[5]

The supplement to Xenophon does not appear until we reach the account of Cyrus' death, which was reported only briefly by Xenophon, because, as Plutarch says, he was not himself present. Here Plutarch turns to two lesser writers, Deinon and Ctesias,[6] and gives their versions, though he says that he has curtailed Ctesias and remarks drily about his narrative – 'Such is the tale told by Ctesias by means of which he puts Cyrus to death as though he were using a blunt dagger.' (*Art.* 11.11) Indeed Plutarch expresses some scepticism about the veracity of these other historians; and he could hardly have supposed that we would think of them as contributing to our knowledge of Cyrus' character, if he disparages them by comparison with the inimitable Xenophon. I do not think that these other narratives were pressed into service because they were felt to contain useful material for the student of character. The explanation should rather take the following line. Xenophon's battle was too well known (and too well done) to bear repetition; and the characters could be sketched adequately from the tactics described by Xenophon. But Plutarch's own story could not pass over the battle of Cunaxa so rapidly; we should note that the *Artaxerxes* is not all that long a *Life* anyway and can fairly assume that the biographer was not overwhelmed with material. He chose therefore to add something from Deinon and Ctesias simply to satisfy his readers' curiosity about the last moments of Cyrus; and felt that he could use them presumably because their works were less well-known. The prime need here was not to let the story of Cunaxa drop too abruptly; as we have noticed before, there are times when the story seems to take over and exercises its own claim. But Ctesias is not merely brought in for this reason alone, to make an unreliable report on a subject not in Xenophon. Plutarch distrusts him for the reason that he over-praised and championed

Clearchus (*Art.* 13.7); whereas Plutarch, for his part, thought rather less of Clearchus, disliking him partly because he was a mercenary, partly because he failed as a subordinate. Thus Plutarch's use of Ctesias is eventually made to bear on the theme of character, though the point does not become clear till we have left the battle of Cunaxa.

In these *Lives* the problems facing Plutarch were different from those in the *Alexander*. There he seemed to have more facts at his disposal than he needed, unless he were to make the *Life* excessively long. Thus his method of using 'minor events' enabled him to cut down on some of the battles and to abbreviate the whole. But, with the *Nicias* and the *Artaxerxes*, he had historical authorities who were supreme in style and who also offered the essential events from which he could construct a character. In order to avoid repetition, he needed his method to amplify and produce variants. There was no intrinsic defect in the method which would prevent this; but the trouble lay in his other sources. In the one case they were too sparse to add significantly to Thucydides; in the other, they were too unreliable, except that they make a diversion and lay a foundation for Plutarch's later criticism of Ctesias. The famous method is still present but offers us less in the way of information about character than Plutarch's reading of Thucydides and Xenophon.

With the Roman *Lives* Plutarch did not have to take account of the fact that the field was already dominated by a classic version. Whatever his knowledge of Latin,[7] he had not read its literature during his formative years and he could not have been described as learned in both tongues, though the compliment might well have been justly applied to some of his Roman friends. Thus his difficulties in composing the Roman *Lives* were of a different order, since Greek predecessors like Polybius and Dionysius were not masters of style like Thucydides. Yet here too the material for a *Life* was sometimes more than the writer felt he could handle, as we see from the *Pompey* (8.6). After describing Pompey's achievements on the side of Sulla, Plutarch goes on to mention that he was sent to Gaul to assist Metellus and achieved marvellous feats against the enemy. 'But though Pompey's deeds at that time were remarkable in themselves, they are outdone by the number and magnitude of his later battles and wars; I was therefore afraid to disturb them [his Gallic exploits], lest, if I spend too long on his early achievements, I fail to deal with his greatest actions and sufferings which above all reveal his character.'[8] There is here no question of rejecting some outstanding actions because they do not show character so well as minor events. Instead Plutarch states a preference for one set of such actions as against another; for him Pompey's character can be adequately rendered by studying his wars against Mithridates and the various stages of the civil war with Caesar. These were subjects which also appealed to historians more than the career of the young Pompey; and perhaps one reason why Plutarch exercised his choice in this way was that the Roman civil wars would not seem as familiar to him as the Peloponnesian War and the expedition of Cyrus.

A remark in the *Galba* seems to point in the same direction. Though he here (2.5) distinguishes between pragmatic[9] history which reports events in detail and his own form of biography, he makes an important qualification : 'not even I should omit those actions and sufferings of the Caesars which are worth mentioning.' As the *Life* shows, he is here heavily indebted to the facts which were to attract the historian, as we see by comparing him with Tacitus, and to the historian's emphasis, for he writes almost entirely of Galba-imperator and barely touches on the rest of his seventy years. Thus the effect of the narrative in this *Life* is, once again, to make him draw close to the material which a historian would use, and one begins to think that the crucial difference between him and Tacitus is one of temperament and values. For Plutarch the year of the four emperors illustrates the difficulties that arise when military spirit fails to obey the ruling power; unless the army is a disciplined body the ruler has no chance to save and organize his people. This simple political lesson would not have sufficed the pessimistic energy of Tacitus.

These stray remarks in other *Lives* show that Plutarch's reflexions on method in the *Alexander* are not to be taken in isolation. It seems fair to conclude that the Alexander-method was always available, though the manner of applying it varied from one *Life* to another. The *Alexander* itself was something of a special case, providing the biographer with more material than he required. In other *Lives* the need for an abbreviating method was less keenly felt. In the *Nicias* the method is really needed to supply variations and additions to Thucydides, though the claim is not justified by the result. And in two Roman *Lives* Plutarch does not seem to have felt any awkwardness about using major events, though in these cases we are less clear about his difficulties than in the *Nicias* and *Artaxerxes*.

## 5.2 THE PROBABLE

It was an accepted practice for ancient historians to decide between different or conflicting versions of the same event by appealing to the criterion of probability (*eikos*).[10] As source-criticism in the modern sense was virtually unknown, writers could do little else than keep in mind the more obvious bias or prejudice of their sources and follow what seemed to be the more likely account. But, in general, they failed to realize that deciding on what is likely or probable is a more complicated task than would appear to common sense; for even the unlikely, provided we can be certain that it has happened, becomes by that very fact likely.[11] And a writer who relied on what is likely in terms of his own society as a means of interpreting the culture of another society would not now succeed as a critic or historian. Plutarch sometimes makes use of this criterion of probability to decide between variants and in this way he uses a technique that historians would have recognized. But his application of it to particular cases frequently reveals assumptions that are peculiar to him or specially characteristic of his thought.

The clearest acknowledgment of his dependence on the probable comes in the introduction of the *Theseus*. He there tells Sosius Senecio that after completing the lives of Lycurgus and Numa he has exhausted the period 'which is accessible to a likely account and gives a firm footing to enquiry that adheres to facts'. But as he has gone thus far, it seems not unreasonable to go back to Romulus and match him with Theseus as the founder of Athens. He then prays that it may be possible to purify what is mythical by means of reason and so come to a view of what actually happened. But in cases where 'the mythical defies what is credible and does not admit the admixture of probability', he hopes that his readers will be indulgent and forgiving to his version of antiquity. To go as

161

far back as this, he suggests, in a comparison with maps, is like filling in the details beyond the limits of the known world.

In this passage Plutarch distinguishes in broad terms between a mythical and a historical period. If we are to take him literally, it seems that only the *Romulus* and the *Theseus* of the extant *Lives* fall within the mythical period. But, as he says himself, he found it difficult to be sure of anything about Lycurgus (*Lyc.* 1), and, in a lesser way, he had a similar problem with Numa. It seems reasonable therefore to treat all these *Lives* as falling within the mythical period; all of them were the subject of traditions which seemed implausible to the ancients, and the tales of this period had therefore to be deciphered in the light of what was likely or probable.

It had long been accepted that historians should not traffic in 'myth', by which was meant an account of events that seems inconsistent with what is known or expected of ordinary human behaviour. Plutarch employs this distinction between 'myth' and 'history' in several places in these *Lives* from the mythical period. Thus, in the *Romulus* (2–3), he contrasts the 'utterly mythical' versions of Romulus' birth with another account, attributed to Diocles and Fabius Pictor,[12] that is said to be credible and have most witnesses supporting it. (There is a suggestion here, as often, that counting heads is a way of confirming what is felt to be the probable account.) The mythical version about Romulus states that Tarchetius, a cruel king of Alba, found a phallus on the central hearth in his house. An oracle was consulted and replied that a virgin should have intercourse with the object; the girl would subsequently give birth to a child outstanding in 'virtue and fortune'. Since Tarchetius' daughter refused to offer herself to the phallus, her place was taken by one of her maids. Eventually the maid gave birth to twins who were exposed to die by a river; however, they were fostered by a she-wolf and rescued by a herdsman; when they grew up they attacked and killed Tarchetius.

The 'more credible' or likely version refers to the familiar story of Amulius and Numitor (though this account is said to have different sub-versions which are only specified in part). The gist of the tale is that Amulius wished to retain power for his family and tried to prevent Numitor's daughter Silvia from marrying. Nevertheless she became pregnant and gave birth to twins who were exposed but saved. This account is felt to be more credible because it sets the birth of Romulus within a familiar context of power-politics and excludes the improbability of intercourse with the phallus, though Plutarch does not comment specifically on this.[13]

It is interesting here to compare the so-called historian's approach to this question, for Dionysius of Halicarnassus allots some space to the versions of Romulus' birth. One account said that the father was a former suitor of Silvia's; another, that it was Amulius himself, but disguised; and a third (evidently the commonest) that it was an image of the divine power (*daimōn*) who presided over a sacred grove which Silvia had entered. Dionysius comments on this like a historian who feels that he is on the verge of a discussion which belongs to philosophy rather than to sober history. 'It is not opportune to take sides on the question; what philosophers have already written is adequate – the question is whether we should reject the story on the grounds that human wickedness has been ascribed to gods . . . or whether we should admit the story on the grounds that all that exists within the universe is intermingled, and that there is a third nature between god and man, the class of *daimones*, which mixes at one time with gods, at another with human being.' (*Ant. Rom.* i 77) Dionysius does not say, as we might expect him to, that the story of a divine father was invented to make the origins of Rome more august. He hints at the possibility that the story is reconcilable with a certain view about the place of *daimones*, intermediary between gods and men; but he does not commit himself either to rejecting the story completely or accepting it. Tentatively, he airs some knowledge of philosophy, but not because he believes in it; he then observes the historian's convention about not letting digressions go too far and returns to narrative.

Plutarch does not express an opinion about what exactly is unlikely in the story of the phallus. But it would be wrong to draw the conclusion that the historian is more prepared to go outside his brief than the biographer (though we have noticed that the biographer follows to some extent the historian's rules about brevity of digression). A passage in the *Numa* (4) is more typical of Plutarch, and it is instructive to compare his remarks on Egeria with Dionysius on the subject of the *daimōn* committing rape. The improbable or mythical story about Numa was that he cohabited with a *daimōn* called Egeria, who loved him. Plutarch gives a long comment on this, the sort of comment which Dionysius starts but refuses to develop. 'It is, I am sure, reasonable that god, who is characterized by love of man rather than love of horses or birds, should want to associate with men who are outstandingly good, and would not disdain or spurn the company of a pious and moderate human being. But it is difficult to be persuaded that a god or *daimōn* can have intercourse or take delight in a human body. Now the Egyptians say, not implausibly, that it is not impossible for the breath of a god to have intercourse with a woman and beget progeny, but that a male cannot have bodily intercourse with a goddess; but they are overlooking the principle that that which is mixed (in intercourse) grants to that with which it is mixed an equality of association. It would be only fitting for a god to have affection for man, and that this should develop into a loving concern with character and virtue (*aretē*).' He then refers to stories about gods associating with poets and concludes: 'Can it be right . . . not to believe that the divine did associate with Zaleucus, Minos, Zoroaster, Numa and Lycurgus, the rulers of kingdoms and organizers of states? Or is it not likely that the gods in all seriousness mixed with these men, in order to teach them and exhort them to the best, whereas they associated with poets, if they ever did, as an amusement? If anyone disagrees, as Bacchylides says,[14] the way is broad. There is also another explanation which has some merit; it is that Lycurgus and Numa and their like, who ruled over insubordinate peoples and introduced great political changes, claimed the repute of being associated with god, as a way of achieving the security of those for whose benefit they made this pretence.'

Now Plutarch seems to leave it open, whether we should accept the justifying rationalism of his first explanation or follow the more sceptical, Polybian argument of the second. But what he does make plain about the first theory is this; a seemingly improbable story can be shown to be compatible with the author's views about virtue (*aretē*) and the attitude of the gods to men who have virtue. We may compare the passage in *Thes.-Rom. comp.* 1.5–7 about Ariadne's love for Theseus, which is explained by the philosophers' definition of love (*erōs*) as 'the service of the gods directed towards the care and safety of the young'. An improbable fact, the relationship between Numa and Egeria, is shown to be probable in the light of the author's philosophical convictions. Thus, in this case, he is near to accepting the authenticity of a tale on the grounds that it fits his theory of values; whether something happened or not in history can be decided by whether it illustrates a philosophical truth or not. In short, in discussing this particular improbability, Plutarch brings in his beliefs, as the historian Dionysius does not. Of course, he does not exclude another possibility, as we see; but he has used the criterion of the 'probable' in such a way that it is only possible to accept if we also accept Plutarch's beliefs.

I have discussed this instance at some length because it is not a story about mundane events but concerns the relationship between god and mankind. This kind of excursus on 'the probable' is not an isolated case among stories from the earlier periods of history. Plutarch felt challenged by those stories which appeared to cast doubt on his own belief that the human body is mortal whereas the soul is divine and immortal. It is for this reason that he is troubled by the legend about Romulus' death, according to which Romulus was taken up to heaven and his body was never found again.[15] After citing some Greek parallels, Plutarch remarks with some sharpness that the authors of these tales 'contrary to what is probable are raising the mortal parts of human nature to the divine along with the parts which are divine' (*Rom.* 28.7). He means, firstly, that we cannot deny that virtue (*aretē*) has a close relationship with the gods; but that the body, being earth, can have no such contact with the heavens. There is a scale whereby virtue does ascend to the peak of divinity, but there is no need to suppose that the bodies of good men accompany their virtue on this journey – this is 'against nature'. Thus in this case the 'myth' is flatly rejected because it conflicts with Plutarch's views about the soul and body. But though he is sure that man's body cannot rise, he is less certain that god needs a body to do what man does. In the *Coriolanus* (38) he refers to a story that a statue uttered distinct words. It seems improbable because it is contrary to our experience; nevertheless we should remember the principle that the divine power is marvellous, quite different from the nature of man; and this principle is here on the side of those who believe the story because they are impressed by the persuasive evidence of history and are fervent admirers of the gods.

In one of these cases, the alleged association of Numa and Egeria, the writer's enthusiasm for virtue makes it possible for him to see reasons for accepting what would seem incredible to others who do not share his philosophical views. His theory determines what is probable. Elsewhere, both in *Lives* from the mythical period and in those from historical times, the criterion of the probable is invoked somewhat differently, as I shall now indicate.

Although it was difficult to write with certainty about Lycurgus, Plutarch gives him the credit for much of the legislation which made Sparta a good state. His character is deduced partly from his actions, but still more from the spirit of his laws. However, one Spartan custom in particular did not meet with Plutarch's approval and made him wonder whether this too should be attributed to Lycurgus. At *Lyc.* 28 he describes the so-called *krupteia*;[16] at certain times Spartan youths, armed with daggers, were sent out into the countryside, with instructions to keep hidden by day and to murder any Helots whom they happened to meet on the roads at night. The practice is obviously repugnant to Plutarch, since it seems to conflict with his idea that the individual state should be a harmonious whole. If Lycurgus is held responsible for the introduction of this form of civil violence, it would be a piece of evidence on the side of those who maintain that the laws of Sparta are designed to make the citizens courageous rather than just. Or, to put the matter in Plutarch's terms, the law-giver's purpose (*proairesis*) would then be defective, if it were to be accepted that he chose the lesser virtue, courage, as his objective, rather than justice. Plutarch states that Plato held this view of the Spartan polity (he is referring here to the argument of *Laws* i),[17] and suggests that he did so because of this objectionable custom. Now the biographer's wish is to save Lycurgus from this criticism, and he does so by arguing that the *krupteia* was introduced at a later date in Spartan history. 'For I would not make Lycurgus responsible for this appalling measure, judging on the basis of his overall gentleness and justice . . .' The principle here is that a particular action or measure is felt to imply a character that is not in keeping with the general impression of Lycurgus; it is not probable that a man, whose other laws were just, would have brought in a measure which seems so unjust. Evidently there was a dispute about the date when the *krupteia* started; and Plutarch is disposed to favour a non-Lycurgan date, as this will save him from having an improbable character on his hands.

There is a similar instance in the *Pericles* (10.7) where Plutarch alludes to the malevolent charge made by Idomeneus,[18] that Pericles was responsible for the murder of Ephialtes, his colleague and political friend. The accusation is reported but is felt to be incredible, since it seems to imply a different Pericles from the hero as portrayed *in general* throughout this *Life*. Plutarch believed that Pericles was calm and moderate in politics; though he acted for the prosecution at the trial of Cimon,[19] he only did so for form's sake and did not make a vehement speech. How then could one who was lenient to a rival be guilty of assassinating an ally? Political motive, as often, is not considered; it is replaced by character-motive. Plutarch concedes that Pericles was not entirely without fault, but asserts that a man with his 'true grandeur' could not conceivably be affected by such 'a cruel and beastly passion (*pathos*)'. Thus his test of veracity in stories like this is to ask whether they are psychologically probable or not; and his criterion is derived from his understanding of the subject's political activity as a whole. Yet the question whether Pericles killed Ephialtes or not cannot be decided by such tests; if the allegation had been confirmed, Plutarch would have been obliged to refashion his portrait.

The charge against Pericles is rejected partly because it shows malice, partly because it seems incompatible with the character as known or judged already. Another example is somewhat different. In the *Alcibiades* (32) Plutarch describes the hero's return to Athens; he felt able to come back as he had led the Athenian fleet to victory in several engagements in the Aegean and could therefore expect to be hailed as the saviour of his country. His ships were decorated with trophies captured from the enemy and followed by the vessels they had taken. So far the story was credible. But Duris of Samos[20] added some picturesque details which did not seem so plausible; according to him, the oarsmen rowed to a song played by the flute-player Chrysogonus and the rhythm of the stroke was called by the actor Callipides. Alcibiades' own ship carried a purple sail, 'as though he were leading a drunken revel'. Plutarch rejects this story partly because it was not mentioned by other writers (Theopompus, Ephorus and Xenophon), partly because it is not

167

probable. But this improbability has nothing to do with Alcibiades' character in general; the reader of this *Life* will find the tale compatible with Alcibiades' known extravagance and fondness for putting on a show. Plutarch finds it improbable for another reason; it is, in his opinion, not likely that one who was returning from exile and misfortune would parade his wealth as well as the symbols of his military victories. Thus the standard of measurement here is the writer's notion of how man in general would behave on such occasions; Plutarch seems to overlook the fact that Duris' tale is probable *ad hominem*. This form of improbability is used to confirm the argument from the silence of the three other authorities, who have more standing as historians in Plutarch's eyes.

There are, of course, many passages where Plutarch reports variant opinions among the sources without taking sides. But where he does make a choice, he is sometimes guided in his interpretation by his sense of what is probable. In some cases stories are deemed probable if they can be used to illustrate a tenet in accord with the writer's philosophy. In others he assesses the likelihood of a tale by considering whether it harmonizes with the character of the man's political activity as a whole, or with how man in general ought to behave in such and such a situation. As a way of deciding the truth or falsehood of particular stories it has obvious defects. But the reader of the *Lives* will usually find that these passages instruct him about Plutarch's own outlook on human nature, even if he sometimes has the feeling that what was probable to Plutarch would not have been so to most people.

## 5.3 TRAGEDY AND TRAGIC HISTORY

These questions of method can tell us much about Plutarch's closeness to or remoteness from historians. But the study of method is only one guide to help us see more clearly the relationship between the *Lives* and historical writing, of which they are an offshoot. Critical theory, such as it was, did not only demand that the historian should tell the truth (and required him, therefore, to deploy the criterion of probability in order to get the facts right); he was also expected to present his readers with a work of literature, in which they might enjoy the fine style or be excited by the dramatic treatment of a subject. Historical narrative, as practised by many of the Hellenistic authors on whom Plutarch drew, was often intended to stir the reader's emotions, to evoke the feeling of pity which moves yet leads on the spectator of a tragedy. Thus Cicero, in asking Lucceius to write up his defeat of Catiline and subsequent exile, indicates that this subject has great dramatic potential (*ad fam.* v.12). Plutarch could not fail to notice that some of his sources had exploited means and effects which might more properly be used on the stage. In particular, he has several observations to make on the subject of tragedy, the dramatic form that was most frequently put forward as the model for the historian. I shall begin with his comments on tragedy[21] and go on to consider whether his own composition is dramatic. We have to do with a particular form of that general problem, whether Plutarch meant to entertain as well as instruct. The question is especially interesting in view of the fact that several of the *Lives* provided the basic plots for the Roman tragedies of Shakespeare.[22]

In the *Lives*, as in the *Moralia*, Plutarch speaks disparagingly of tragedy. His account of how it started makes us see it through the eyes of the legislator-hero Solon (archon 594 BC). 'Thespis and his followers were at this time beginning to develop tragedy; as it was a novelty it attracted the many though it had not yet become established as a competition. Solon was by nature fond of stories and learning new things, and now that he was old he would restore himself by relaxation, amusement, drinking and music; he came and watched Thespis taking a part himself, as was the custom with the ancients. After the show he asked Thespis if he was not ashamed to be telling such lies in the presence of so many people. Thespis replied that there was nothing so terrible about saying and doing these things in play; whereupon Solon struck the ground with his stick and said, "By praising and valuing this play we shall soon find it counting as something serious and worthwhile".' (*Sol.* 29.6–7) Though Plutarch reports the view of Solon without any comment of his own, there is little doubt that he would agree with Solon's criticism. For Plutarch, as we have seen, what is done or said in play (*paidia*) can be an important clue to character; but play has its own rules of dignity, just like serious matters, and it is not the case that anything is allowed the hero when he is relaxing after the performance of fine things (*kala*). Further, the criticism that tragedy is a lie is an indictment with two heads, and these charges are formulated elsewhere. Tragedy is mendacious[23] in respect of its subject-matter, for its plots are drawn from fiction, not from the events of real life; and the actors have to lie in that they purport to be persons other than they are.

Thus the institution of tragedy meets with objections from Solon in which he is speaking with the author's voice. It is evident that the later prestige of tragedy is not seen as socially or politically helpful. We can contrast it with other institutions of which Plutarch does approve. He commends the Roman triumph[24] (though quite how he failed to see the mischief caused by its prestige is astonishing) on the grounds that it called forth the enthusiasm of the young to serve their country; glory would, it seems, be a spur to virtue (*aretē*). Again, he sees much to praise in the political device known as ostracism[25] and values it as a means of ensuring that state-harmony would not be disrupted by the struggles between political rivals. But there is no indication that tragedy has anything of value to contribute; and it seems that it may do harm. Secondly, Plutarch does not speak of tragedy with the sympathetic insight shown by Aristotle[26] when he asserts that tragedy is more universal than history. Plutarch can never forget that tragedy is based on events that never happened, though he does recognize that the appeal of tragedy resides in putting before us characters who are credible human beings. Yet he does not use this persuasiveness as the foundation of a theory, but sees it as the device which makes an audience accept moral or theological false-hoods. If he had been prompted to formulate a comparison of history and tragedy, he would probably have said that the former is concerned with truth, the latter not.

Explicit references in the *Lives* to tragedy enable us to see that Plutarch's hostility covers more than his sense of outrage at the violation of fact and the dressing-up of actors. He objects to theatricality and sensational display, and feels that these elements were present in Pompey's divorce and remarriage in 80 BC. Pompey married Aemilia, who was already pregnant; and divorced Antistia, whose father had been assassinated because of his political leanings to Sulla and Pompey, and whose mother now committed suicide. Plutarch here refers to 'the tragedy connected with this marriage' (*Pomp.* 9.3). He means, I think, that there was a horrible unreality about the whole proceedings; and perhaps these deaths within the family of Antistia reminded him of tragedies in which several members of one family succumb to a curse. Again, some of the changes and catastrophes in tragedy come about because of orders from a god. Plutarch is thinking of this kind of dramatic effect when he writes of Themistocles using 'divine signs and oracles' (*Them.* 10.1) in order to win over the multitude to his point of view. In this case Themistocles makes use of the supernatural to recommend a good policy, the evacuation of Athens; the end is good, but the words used to describe the means – 'raising a device as though in a tragedy' – serve to point out the extreme pressures under which he was acting. A similar point is made about the means employed by Lysander to bring about a change in the Spartan constitution (*Lys.* 25).

The condemnation of tragedy as unreal and sensational, the scene of false values, appears in many incidental references in the *Lives.* Yet Plutarch as an educator knew that the classic Greek tragedies formed part of the curriculum and could hardly be excluded. In his treatise, *On reading the Poets*, he keeps up his criticism of poetry, including tragedy, but offers also a partial defence. Poetry can be useful, even though it does refer to myth or the unreal, if we regard it as a propaedeutic to philosophy.[27] Some of the strange sayings and doings in tragedy can be explained in the light of philosophical doctrine. It seems here that Plutarch is not concerned with explaining or defending a particular tragedy or poem *as a whole*; it is rather that he is anxious to explain particular lines or sentiments that strike him as offensive. The Homeric line,[28] 'That is how the gods have spun the fates for wretched mortals, to live in pain and suffering', seems wrong to Plutarch, as it suggests that the gods intend mankind to suffer and be uncomfortable. He can save Homer for the curriculum and the young from corruption by the following explanation; we should not suppose that wretched is an epithet referring to all men, but that 'wretched mortals' refers to a particular class of mankind. If they are wretched, they will have become so through their own fault; their pain and suffering is a penalty meted out by the gods as a suitable return for their misdeeds. Thus the sentiment is made acceptable through an untenable rendering of a Homeric formula. The poetic criticism practised by Plutarch is that of a philosopher who is used to turning to the poets for quotable examples and who is prepared to rewrite or bend what seems to him false doctrine.

In the light of his critical remarks about tragedy, it is no surprise to find that Plutarch speaks harshly of 'tragic history'. It is not my intention to discuss the origin of this kind of writing but to indicate the relevant passages in the *Lives* and isolate the ground of his complaints. The *Themistocles* ends with a discussion of where the hero was buried. Anyone, he says, would recognize that Phylarchus[29] has made up *his* story; 'he uses machinery as though history were a tragedy, and he brings forward Neocles and Demopolis, sons of Themistocles, because he wants to make a scene and affect the reader' (*Them.* 32.4). We cannot be sure why exactly Phylarchus is reprehensible but we can guess; firstly, Plutarch has already said that Neocles died young, and as he was one of the older children his death had, perhaps, preceded that of his father. But the more objectionable element in Phylarchus was the emotional pleading put into the mouths of the children, presumably to ask the Athenians to allow the burial of their father's remains. This obvious fake, which might have been criticized as rhetorical, is here set aside as so much tragedy; an attempt to draw tears from the reader at a dramatic point in the story, when the hero has died. Philistus also is criticized for writing an emotional set-piece about the burial of Dionysius, which was evidently an occasion when no expense was spared. But the grounds of Plutarch's rebuke are now somewhat different. Lavish expenditure at a tyrant's funeral can encourage a wrong sense of values; what is really admirable is a funeral like that of Pelopidas, which was not adorned with ivory, gold and purple, but was attended by numerous devoted admirers. Such is the true reward for virtue, shown by popular enthusiasm. Ostentatious expense is a veil which the biographer has to put aside in order to see whether there is any loyalty in the hearts of men (*Pel.* 34.1).

Other criticisms about tragic writing are directed at Theopompus and Duris. The former (*Dem.* 21.2) is accused of misrepresenting the state of public opinion at Athens after the defeat at Chaeronea in 338 BC, when Alexander's victory put an end to Demosthenes' policy of resistance. According to Plutarch, the people did not turn against the politician but asked him to speak the panegyric in honour of the fallen. By this gesture they showed that they were steadfast adherents of Demosthenes' policy, even though it had failed. But Theopompus[30] portrayed the Athenian people as humiliated and is said to have written 'tragically' on the subject; probably his account of Athenian despondency was meant to make the reader agree with Theopompus' hostile view of Demosthenes. Plutarch, we know, objected to the malice of Theopompus and disagreed with him entirely about the character of Demosthenes, whom he interpreted as a man of steady purpose, not a fickle political opportunist. He considered that Theopompus had got his facts wrong and had used the distorting medium of pathetic writing to set people against Demosthenes. The case of Duris (*Per.* 28.2) involves a similar disagreement about the facts of the matter. For Duris maintained that Pericles was guilty of war-atrocities against the people of Samos, and wrote in detail about their sufferings in order to denigrate Pericles and Athens. Plutarch did not believe that the crimes had ever occurred, since he found no mention of them in more reputable sources.[31]

In no case, it seems, is 'tragedy' used to refer to a serious vision of human life. It denotes an exaggerated pathos, which is founded on wrong facts or erroneous values; Plutarch thinks of such writing as tragic for two reasons; it is partly that tragedy as such contained many false views; partly that a certain kind of history had (not unnaturally) come to be called tragic because its pathos and theatricality resembled scenes from the Greek tragedians.

These considerations make it highly improbable that Plutarch intended to compose his *Lives* (whether all or some only) as tragedies. In his view this would have meant using the sensationalism and pathos of 'tragic history', a form of writing which he found repugnant. To do so would have interfered with his concentration on virtue; he describes and collects instances of virtue because he is full of admiration for them, and believes that they will appeal to well-disposed readers without there being any need for dramatic effects. His temperament and imagination were those of an optimist. It is true that he refers to the difficulties that confront the achieving of virtue; there are, for instance, several passages on the perversity of fortune, but the reader is not encouraged to see in fortune the persistent adversary of virtue. One's impression on finishing the *Coriolanus* is that the author felt that the hero's deficiencies of character could have been made to come right if only it had been possible for him to apply to a moral philosopher. The death of Phocion[32] is described movingly – there is a feeling that the Athenians were ungrateful to this man's virtue – but Plutarch's criticism of the Athenian people is moderated and hardly resembles the pathos of the authors he attacks for being 'tragic'. Their pathos was dictated by a feeling of hostility to one side rather than by the sympathetic search for virtue.

His mind did not have a dramatic cast and the pace of a narrative is constantly slowed by digressions which admittedly instruct but often weaken one's attention to the story as a whole. Secondly, it is clear that ideas of accusation and defence are sometimes prominent in his judgments about people. Brutus, for instance, is said to have done only one thing for which no defence could be offered (*Brut.* 46.2); he promised his troops that if they won they would be allowed to sack two Greek towns. Now the role of barrister, whether as prosecutor or defendant, could easily provide a story with a dramatic structure. But though Plutarch refers to accusation and defence he does not approach his cases with the energy of a barrister bent on making his case prevail. His attitude is, rather, that of the judge who wishes above all to be fair to everyone. The bad impression of wrong conduct or character is not ignored (since Plutarch was honest) but softened; such character or conduct could not make a tragic flaw. And Plutarch's tendency was to see faults and errors as blemishes on virtue rather than as the triumph of vice.

The *Brutus* shows both his failings and his success in stirring our dramatic expectations. This *Life* is, to a large extent, the story not of one man but of two, Brutus and Cassius; several passages give material which offers a comparison between the greater and the lesser virtue.[33] But this comparison is not invidious or intended to discredit Cassius. In fact Plutarch rescues Cassius from the charge that he became an enemy of Caesar out of personal malice, and brings forward evidence to show that his political purpose was, like that of Brutus, a hostility to the tyrant not the man. The two heroes are thus put more nearly on a par; the effect of the other references to them is to present a mild contrast between the purpose (*proairesis*) with great virtue (Brutus) and the same purpose with somewhat less (Cassius). But it is doubtful whether Plutarch himself imposed this pattern on his material. It seems, rather, that the sources he used had already drawn a contrast between Brutus and Cassius, which Plutarch thought should be less extreme. Though there is drama of a sort in these sections of the *Brutus*, the *Life* as a whole is a lost opportunity, dramatically speaking. Antony and Augustus are left as cardboard figures on the edge of the narrative; and the key question, which every reader will ask, about the relevance of Brutus' virtue to the political conditions of the age, is not really faced. Plutarch merely alludes to his view (which is also expressed elsewhere) that the times needed autocracy, not the republic for which Brutus fought. But he does little more than make this comment in passing.

There is, however, some evidence that points in the other direction and suggests that Plutarch did at times compose with tragedy in mind. The latter part of the *Crassus* (16–33) deals with the Roman's expedition to Parthia and his defeat there. A good half of the *Life* is devoted to a year or two in the hero's career, an indication, as we have already noticed, that the biographer has emphasized those events which would seem important to a historian. The *Life* concludes with a description of how Crassus' head was brought to the Parthian court during a performance of Euripides' *Bacchae*. A human head is useful as a stage-prop for this play, when the chorus bring on the *disiecta membra* of the torn Pentheus, and one of the actors did so use the object and earned a talent for his sense of realism. Plutarch remarks that 'this was the final end of Crassus' campaign, like a tragedy'. The terminology is explicitly borrowed from drama and might therefore lead us to suppose that the whole of this Parthian campaign is presented as a tragedy. Indeed, this part of the narrative begins with a sense of doom and foreboding, evidenced by curses and unfavourable omens (*Crass.* 16.6). But the character of Crassus himself is presented in the usual fragmented way; he is seen as over-ambitious, but also displays great courage in defeat (26–27). There is a suggestion that Crassus failed as he deserved but, as often, Plutarch shrinks back from full condemnation. In view of this it seems more likely that the remarks on tragedy in *Crass.* 33 refer to the particular grotesque episode at the end of the Roman's life; it was the extraordinary and sensational use of the severed head which reminded Plutarch of the excesses of tragedy.

On the other hand, the *Demetrius* seems to be a more likely candidate for biography-as-tragedy, since allusions to tragedy persist throughout the *Life*, whereas in other *Lives* they are occasional. It has been argued[34] that the *Demetrius* is therefore an instance of tragedy, conceived on the lines of Plato's account of the 'descent from aristocracy through timocracy to tyranny in *Republic* 8 and 9'; and Demetrius himself certainly undergoes a moral decline 'from justice through ambition to the pursuit of pleasure'. The references to the tragic element underline the writer's adverse judgment on this subject, as when he speaks of Demetrius' extravagant clothes as a tragic spectacle (*Demetr.* 41.6). It seems, then, that Plutarch might agree that Demetrius is cast as a tragic figure, and the formulation will do as long as we remember that tragic here has the author's disapproval as well as Plato's. It is not the case that Plutarch has here described a tragic hero in the sense studied by Aristotle, or as we now use the expression. And though this element is present in the *Demetrius*, to talk of this *Life* as 'a Plutarchian tragedy' is hardly convenient or accurate, as the phrase needs to be translated into other English; and my judgment is that the *Demetrius* is in fact less dramatic in our sense than other *Lives* which have better heroes.

Plutarch's expressed dislike of tragedy reveals his scorn for what we could call melodramatic twists and turns, false pathos and theatrical ostentation. Yet there are features in the *Lives* which can only be described as dramatic, though Plutarch does not always put them to that use. It is common to find that expeditions which ended in disaster are preceded by accounts of inauspicious omens. The omens of Crassus (16.6) come to mind; and similar instances occur in the *Nicias* (13) and *Dion* (24). The effect of these passages is to prepare the reader for the disaster which happens in the end; but this is not to say that the effect was always so intended. I think, rather, that Plutarch recorded these items because they were in the tradition; he saw no reason to disbelieve them, and he himself believed that they were pointers to coming events if only they could be read. What he objects to is the sort of factitious connexion made by Timaeus (*Nic.* 1.2) between the mutilation of the Hermae and the defeat of the Athenians by the Syracusan Hermocrates. The signs and omens that Plutarch treats with respect are sometimes open to the objection that they have become significant through hindsight. If Dion had achieved lasting eminence after his victory, we would not have heard about the sundial on which the hero stood while addressing the Syracusans after their liberation. The seers 'were afraid that his affairs might be subject to a quick reversal' (*Dion* 29.3–5). Their fear, of course, was substantiated by the event. 'Facts' like this will strike the modern reader as not so very different from the etymological inventions of Timaeus. The authentic and the spurious omen both subserve a common end, which can reasonably be called dramatic.

But though we are right to detect this element in the *Lives*, Plutarch did not think highly of this kind of literary aim or count it as one of his prime objectives. Compared with other writers, he does not compose dramatically or make much of his opportunities. The *Marcellus*, for instance, offers the famous story of how the Roman general wept before the liberation and destruction of Syracuse. Livy's[35] version exploits the obvious resources of the incident; the general wept, partly from excitement at the glory that would soon be his, partly at the thought that a beautiful city would soon be destroyed by his infuriated troops. He is made the vehicle for the author's melancholy thoughts on the glorious past of Syracuse. The same fact of the general's emotion forms the starting-point of Plutarch's narrative (*Marc.* 19); but though he is commended for his moderation, the scene is treated in a dry, not to say brisk, manner. The biographer's purpose is to offer an instance of mercy or self-control in victory, and he does not attempt to move his readers by presenting the scene through the mind and emotions of Marcellus.

It might be said that Livy's use of this incident is meretricious and that history, or biography, for that matter, does not need this artificial heightening. Yet Livy is capable of authentic touches of drama that are beyond the reach of Plutarch. Both writers refer to Marcellus' plundering Syracuse of its statues to adorn his triumph. Livy reflects that Marcellus was entitled to do this by right of war; but he thereby set a precedent for that indiscriminate ransacking which had even deprived Marcellus' own temple of some of its trophies. The irony is not so much a criticism of Marcellus, but is an expression of Livy's own pessimism, his feeling that the conquest of the world has brought some foreign and less admirable ways of acting and thinking. The admiration of Greek art has led to the downfall of Roman virtue. Plutarch, for his part, seems to make something positive out of the fine statues brought by Marcellus, though he alludes briefly to some adverse comment. He makes an antithesis, too, between Marcellus and Fabius, who did not take the statues of gods away from Tarentum, but left them there to threaten the defeated town. But he tells this tale so obscurely that the reader needs to go elsewhere to learn that it was a grim joke on the part of Fabius.[36] Even so, the antithesis is of passing interest only – like so many items in Plutarch, it is perhaps meant to start a discussion rather than affect us because of its artistic form – and does not seem to be *dramatically* related to other passages. Livy, on the other hand, turns the event into evidence for his views on Rome's decline, though he states this indirectly.

For the sake of brevity, I will limit this account to one more case, where again it is instructive to compare Livy. The *Titus* (10) tells how, at the Isthmian games in 196 BC, a herald proclaimed that the Roman senate and Titus granted their freedom to the Greek states. The audience was so astounded that it would only believe its ears when the news was announced a second time. This dramatic occasion is described at some length by Plutarch, but even so there is no attempt at imagining the stunned reaction of the Greeks. For that one must go to Livy, who makes his readers see by vividness (*enargeia*) the various moods among the listeners. Their impression of doubt turning to exultation as the news is repeated is enhanced by the description of the Greeks' behaviour after the games – they crowded round their benefactor and even endangered his life. But Plutarch's sequel, though it seems a promising item, ends differently. He cites a strange piece of evidence for the sheer volume of applause that eventually greeted Titus' good news; the fact that some crows were flying across the stadium and plummeted down in mid-flight because of the noise. But instead of going on at once to describe the enthusiasm of the Greeks, Plutarch breaks off to discuss the reasons for this phenomenon. What drama there promised to be is replaced by scientific theory.

Plutarch's explicit criticism of 'tragedy' and 'tragic' writing is not just a piece of theory but seems to be his own practice as well. He avoids what he would call false pathos and does not develop the dramatic potentialities within a story, though they are often suggested. This lack of fabrication in the story is, I suspect, the very feature which has appealed to many modern readers; on its positive side this counts as a discursive readiness to start a number of subjects for investigation, most of which is left to the reader to do for himself. But this means that it is hardly possible to speak of Plutarch the artist though it is common to read of tributes to his art.

## 5.4 FORTUNE

Like many of the historians whom he read for his character-material, Plutarch makes a certain amount of play with the idea of fortune or chance (*tuchē*).[37] As a literary and compositional motif this idea is not confined to the historians but occurs in other genres in Hellenistic literature. It is always difficult to judge whether a writer is referring to belief in a divine power, fortune with a capital F, so to say, which is held to distribute success or failure in a capricious manner; or whether he is simply referring to the idea that certain events are irrational or unexpected. As fortune and related words occur frequently in the *Lives*, I shall attempt to discover whether Plutarch puts the idea to a serious purpose. Though I have in the main limited the discussion to passages in which the word fortune (*tuchē*) is used, it is as well to remember what Plutarch has to say about the idea in the *Moralia* (22D–24C). He there indicates that our reading of earlier writers can only be on the right lines if we sometimes allow that when they write 'god' they mean fortune, a theory which enables him to explain away apparent blasphemies in the poets. It is then possible that other words too would be interpreted by Plutarch as referring to fortune or chance.

It is important, though far from easy, to establish the senses in which he uses the word fortune. Since the etymology ('happening') is not much of a guide, it is more instructive to study his usage. We noticed earlier that his main interest is the construction of character, in which the notion of choice (*proairesis*) is a significant factor. Acting from choice is contrasted with and preferred to acting because one has to, from necessity. But this is not the only contrast used to build up character. Choice is also opposed to chance or fortune; thus, in the *Aemilius* (1.6) we are told that Aemilius and Timoleon are alike 'not only in their choice, but also in their good

fortune'; in fact, says Plutarch, it is debatable whether they succeeded more by good fortune than by virtue, a question which I
shall consider later. The *Dion* (2.1) deploys the formula of choice
or chance more explicitly; Dion and Brutus are said to have been
more alike in their accidents than their choice. Plutarch here means
that they are not so easy to compare in the role of enmity to a
tyrant, because the objects of that enmity were not equal; the
tyranny of Dionysius was *de facto* more objectionable than the
autocracy of Caesar, which, in Plutarch's view, was a form of rule
necessary to the age. The two are comparable in their accidents,
firstly, because they died before they could achieve their purpose;
and, secondly, because their deaths were foretold by apparitions.
Accident, or fortune, is here used to refer variably to different
things; the fact that events do not always go as planned because
they are frustrated by the opposition of others, as in the battles of
Philippi; and the apparent fact, which seems hard to argue away,
that some events are so remarkable that one has to invoke a non-
human or supernatural cause.

Whether any alleged piece of fortune is of the first or second
type is for the moment not relevant. It seems to follow that man
is looked on as a sum both of his actions, which are the prime
source for discovering his choice and virtues, and his accidents
or bits of fortune. There is a more elaborate account in the
*Demosthenes* (3.4). Plutarch here begins with the comment that
the god (*daimōn*) gave Cicero and Demosthenes many shared
characteristics, such as their ambition, love of liberty and their
timidity. At the same time, he says, they have many accidents in
common. 'I do not think you would find two other speakers who,
from being inglorious nobodies, became great and powerful; they
were in conflict with kings and tyrants; lost their daughters; were
exiled from their countries; returned in honour; fled again and
were captured by the enemy; and ended their days at the very
time when their countries' freedom came to an end.' He goes on
to say (and the point has some resemblance to his comment in the
*Aemilius*) that nature and fortune might well dispute which has
done more to make the men alike. The distinction is, broadly speaking, between events, which can be seen as the consequence of one's
own planning, and happenings to oneself, which are not of one's
own choosing but are caused by the purpose of others or by non-

human factors. Cicero did not choose to be a contemporary of Caesar (though he did choose to oppose him); he did not choose to lose his daughter; and he did not choose exile, which was imposed on him by others. Of several items in this list we can say that one man's happenings are the events of other men, since he suffers what they both choose and are able to effect. We can also think of the contrast as one between active and passive events. Though heroic man proposes, his success or failure will depend on the arrangements made by other men and, sometimes, by the divine powers.

The idea that a life is a sum of character or nature on the one hand and fortune on the other is not just an introductory flourish to arouse interest at the beginning of a biography. The formula was used to sum up the minor figure Philistus[38] (*Dion* 35–36). We are told that we should neither praise him for his actions nor delight in recounting or exaggerating his misfortunes. By his actions Plutarch means his support for the tyrant Dionysius and his hostility to Plato, which are evidence of a choice or policy that is ignoble. His misfortunes here refer to the manner of his dying, which according to one authority involved torture at the hands of his captors. Thus here too the formula is a neat way of embracing events for which one can be held responsible and other events which one cannot help.

If it seems surprising to find that Plutarch thinks in this way, we should first remember that, compared with some, he is sparing in his use of the idea of fortune. The *Sertorius* (1) seems to indicate that other writers had specialized in collecting examples of accidental resemblances. There were said to be two Actaeons,[39] one who was torn to pieces by his dogs, the other by his lovers; and one might make the defeat of Carthage the common ground in a study of the two Scipios. Plutarch is mildly humorous at the expense of this kind of comparison, for he goes on to say that you might also argue that the generals with most guile were all men with one eye – Philip, Antigonus, Hannibal and Sertorius. His own purpose is quite different, as he makes clear; for his brief comparison of Sertorius with these other generals is designed to show his superiority to them in terms of virtue. So this kind of accident is dismissed with a quiet smile.

Though he retains the idea of fortune, as we have seen, he

rejects trivial meanings and tends to explain it as something which can be used to throw light on character. The story of the matrons' embassy to Coriolanus brings out a distinction between events which are normal or expected and those which seem surprising or miraculous. The Roman state, faced with the implacable anger of Coriolanus, made use of the customary diplomatic means to persuade him to withdraw his army. When these failed, the senate, feeling hopelessly outnumbered by Coriolanus' army, decided against fighting in the open and in favour of armed resistance from the walls: 'they put their hopes in the passage of time above all and in those unexpected things which come about by chance.' The next event was the embassy of the ladies to Coriolanus; their persuasion was effective, though no one could have expected that such a mission would start in the first place, let alone succeed.

The language of the passage translated above leads us to think of a contrast between 'expected' events and 'unexpected events which come about by chance'. Embassies composed of Roman politicians and priests are expected, whereas those consisting of Roman matrons are not. We might then suppose that the first class can tell us something about choice (*proairesis*), while the second class may seem caused by divine prompting; the agents will then no longer be agents but the passive puppets of a moving force outside themselves. But Plutarch does not draw this conclusion. In his view, unexpected events are only caused by outside powers in the sense that these can supply the initial impulse without which the action could not have taken place; but the action is still voluntary. Thus an expression like 'a god made me do it'[40] should not make us think that the human agent is merely an instrument of the divine; it only means, according to Plutarch, that the *idea* of feasibility came from the god, whereas we can still admire the matrons for what they actually did. In this way, a class of events which seems at first unexpected or odd, is shown to be relevant to the study of character.

Even with these restrictions on chance or fortune, it is still the case that a man's career can meaningfully be described as a sum of character-events and fortune-events. Character-events, such as Pericles' treatment of the assembly or Nicias's conduct as general, point to the virtues or lack of them. Fortune-events are often no more than a shorthand for the success or failure of these virtues in the sphere of action. Virtue may have good or bad luck; and though virtue itself cannot be cast down or brought to nothing, luck deserves the biographer's attention for the light it throws on the hero's reaction to his circumstances. We should not, therefore, marvel at good or bad fortune as something inexplicable or perverse, but treat it as an opportunity to study the use of fortune; and this is an important theme in several *Lives*.

Plutarch believes that man is capable of aspiring to the highest, but that human nature is weak, as he puts it; virtue cannot guarantee that it will succeed. There *are* sudden ups and downs, but we should not therefore bow the knee to the caprice of fortune; we should accept that there will be mutability and study how to compose ourselves before it. He has this point in mind in his excursus on the tyrant Dionysius (*Tim.* 14–15). He refers to Dionysius' exile in another passage (*Dion* 50.4) as 'even to this day the most conspicuous and greatest of the examples of fortune's power'. Dionysius, according to Plutarch's version, was deprived of his power unexpectedly, against the odds, and his downfall may therefore seem to illustrate the principle that all human affairs are full of change and uncertainty. But to let the matter rest there is to share the views of 'the many', who are too ignorant to look behind the surface of things. The important task is to see how Dionysius reacted to the loss of his position; and what Plutarch knew of the tyrant's exile in Corinth suggested that he had derived some benefit from his meetings with Plato. The man who said 'Do I not seem to you to have been helped by Plato in that I put up with the change of fortune as I do?' (*Tim.* 15.4) clearly had some fine qualities. Though Dionysius is not a hero (he is a tyrant, not a 'politicus'), he is described as not without good qualities; and Plutarch's account of his exile seems to bear this out.

The career of Marius is another case which provides material for reflexions about the right attitude to fortune. Even at the end of his life Marius was still hungry for power; and though he had lived long and had been consul seven times, 'he was still bewailing his fortune as though he were dying before his time, in want and without achieving what he deserved' (*Mar.* 45.12). Though Plutarch makes Marius describe his own vicissitudes and add that a prudent man would no longer trust himself to fortune, he seems to think that Marius' attitude at the end belies this statement. The right attitude is, by cultivation of the memory, to recollect one's blessings, as Plato congratulated himself on being human, Greek and an associate of Socrates. Still to be looking forward at the end of one's day, is to trust in the hazards of hope. This kind of hope is a pathetic resource for those with bad memories : 'such people are stuffed full of hopes and look towards the future while neglecting the present.'

The prudent course is not to trust in fortune and to show this by one's behaviour. Perhaps the most outstanding example in the *Lives* is Aemilius, the conqueror of Perseus and of Macedonia. When it seemed that he had reached the heights of worldly ambition, at the very moment of his triumph he suffered a heavy loss, the premature death of two of his children. The private calamity could well seem to prove 'the cruelty of fortune'. But Aemilius did not succumb; he knew that courage is for use not only in war but in all circumstances of life. He addressed the Roman people on the subject and admitted that he had always been suspicious of fortune. But now that his family had paid this token of suffering to the malevolent power, he could feel that Rome's (good) fortune would be left intact. We have here the idea that some forms of success attract the evil eye, not of the gods, presumably, who approve of virtue, but of bad spirits. Success on the grand scale demands therefore a compensatory setback or disadvantage; and it is only prudent to resemble men like Aemilius and be able to react appropriately to the disaster which seems bound to come.

These instances are typical of Plutarch's attitude towards fortune. It is, in his view, a separable element when we examine a life; but it is important not to regard ourselves as the plaything of circumstances or another power, but to display our positive moral qualities. In this way what happens by accident or fortune is woven into the moral fabric of the *Lives*. One would not *choose* certain kinds of fortune if that were within our power. But though bad fortune can prevent a good choice (*proairesis*) from achieving its end, it is the attitude to failure (or success, for that matter) that is decisive. To say that a man had 'virtue and good fortune' had been (in Roman oratory, for example) a device for recommending a successful general, and Cicero uses the formula in several speeches. In practical politics it would not be much of a recommendation to

say that one's candidate had the virtues but had always been
unlucky. But Plutarch's aim is to encourage virtue, and certain
virtues can be demonstrated whether fortune is good or bad.

So far I have been concerned to show that Plutarch restricts the
scope of fortune or exploits the idea in such a way that we are at
once aware of its relevance to the study of character. Nonetheless
there are some *Lives* where the idea does not merely occur in
isolated passages, but seems to be used compositionally as a way
of giving some structure to the whole *Life*. I shall conclude this
survey by examining some of these cases.

Perhaps the idea is most noticeable in the *Lives* of Aemilius and
Timoleon. The *Aemilius* (1.6) begins with the remarks that the
careers of these men leave it in some doubt whether they succeeded
by good luck or by judgment. Plutarch is here referring to the idea
that successful men can be regarded as having virtue which has
been so aided by good fortune that it becomes difficult to dis-
entangle which has done more. Virtue and good fortune are
engaged in a sort of friendly competition to decide which of them
shall grant more to the lucky recipient. Plutarch had used a variant
of this idea when he composed the epideictic speeches about
Alexander, which are thought to be early compositions.[41] His theme
there is that Alexander had virtue which was dogged by bad
fortune. The fact that other variants of the theme occur in the
*Lives* should make us wary of dismissing this way of interpreting
a character or life as no more than a rhetorician's plaything, to be
taken up or discarded just to make a speech; Plutarch does in fact
use the idea for a serious purpose.

Certainly, there are other references in these *Lives* which suggest
that Plutarch had the idea of 'virtue and good fortune' in mind
throughout the writing of both. He was aware that both men had
been described as men with good fortune – Timoleon, in fact, had
ascribed all his successes to fortune and had even set up a shrine
to a form of the goddess – and so it was natural for Plutarch to
raise the question whether good fortune was the major factor in
their careers. As we might expect, the question is easily answered,
for Plutarch asserts that both men owed their achievement to
virtue. We should think of Timoleon's success not as the work of
fortune, but of virtue enjoying good fortune[42] (*Tim.* 36.5). And this
virtue is shown, as we have already seen, by both men's steadfast-

185

ness in the presence of good or bad fortune, their refusal to be elated or cast down.

Why, then, does Plutarch raise the question at all, if he makes it so plain that virtue alone is what really matters? I am inclined to think that the scheme seemed particularly relevant to these *Lives* because the material from the sources was rich in this sort of suggestion. Plutarch himself does not believe that you can meaningfully say that fortune is more responsible than virtue for a good man's success, though he does appear to invoke fortune as a way of accounting for relative failure. His initial question is therefore somewhat of an Aunt Sally, but it enables him to punctuate the narrative with reminders that virtue is all-important. In the *Aemilius* these occur fairly early. Thus Plutarch looks on Aemilius' easy crossing of the Adriatic as a piece of good fortune, but then waxes lyrical about his virtues as a commander: 'I cannot allocate any remarkable achievement to the man's so-called good fortune, as one can with other generals, unless it be the avarice of Perseus . . .' (*Aem.* 12.2) The suggestion is that his biggest piece of good fortune was a virtue-defect in his adversary; which is again typical of Plutarch's habit of mentioning fortune only to make us see the implications for the study of character. It seems to be Plutarch's view that writers came to emphasize the good fortune of Aemilius because they were dazzled by the speed of his victory over Perseus. Events seemed to run favourably for the Roman. Much the same point is made about Timoleon's liberation of Syracuse from tyranny. Luck of a divine kind seemed to have a hand in his appointment (*Tim.* 3.2) and he was helped towards his goal by all sorts of favourable turns. The reader notes various items of good fortune as well as instances of virtue as he proceeds with the story. Here it was the relative ease of accomplishment, as well as Timoleon's own gesture towards fortune the goddess, which had created the emphasis on the friendly competition between virtue and good fortune. There is much of the panegyric about this, as we can see by glancing at Cicero's idealization of Pompey.[43] Even so, the reader of Plutarch hardly needs to wait for the explicit solution (*Tim.* 36.5). Yet the references to fortune do give a framework to the narrative, which is often lacking in the *Lives*. Perhaps we are being reminded, too, that for virtue to succeed and prosper, one does need divine good luck or fortune, as Plato put it (cf. *Dion* 1.3).

A different version of this scheme is applied to the career of Lucullus. The first part of his *Life* covers the hero's exploits against Mithridates and his generalship in the east. He seems here not only to display the virtues but also to be assisted by good luck; events run well for him and even the weather seems to be on his side. His absence from Italy during the civil wars fought by Sulla is counted as part of his good fortune. The dividing-line comes after the siege and capture of Nisibis (68 BC). 'Up to this point one might say that fortune followed Lucullus and was his fellow-general. But from now on it was as though the wind had died down; he met with opposition and resistance in everything. He displayed the virtue and spirit of a good leader, but his actions had no grace or glory at all. With all his difficult and vain contending he came near to losing the glory he had already earned.' (*Luc.* 33.1) The passage serves to divide this *Life* into two parts; in the first the general has virtue and good fortune, whereas in the second his virtue is still present but has now to contend against fortune as well as men. If Plutarch had done no more we would have had a picture of one whose ultimate failure was not due to himself but to fortune; bad luck can be a means of exculpation. But Plutarch at once makes it clear that there were faults in Lucullus which to some extent caused him to *earn* his bad luck, the result of which was that he was not able to finish the war he had waged for so long. He failed to cultivate the troops; though flattery is a vice, cultivating others is a quality that the politician should not overlook. Secondly, he was 'unharmonious' in his dealings with his social and political peers. These political defects are, of course, central to Plutarch's main interest in the *Lives*; in this case they are mentioned to explain why Lucullus' campaign remained sadly incomplete and why he was replaced as a general. It is undeniable that he has both good and bad fortune at different times in his career, and this *Life* is composed round the dividing-line. Nevertheless we hear most from Plutarch about these failings in Lucullus which may help to explain why his bad luck was merited. We are left with the notion that *some* at least of the bad fortune was the fault of Lucullus himself.[44]

The case of Sulla is more complicated. Here we have a general who in some ways resembled Timoleon; he attributed his success to fortune or various divinities which were felt to have a close association with good fortune. 'Sulla the fortunate' seems to have

187

been a nickname invented by his enemies, but the victim was quick to accept the insult and turn it to his own advantage. He thereby put himself forward as one who enjoyed the special favours of the gods.[45] This was a theme developed at some length, it appears, in Sulla's memoirs,[46] which, either directly or indirectly, are the principal source on which Plutarch drew for his narrative. Sulla had done much to exaggerate the divine assistance given by fortune, and had, for instance, minimized the casualties on his side; a lucky general is one who wins easily and without much damage to his troops. This approach in one of the sources was admittedly partial and might have led Plutarch to see in Sulla a figure like Aemilius or Timoleon – a case of virtue enjoying good fortune. But he does not adopt this solution, since there was much to condemn in Sulla's character; his arbitrary misuse of power and his addiction to low company and forms of pleasure that distressed Plutarch. Hence he retains in the narrative those items of good fortune which, in Sulla's view, showed him forth as one favoured by the gods; but states his reservations about Sulla's character soon after mentioning the legend about Sulla the fortunate. 'He was by nature of a harsh disposition and given to exacting vengeance; but he moderated some of his violence by calculating what was expedient.' (*Sulla* 6) One cannot say that Plutarch's Sulla is a case of virtue prospering, though Sulla's own emphasis on his good fortune is reflected in the story and makes a remarkable, not to say sensational, *Life*.

Thus the idea of fortune, whether good or bad, can be combined in various ways with virtue to form a structure and interpret a character. The short comments, such as those on Cicero and Philistus, asserting a division between acts exhibiting virtue and pieces of good fortune, can be expanded to enfold and present a whole career. Even so, the most characteristic feature of Plutarch's approach to the idea of fortune is his insistence that one must make the right use of fortune. Success or failure in the world of action does not happen without the intervention of fortune. We cannot obtain good fortune merely by having virtue, though one suspects that, in Plutarch's view, if political matter were less awkward, this would be the case. Success and failure provide the biographer with an opportunity to discriminate a particular function of virtue; the ability to recognize that good fortune is not bound to last and to be prepared by courage for a change to the worse; and the ability to see that the virtues can still be used to endure bad fortune. The model examples are Aemilius and Phocion, the one steadfast in personal loss, the other in political defeat. But conduct like that of Perseus, who is portrayed as feeble in his defeat, is deplored. The virtues of a Plutarchan hero, then, equip him both for success and failure and enable him to know either fortune for what it is.

## 5.5 MALICE

Of all the factors which influence the narrative in the *Lives*, Plutarch's own attitude to the heroes is the most important. He has a willingness to see the best and follow it, and he expects his readers to come to his work with a similar disposition. He does not deny that there are faults when the evidence seems to him to be clear, but he is on the whole prepared to regard them as minor blemishes, not as disfigurements. To put the matter in his own terms, he writes without malice (*kakoētheia*).[47] This translation of the word is not wholly satisfactory, but has become part of the tradition about Plutarch, because of its closeness to the Latin title of his work on the subject – *De Herodoti malignitate*. In this case, as in others, we have a treatise in the *Moralia* which helps to shed some light on the way in which the idea is relevant to a reading of the *Lives*. I shall begin with a discussion of the work on Herodotus and then consider how the absence of malice makes itself felt in the *Lives*.

The work on Herodotus is, presumably, a late composition, a by-product of reflecting about the historian as a consequence of using his work for such *Lives* as the *Aristeides* and the *Themistocles*. But we do not know for certain whether this is so; what is certain is that the *Malice of Herodotus* does not represent a cool, scholarly meditation, based on a careful reading of the text. Plutarch quotes chapter and verse for the headings of his indictment, but the fact that his quotations are right should not make us blind to his strange interpretations of them. The high-pitched, rhetorical tone is extremely distasteful to a modern reader; add to that the polemical wrong-headedness, and it will then be appreciated that we have a piece of writing which seems to presuppose a different character from the author of the *Lives*.

Plutarch finds that the malice of Herodotus is especially objectionable because most readers are taken in by his agreeable style and draw the inference that the author's character is honest and straightforward. But for Plutarch, who is convinced that malice is there in Herodotus, the style merely conceals the animus. Just as, in Plato, the worst form of injustice is to be unjust while having a reputation for justice, so it is with malice. The apparent good nature of the historian is a mask donned by one who slanders mankind. Plutarch considers that Herodotus belittled his compatriots, the Boeotians, for the part they played in the Persian wars. In absolving the Boeotians from these allegations, Plutarch can therefore have the best of both worlds; he can display piety towards his ancestors and, at the same time, show his respect for the truth.[48] There is, in this case, no conflict of interest between love of truth and love of one's friends. But, as a moral phenomenon, malice is less well charted than justice; and so Plutarch begins by outlining some of the characteristics which will enable us to tell whether or not a narrative is malicious.

First is the use of harsh or unkind words to describe character when these could be avoided. To speak of Nicias as 'possessed by a god'[49] would be, on the writer's part, a lapse that gives offence, since it would be proper and more considerate to say that he was 'too fond of paying attention to the gods'. The same applies to characters who, in the *Lives*, are less worthy, such as Cleon.[50] It would not be right to say that Cleon is 'audacious and mad', but that 'his speeches have no weight'. Next come two charges which are closely related; including failures or bad actions when these are irrelevant to the main theme, and omitting fine actions when these ought to be in the record. To write in this way is to show that one has failed in the historian's task of allocating praise and blame. Again, when there is a conflict of reports or evidence, it is malicious to express a preference for the less creditable; one ought to choose the version 'that is better at seeming to be the truth'. The language here seems to suggest that the more plausible version will also be the more creditable for the person whose actions are scrutinized. Plutarch has in mind the question whether Themistocles knew about the treachery of Pausanias and his dealings with the king's generals; though the facts are uncertain, it is more likely that Themistocles did not know, as Thucydides says nothing about it.

Thus, in this case, the less creditable version is omitted altogether; the argument from silence is not a good way of deciding questions, but even so this is a remarkable instance. After all, even Plutarch might have seen that there could be many reasons why Thucydides does not refer to the matter. The next sign of ill will is a variant on the above; when the facts are not in dispute, it is malicious to attribute a less creditable cause or motive. To say that Pericles started the Peloponnesian War because of Aspasia or Pheidias; to explain Thēbē's assassination of her husband Alexander as caused by womanish emotion, not because she came to hate tyranny out of principle; to disparage Cato's suicide as the act of one who feared death at Caesar's hands:[51] all these are instances of putting a false interpretation on the known facts. Great exploits are thereby belittled and will be of little or no use to the moralist.

Plutarch goes on to mention other characteristics but those mentioned are in my view the most important. This description of the forms of malice is the prelude to a progress through the work of Herodotus. One or two incidents are taken from each book and the historian is then found guilty of malice on one or more counts. The whole treatise has been a problem to modern scholars, especially for those who admire both writers; it seems strange that Plutarch should have read the father of history in so perverse a fashion. We may grant that Plutarch the patriot was upset by Herodotus' version of some events in the Persian wars, but find it hard to see why he should settle on malice as the explanation. Herodotus had often been cited as mendacious,[52] but the charge of malice is new. There seems to be no reasonable explanation except that when Plutarch becomes excited he goes well beyond what is allowed in his critical brief and overstates his case.

But my reason for discussing this work on Herodotus is to see whether it can help us in any way to understand the author of the *Lives*. The list of characteristics given above includes one or two items which are inconsistent with what we find in the *Lives*. We are told that it would be malicious to refer to Cleon as 'audacious and mad', though Cleon is not treated at all leniently in the *Nicias*. Here, as elsewhere, Cleon is portrayed as an example of the demagogue-politician, and it is not surprising that his conduct is described in terms that show the gap between him and the ideal 'politicus'. But the Plutarch of *The Malice of Herodotus* seems

willing to show mercy even to Cleon. There is, too, some dis-
crepancy between the comment on Pericles in this work and the
treatment of him in the *Life*. The treatise says that it would be
wrong to maintain that Pericles started the war because of Aspasia;
the alternative, which is preferred, is to invoke the ambitious
*philotimia* of Pericles, who was eager to check Spartan arrogance.
Yet, as we have seen, ambition is not an unqualified good in the
*Lives*; and in the *Pericles* the disreputable causes of the Peloponnesian War *are* mentioned, and Plutarch's conclusion there is that
the truth is unknown. It is possible, then, that the treatise preceded
these particular *Lives*. But we can hardly say that this is likely on
such slender evidence, since when Plutarch is writing polemically,
he is apt to be carried away by the cause of the moment.

There is no fundamental inconsistency of attitude between the
treatise and the *Lives*; there is a similar determination to set greatness up and let it stand without feet of clay. What seems to have
incensed Plutarch above all is that Herodotus' malice was at
variance with the style. Though he admires the style of writers like
Thucydides and Xenophon, he does so because they have the
quality of vividness which transports the reader to the scene of
action. He would not himself, I think, take much delight in the
qualities which can attract a modern to Herodotus, who writes at
times as the amused spectator, though with a strong sense of
obligation to put down different versions of the facts.[53] The earnest
moralist in Plutarch, drawn by a spirit of reverence towards the
great, would not find it easy to understand one who was sympathetic to the Greek side but at the same time knew quite well
that different cities offered different versions of the Persian wars.
Though Plutarch does not mention this difference of outlook, it is
one of the causes which led him to inveigh against Herodotus; it
is significant that he admires the austere Thucydides, who is
extolled as a historian, though not for the reasons for which he
is respected today.

In the *Lives*, Plutarch's shrinking from malice shows through in
various ways. To take a few examples, it is not uncommon to find
that he is reluctant to use the obvious terms suggested by the
tradition, if that conveys a suggestion of hostility or disparagement.
We are now quite accustomed to speak of the 'conspirators' when
we wish to refer to the group which plotted against Julius Caesar,

and we do not think of ourselves as taking sides for or against the members of the group. But Plutarch, it is clear, felt uncomfortable about this way of talking, and shows this reserve at an important point in the story of the assassination. He mentions Caesar's lengthy conversation with Popilius Laenas, who has just wished the conspirators well, and goes on to describe their fear of betrayal. 'But the conspirators – to call them by that name – could not hear what was said . . .' (*Brut.* 16.3) Plutarch is here unwilling to use the obvious word and apologizes for bringing it in; had he looked for some euphemism, the result might have been to underline his sense of discomfort even more. The reason for this manoeuvring is as follows. In the abstract Plutarch admires Brutus (and Cassius,[54] to an extent) as one who acted out of conviction to achieve a good end, the removal of a tyrant and the restoration of liberty. (In fact, though the choice [*proairesis*] is admirable, the autocrat was not objectionable in practice). A term like 'conspiracy' implies underhand or furtive methods and might therefore seem to disparage the virtue of the hero, who may need political subtlety but ought to be open in his actions.

Though Plutarch himself does not speak of malice here, it seems from his apology that he is half-anticipating some such accusation. A passage in the *Crassus* (2.4) has a similar apology as well as an explicit reference to malice.[55] Plutarch is writing about Crassus' great wealth : 'most of this, if one must tell the truth harshly, he acquired through fire and war. The misfortunes of the Romans were his personal income.' The allusion is to the proscriptions of Sulla and to the fire-hazards in Rome, both of which gave Crassus the opportunity to buy property at a low price. The phrase 'through fire and war' is felt to be too trenchant a way of putting the facts and is therefore used with an apology. Crassus, indeed, has more faults or blemishes than many other heroes, but as a hero he has to be treated with proper decency. The truth about his faults has to be indicated, but it should not provide the opportunity to undermine his virtues entirely. It is, of course, possible that the vivid phrase had already been applied to Crassus in the sources; but whether it is a borrowing or not does not matter, since Plutarch feels that as a piece of adverse criticism it is very near to the limit.

The treatment of the Hellenistic heroes Aratus and Cleomenes[56] (though Plutarch, it should be noted, knows them only as Hellenic), was something of a problem. Plutarch admired both men and thought that both deserved to be commended in a biography. Yet the two Greeks had pursued opposite policies; Aratus, in Plutarch's eyes, began as the liberator of Greek cities from the external interference of Macedonia, but later was responsible for inviting Macedonia back into Greek affairs. This policy was designed to counteract the influence of Sparta and protect the Achaean League against Cleomenes. The modern historian can approve the episode as a political move, since he contrasts the forward-looking federation of the Achaean League with the old-fashioned city-state imperialism of Sparta. But this kind of political thinking was foreign to Plutarch. It seemed to him that Aratus of Sicyon might well be accused of inconsistency; how could the liberator fail to respond to a man like Cleomenes, whose domestic policies were intended to bring back the old Spartan values and remove corruption from the State? Plutarch, therefore, feels that both men are admirable since both can be shown to have acted in ways that befit the 'politicus'; yet the action of Aratus in turning to Macedonia seems to be a slur on his character, as Plutarch feels that he, of all men, should have preferred Cleomenes to Antigonus the Macedonian, who was abused by Aratus in his memoirs.[57] Consequently, Plutarch could not, in honesty, fail to make some adverse comments on Aratus; but he hastens to make it clear that he is not 'accusing' the Achaean, but writes in sorrow rather than in anger. It is a sad reflexion on the weakness of human nature that even with a man of Aratus' stature, it cannot perform actions that are fine without qualification.

Plutarch's benevolence is well illustrated by the way he uses the famous comment on Philopoemen, who was called 'the last of the Greeks'.[58] He accepts the verdict as a straightforward expression of praise, the more significant as it came from a Roman (*Philop.* 1.7). He would find it impossible to believe that this was perhaps the remark of a *cynical* Roman, alluding to Philopoemen as a local patriot who aimed at personal advancement through promoting the interests of his own homeland. In the *Aratus* (24.2), however, while not denying Philopoemen his tribute, he extends the phrase to cover an exploit of Aratus, the liberation of Corinth from the Macedonian garrison. This, he feels, was the 'last and latest *Hellenic* action', fit to be compared with the great deeds of the past. He means that there may still have been great men, like Philopoemen, since that date, but that this was the last instance of Greeks cooperating as effectively as they had in the Persian wars. We are told that the exploit shows both daring and good fortune, a reminder of the adage that for virtue to be effective 'divine good fortune' is necessary.

The anger of the treatise on Herodotus is directed against surreptitious malice. There *is* adverse criticism in the *Lives*, but it is always explicit and nearly always temperate. To describe this attitude as an avoidance of the sin of Herodotus, may seem to be comparing like with unlike. Yet it is apparent that hostile disparagement is called malice whether the criticism is overt or concealed. In Plutarch's view malice is to the writer or biographer what envy is to the contemporaries of a hero, the posthumous form of the same disease. It is a pity, though not a surprise, that greatness of character does at times attract envy. But one of the biographer's functions is to rescue the hero from this sort of misfortune; his own good will is a proper response to virtue.

Plutarch was not much interested in source-criticism but he had a quick eye for a hostile witness. The *Life* of the younger Cato is instructive here. The sources provided a good deal of so-called information deriving from the propaganda and slanders of the late Republic. Cato was accused of drunkenness, meanness, avarice and licentiousness,[59] character-traits which are all based on 'evidence' reported by Plutarch. But he clearly does not accept the charges and seems to report them, so to say, because they are there; the truth is served, however, not just by repeating the stories against Cato but by disbelieving them as well. With these allegations we should contrast the criticisms which are Plutarch's own,[60] though, as always, he is not vehement. He thinks that Cato made a mistake by refusing to let Pompey marry into his family, as this led to Pompey's alliance with Caesar and ultimately to political change. Cato might have tried to save the state by a less rigorous approach (cf. *Phoc.* 3), as is expected of a good statesman. Apart from this, the other main stricture is on Cato's deportment while praetor. Plutarch seems to think it was wrong of Cato not to wear shoes, since this is unbecoming in one who holds office (*Cato ii* 44.1). Though Plutarch's chief interest is in the use of power, office as such is felt to have a dignity of its own. Thus, in this *Life*, we can see that Plutarch's own criticisms are based on the high standards demanded of the ideal politician.

It was suggested above that a writer's malice is in a sense a variant on the envy felt by contemporaries. But this comparison should not be pressed too far. Some forms of contemporary envy are perhaps more excusable; it is, for instance, regrettable that the many should misconceive the virtues of a Fabius, but one cannot expect anything better from their ignorance. They need to be cajoled before they can act and feel with a semblance of order and reason. But one hero's hostility to another, like Fabius' resentment of Scipio, is a different matter; heroes have virtue to a greater extent and should conform to a higher expectation. Writers ought to measure up to the heroic rather than the popular standard. They are in a position to see greatness for what it is and should not malign it. Plutarch does not, for instance, attempt to see why Theopompus judged Demosthenes harshly, but feels aggrieved that the historian did not look at the facts with the same moral perception as himself. The hero, of course, is greater than the writer as action is superior to theory. Plutarch's sense of man's inadequacy allows him to let someone like Aratus off. But he does not seem so ready to forgive writers their hostility and malice, as he feels that they, like himself, are secondary onlookers and should respond positively to the virtues. To deny that they are there or misrepresent them is culpable trivialization. Though this train of argument is not made explicit in the *Lives*, it seems to me to be implied by Plutarch's known attitudes.

# 6

## *'Political' Philosophy*

Plutarch's own philosophy, including his study of Plato and his attacks on Stoicism and Epicureanism, would require lengthy and detailed discussion. But many of the topics that come under this heading are not of immediate concern to the reader of the *Lives*. For example, the interpretation of the *Timaeus*[1] is of great interest to the historian of Platonism, but is hardly relevant to an account of the biographer. In Plutarch's day philosophy was held to embrace three subjects; cosmology and science, logic and theory of knowledge, and ethics including politics. Only the last of these concerns us here, since the *Lives* are a study of what is the good for man in political society; the theme is the life of action and the ways in which action can be assisted by right theory.

In section 1 I discuss the references to what Plutarch calls 'early political philosophy', by which I mean the allusions to men who showed political wisdom before the time of Plato. Plato himself is of central importance in any account of Plutarch. Hence, in section 2, I illustrate Plutarch's general attitude to the philosopher he revered most, and go on to discuss the way in which he read Plato, using as evidence his quotations from the dialogues.

No one can fail to notice that the *Lives* dwell repeatedly on the importance of philosophy, and speak – sometimes with tantalizing brevity – of the association between some men of action and their philosopher contemporaries. Plutarch thereby insists that philosophy is of use; it is not remote from public life and should not be neglected. Section 3 is an attempt to analyse what is thought to be of value to the hero in the various relationships.

## 6.1 EARLY 'POLITICAL' PHILOSOPHY

The modern academic study of Greek philosophy postulates a development in three broad stages; the pre-Socratics, Plato and Aristotle, and the post-Aristotelian period. Interest in the pre-Socratics turns largely on their cosmology and their discussion of the questions, what is ultimate substance and what is meant by change? Some of their fragments do exhibit a concern with ethical and political questions, but these have not been regarded as typical of pre-Socratic interests. In effect, then, modern enquiry has accepted Cicero's formulation,[2] that 'Socrates called philosophy down from the heavens' and turned its attention to man and society, for this statement assumes that before Socrates philosophers devoted their energies to studying nature. There is no reason to question the validity of this approach to Greek philosophy; yet it will be found that Plutarch in the *Lives* conveys a rather different picture of philosophy before the time of Socrates and Plato. In a number of passages he puts the main emphasis on what must be called 'political philosophy' and seems to suggest that this was the first stage, preceding the development of cosmological theory. At first sight this is surprising; and, probably, it can only be explained by Plutarch's eagerness to insist that action and moral philosophy should always be on close terms with each other.

In the earlier period before Socrates one figure stood out; Solon is regarded not merely as a legislator-hero but as a political thinker as well. The evidence for his thought was to be found in his poetry, in which Plutarch detects a change in attitude. To start with, he says, Solon used poetry as a diversion, for no serious purpose; but later on he brought philosophical maxims into his poetry and introduced his political actions, not just for the sake of telling the story, but as a way of defending his record and exhorting the Athenians. Thus his 'philosophy' was devoted towards an immediate, practical end. Plutarch goes on to say that 'like most of those who at that time were wise (*sophoi*),[3] he took most delight in the political side of ethical philosophy' (*Sol.* 3.6). In this respect he draws a contrast between Solon as a political thinker and Solon the cosmologist, whom he describes as over-simple and old-fashioned. Plutarch's evidence for Solon as a thinker about nature comes from four lines of poetry which he quotes. 'From cloud comes the might of snow and hail, from bright lightning comes thunder. The sea is stirred by the winds, but if no wind moves it, it is the most just of all things.' Evidently Plutarch looked on this passage as a halting versification of the principles of coming-into-being. According to him, only Thales had developed wisdom (*sophia*) to cover more than practical needs; others were given the name wise because of their 'political virtue'. No one now would think that Solon was touching on the subject of nature (*phusis*) in the lines just quoted. The whole passage is a good illustration of Plutarch's tendency to import serious philosophical interpretations into his reading of poetry. It is worth noticing, too, the implication that political wisdom is relevant to man's needs; it is not free speculation for the sake of the truth alone, but is concerned with the values and objectives of society here and now.

The reason for counting Solon as a political philosopher is that he was traditionally regarded as one of the Seven Sages. Plutarch also wrote an account of the famous banquet at which these sages were present, the *Banquet of the Seven Sages*.[4] In this work the sages are invited to a feast by the tyrant Periander and deliver themselves of homely political wisdom, often in the form of proverbs, not all of which is calculated to find favour with their host. But one of the serious purposes behind the *Banquet* is to portray an association between thinkers and a ruler; one of the lessons to draw from the work is that power needs the presence of philosophy as an educative influence. Plutarch writes briefly of this meeting in the *Solon* (4); but he there gives more space to the argument between Anacharsis and Solon about the function of written law as a curb on injustice. Solon does not do too well in this discussion but this is not intended to lower his status as a political thinker. He hoped to make his laws effective, but events turned out as Anacharsis[5] said; law would subdue the weak but would not keep the strong in check.

Solon seems to be an important instance of early 'political philosophy' in the *Lives*, but he is not the first. The *Theseus* mentions Pittheus,[6] Theseus' grandfather, as a wise man of the day. The sort of wisdom evinced by Pittheus is compared with the maxims found in Hesiod,[7] relating to the practical conduct of everyday life. Plutarch sees this as wisdom concerning the management of one's *oikos* (household), as prefiguring therefore the concern with the ends of the state which is the mark of political philosophy when fully developed. Plutarch got this 'information' from Aristotle and he also quotes Euripides as evidence for the view that Pittheus was an educator (*Thes.* 3.2–4).

There is no formal link connecting Pittheus with Solon, no attempt to create a philosophical succession among the early sages. But Solon is given a pupil, Mnesiphilus,[8] who is mentioned in the *Banquet of the Seven Sages* as an admirer. He appears too in the *Themistocles* (2.5–6). Plutarch begins by rejecting the view that Themistocles was instructed by Anaxagoras and Melissus, as to him this does not make chronological sense. 'One might pay more attention to those who say that Themistocles was an admirer of Mnesiphilus, who was neither an orator nor one of the so-called philosophers of nature, but practised what was then called wisdom, which was in fact political skill and intelligence about how to act. He had made this his subject and continued as it were in succession from Solon.' The formal language here suggests that Plutarch is thinking in terms similar to those used in doxographies of natural philosophy. He hints that there was a 'political' school beginning with Solon and ending with Mnesiphilus. After the latter this political wisdom was diverted from action to rhetoric and its exponents became known as sophists. Plutarch disapproves of sophists; but here he sees them as practitioners of a form of political thinking which was diverted from its proper functions.

There is no satisfactory explanation for this passage which transforms Mnesiphilus into a political educator. The tradition knew Mnesiphilus as the Greek who advised Themistocles at a crisis in the wars against Persia. Themistocles saw that the advice was good and put it forward as his own plan. Thus the story, as told by Herodotus,[9] seems to illustrate the cunning of the great Athenian and may have started as a piece of gossip in order to denigrate him. In the *Malice of Herodotus* Plutarch treats the tale with scorn, as evidence of Herodotus' own intention to do Themistocles down. But, in the *Life*, though the anecdote is not repeated, the relationship between the two is taken seriously. Plutarch fosters the mere idea of an affinity between the hero and the thinker and is ready to make the most of slender evidence.

Two other passages concerning this early, pre-Socratic period are of interest. In the *Lycurgus* (4) Plutarch writes of Lycurgus' visit to Crete and his imitation of Cretan political customs. While he was in Crete he met one of those 'who were considered to be wise and to have political skill' and persuaded him to go to Sparta. This was a man called Thales[10] who had a reputation as a lyric poet but in fact, writes Plutarch, was concerned with the same objectives as the best law-givers. 'His poems were designed to promote civic obedience and to call the citizens to concord . . .' This early poetry, then, is valued because it is thought to contain political truths. A similar point is made about Lycurgus' regard for Homer. According to Plutarch, Lycurgus appreciated that the Homeric poems were 'political and educative' and was responsible for having the scattered lays put together. The early poets, Homer and Thales, are looked at as political thinkers like the philosophers of later times.[11]

Plutarch's account of Damon the musician is as difficult to unravel as his version of Mnesiphilus. He begins by saying that Damon instructed Pericles in music and then proceeds to turn Damon into a political adviser. 'It seems that Damon, being a consummate sophist, took refuge in the name of music as a way of concealing his (political) skill from the many. In fact his relationship with Pericles was that of trainer and teacher to political athlete.' (*Per.* 4.2) But Damon did not get away with his subterfuge. His political influence was noticed and he was exiled. Plutarch does not think that Damon did as much for Pericles as the philosopher Anaxagoras. But, clearly, he is prepared to interpret the tradition about him as a sign that he was a political thinker who tried to hide his profession under another label.

We are left wondering why Plutarch should have put this interpretation on the musical activities of Damon. Is this not a case of carrying an understandable enthusiasm for the influence of political thinkers too far? In describing Damon as a consummate sophist, Plutarch perhaps has in mind the description of the sophist in Plato as a master of evasion and concealment (though the tone of this passage is not exactly hostile to Damon). I think it possible that Plutarch's judgment was affected by the famous speech attributed to Protagoras by Plato.[12] The philosopher presents the sophist as a solemn figure concerned with safeguarding his reputation and with emphasizing the value of the sophistic art. In early times, according to Protagoras, men who were really sophists – for the sophistic art is said to be very old – did not wish to admit openly to their profession. They called themselves poets or musicians or teachers of physical exercise as a way of avoiding attention. But they failed to get away with this pretence; and as it is absurd, Protagoras continues, to practise evasion unsuccessfully, he has chosen a different solution. He admits that he is what he is and has not suffered any hurt in consequence, though he is obliged to Socrates for his tenderness about not damaging his reputation.

This whole passage pokes fun at sophistic pretentions – I think particularly of the claim that the sophistic art is old – and at Protagoras' concern with respectability. Plato enjoyed making him admit to what he is; it is a quiet Platonic joke that the sophist, that bare-faced pretender, should be portrayed as telling the truth, namely that he is a sophist. But I doubt whether Plutarch read the passage in this humorous sense. The idea that thinkers had concealed their activities by professing other subjects would appeal to Plutarch, especially as he was used to looking on poetry as a repository of philosophic truths. I would suggest therefore that he saw Damon as the kind of sophist mentioned in Protagoras' speech. The fact that he did not call himself one need not mislead the initiated reader who knows his Plato. If this is the case, then it follows that Plutarch read this section of the *Protagoras* in a rather literal-minded way. Other evidence also seems to me to point in the same direction.

These are indications, slight in themselves but cumulative, which suggest that Plutarch read into this early Greek period a concern with political philosophy that is either not there at all or is less than he thinks. Socrates himself appears in the *Lives* only in passing references. Plutarch thinks highly of him as an educator and regards him as a good influence on Alcibiades.[13] But he does not take up the charge that Socrates corrupted the young; quite apart from finding a relevant opportunity to discuss this, he would have felt the charge to be not worth refuting in detail. This respect for Socrates is shown by a comment at the end of the *Phocion* (38.5); the Athenians came to realize that their error in putting Phocion to death was as gross as the execution of Socrates.

Though Plutarch seems to exaggerate the significance of 'political philosophy' in the earlier Greek *Lives*, he does not regard it as a *sine qua non* for the good life, politically speaking, since he thinks that one can arrive at right political decisions without having had the benefit of formal philosophical instruction. If he had not thought in this way, Plutarch would probably have found it difficult to admit his early Romans as 'politici'. He does find that early Rome would have gained from more contact with the Muses – he certainly makes this point about Coriolanus – but does not deny it political wisdom. Numa, in fact, is treated with great respect. This is not because Plutarch has accepted the tradition that Numa was a pupil of Pythagoras, which he finds difficult on grounds of chronology. But he speaks of him as the type of the philosopher-king admired by Plato, who is said to have written many years after Numa lived. The reality, therefore, had occurred before the theory. Numa is taken as the kind of legislator-hero like Lycurgus, an incarnation of political wisdom. He is, of course, exceptional, but other Romans too are portrayed as having this sort of political wisdom to a great extent. The lesson is that unaided nature can succeed, but nature is likely to do better if it is assisted by 'political philosophy'. Power and philosophy should consort.

6.2 PLUTARCH'S READING OF PLATO

Plato was the philosopher whom Plutarch admired most; he quotes from him more than from any other author, and the nature of the references seems to indicate a close familiarity with the text. Even where Plutarch puts his quotations to doubtful use, it is arguable that the application is in a general way Platonist. I shall here indicate what elements of Platonism are appealed to in the *Lives* and discuss what inferences we can draw from Plutarch's comments on his references to Plato. It is not enough to know that he is given to quoting him; we want to have an idea of his accuracy and judgment in order to be clear about the relationship between reader and master.

Plutarch's admiration for Plato in the *Lives* is not based on theoretical grounds alone. He is described, in language which has a religious flavour, as 'the guide[14] to virtue' (*Dion* 1.3). By itself this comment would not take us very far, but it is evident from other passages that Plutarch reverenced the life as well as the doctrine. According to the *Nicias* (23) Plato's influence was all-important in gradually persuading ordinary people that the scientific explanation of celestial phenomena is not unreconcilable with a religious attitude towards god. Plutarch thinks that Protagoras was exiled and that Anaxagoras was imprisoned because of popular resentment directed at the theories of 'natural philosophers'; for good measure in his illustration he throws in the trial of Socrates, though he admits that Socrates had nothing to do with such explanations. He is writing loosely, fired by the idea that philosophy had come to seem irreligious. 'But then, late in time, Plato's shining reputation – because of the way he lived and because of the fact that he subordinated natural necessity to more valid principles – removed the suspicion attaching to these theories and made it possible for (scientific) learning to find its way among all men.' (*Nic.* 23.5) The respectability of Plato's life and beliefs is here portrayed as a friend to science. Plutarch, however, does not mean the disinterested search for scientific truth. He is thinking of a particular case, the correct explanation of eclipses, knowledge of which can be useful to the 'politicus' and to those whom he governs.

Nevertheless it is a slight shock to some modern ideas of Plato to find him described in this way. But modern pre-conceptions about Plato can derive some support from the description of Archimedes' mechanics. Though Plutarch speaks of the great prestige of this subject, he thinks of it as a kind of accidental development of geometry. He says that the subject started to make progress under Eudoxus and Archytas, but Plato complained that they were corrupting geometry by solving problems in the medium of perceptible objects instead of referring to invisible lines and planes. Thereupon mechanics was rejected by geometry and became one of the military arts. It did not advance in prestige until Hiero of Sicily persuaded Archimedes to 'divert his art from ideas to physical objects and make theory more accessible to the many by attaching it through perception to the things we need and use' (*Marc.* 14.8). In this curious passage, Plutarch does not blame Plato for this attitude to mechanics; he himself thinks that Archimedes belittled his engines as a by-product of his geometry, and to that extent Archimedean mechanics is not held to be in conflict with Plato's requirements. But Plutarch manages to have it both ways; he admires geometry and at the same time considers that the usefulness of mechanics resides, not in adding to the amenities of life, but in holding up to the ignorant a clear and visible pattern of the invisible principles. The fact that Archimedes' engines were of military use to his king is not felt to be so important, though Plutarch does describe various incidents in some detail. He respects Plato for valuing geometry but acknowledges that most of us need visual help in understanding its difficult principles.

In both these passages Plutarch is concerned with the relevance of philosophy to how we live, even if his attitude to mechanics seems at first to smack of that other-worldliness of which Plato is often accused. This idea of relevance is more apparent if we think of ethical theory, since Plutarch shares with many others the view that the point of philosophizing about the good life is to become good oneself. This explains his admiration for the way Plato lived, since the philosopher is seen as having practised what he preached. Plutarch does not say much in detail about Plato's life. But it is evident from the *Dion* that he admired his sobriety and restraint; his conduct at the court of Dionysius is put in strong contrast to the self-indulgence of the courtiers and sycophants who surrounded the tyrant.[15]

There is little in the way of criticism of Plato. The most significant point is made indirectly during an enthusiastic piece on the legislator Lycurgus. Plutarch asserts that the Spartan state, as created by Lycurgus, provided later theorists with their model. Lycurgus acted whereas Plato, Diogenes and Zeno 'merely left writings and theories behind them' (*Lyc.* 31.2). Here he is exploiting a favourite antithesis, between action (*ergon*) and theory (*logos*), in order to emphasize that good politicians do what theorists recommend; Lycurgan Sparta, that is, is Plato's *Republic* come to life before the theory. Though he is here concerned to applaud the active statesman rather than berate the thinker, he is in effect continuing to make the same point as in his rhetorical speeches on Alexander. In those speeches the argument that Alexander did what others merely preached has been treated in modern times as a sophistic paradox. This may be true of some details; but the underlying idea is one of Plutarch's cherished convictions. In the *Lycurgus* passage Plutarch is carried away by his genuine enthusiasm for Lycurgus into making a statement that seems derogatory to the author of the *Republic* and the *Laws*. But it was not his intention to criticize Plato so much as to say that even in Plato there was imperfection. He recognizes in the *Dion* that Plato did try to change Dionysius for the better; and Plato himself, in writing of his visit to Syracuse, says that he did so lest it be thought that he was all theory, not action.[16] The criticism of Plato the writer is therefore couched in Platonist terms.

In the rest of this section I shall discuss the references to Plato's works; we do not know whether Plutarch actually consulted them to verify quotations or phrases, but we have enough evidence to come to a conclusion about the way he used certain passages.

In several places there is a reference to what was, for Plutarch, one of Plato's cardinal doctrines – that power should be held and exercised by philosophers. A passage in the *Dion* (1.3) states the principle in a colourless way; the actions of Dion and Brutus are alleged to prove the truth of Plato's view, 'that power and good fortune must be conjoined with wisdom and justice before political actions can be fine and great'. Neither Dion nor Brutus, however, meets with the entire success that is expected of the philosopher-king. A passage in the *Numa* (20.8) seems closer to the language used by Plato, though it is not clear whether we can say which part of the *Republic* Plutarch has in mind.[17] He cites Numa as a proof of Plato's dictum 'that man's only escape and respite from troubles will be when by some divine good fortune royal power is united with a philosophical mind and makes virtue dominant and superior to badness'. Numa, like Lycurgus, is rated highly for having achieved what Plato described much later on. Plutarch here introduces the reference to Plato with the reflexion that Numa's reign was not weakened by hatred or envy; Numa therefore is untouched by that hostility which Plutarch's statesman is likely to incur. This absence of envy was a sign that Numa's Rome was a harmonious state and suggested to Plutarch that Numa himself should be considered a perfect ruler. But the only evidence for Numa's philosophy is Plutarch's own extrapolation from his reputed legislation. Whatever one thinks of Plato's dictum, he clearly supposed that his ruler-to-be would need formal instruction or education in philosophical principles. In effect Plutarch is here diluting Plato's observation, since he is, as always, anxious to point out that the philosophy of which he speaks is directed at action. But the reader would be happier if he could point to other influences than Egeria.

It is not surprising that a law-giver like Numa should eventually be given this accolade from the text of Plato. But that Cicero should be so complimented is more difficult to accept. We are told first of Cicero's incorruptibility as quaestor in Sicily and governor in Cappadocia. Plutarch then writes of his greatest triumph: 'in Rome itself, when he was appointed consul, he had in fact the power of a dictator and used it against Catiline. He is a witness on the side of Plato's view, that states will have a respite from troubles when great power and wisdom and justice all combine, as the result of some good fortune.' (*Dem.-Cic. comp.* 3.4) One feels here that the writer's enthusiasm for Plato's principle has made him lose all sense of historical judgment. He has remembered Cicero the student and translator of Greek philosophy[18] – he feels sympathy for the Roman who was called the idle Greek – and has overlooked the fact that the death of Catiline did not mean an end to Rome's political troubles. The reference to Plato's dictum is worthy enough; what is doubtful is the application to the case of Cicero. Though Plato's thought is not falsified in essence, it is diluted because Plutarch is ready to claim as an instance of philosophy one whose political conduct was good (Numa) and to exaggerate the effect of Cicero's philosophical study on his political behaviour. He seems to assume that Cicero was good because he had done philosophy and that Numa was philosophical because he was good. This antithesis is in the manner of a Plutarchan comparison but is not inaccurate.

Both the *Lycurgus* and the *Numa*, the former especially, are full of Platonist ideas. These legislators are praised for having created a condition of health in their respective communities, and in both *Lives* the original state of sickness is described by the same Platonist metaphor. In the *Lycurgus* (5.10) Plutarch says that at the time of Lycurgus' reforms the office of the Spartan kingship was 'inflamed'; and the legislator restored health to the body politic by tempering the kingship with the council of elders (the *gerousia*). The *Numa* (8.2) employs the same metaphor to describe the condition of Rome when Numa became king: 'Rome then was what Plato calls an inflamed city.'[19] We should note that the reference is now to the whole state, not to one office within the state. Early Rome, according to Plutarch, was too hard and warlike; the city was founded by an act of daring, had sustained itself by military ardour and

needed to be moved in the direction of peace. We might expect
Plutarch to be referring to the *Republic*, where Socrates is sketch-
ing the 'minimum state' in order to see where justice and injustice
reside. Glaucon complains that the members of this state will have
a basic or merely primitive existence; and, in reply, Socrates says
he will accommodate the citizens more lavishly and proposes therefore to sketch an 'inflamed city'. Thus the 'inflamed city' of the
*Republic* is a state that has more than the necessities of life; it has
luxuries and some degree of wealth. The contexts of these passages
show that Numa's Rome is not 'inflamed' in the same way as the city
described by Socrates, for the latter is certainly talking about amenities, not about an excess of military spirit. It would seem, then, that
Plutarch was here thinking of the passage in the *Laws* (691e), where
Plato speaks of the 'inflamed office' of the Spartan kings, which the
law-giver chastened and improved by setting up the *gerousia*.
'Inflammation' would easily lead Plutarch to think of excess of heat,
which he would locate in the spirit (*thumos*) of the early Romans;
their wars and conflicts would seem to him to prove the point.

In the *Numa* Plutarch is certainly thinking in the spirit of the
*Laws* passage, even though the form of words might take us first
to the *Republic*. There is, however, a feature of Plato's manner
that Plutarch seems to overlook; Socrates is in deadly earnest
throughout the dialogues but he combines it with a playful banter
which is alien to the solemnity of Plutarch's whole approach. We
have already seen that the failure to see a joke may be the reason
for describing Damon as a sophist. In discussing the influence of
Aspasia on Pericles, Plutarch refers to the first part of the
*Menexenus* as a joke, but seems nonetheless to regard this work as
evidence that Aspasia had a name for rhetoric. It is a doubtful
view. A passage in the *Lycurgus* also seems to show neglect of
Socratic humour. Plutarch gives first a number of sayings which
show the Spartan gift for trenchant utterance, and concludes, 'these
disclose what their sayings were like; some people have actually
said, without absurdity, that love of wisdom (*philosophein*), even
more than love of exercise, is the essence of laconizing' (*Lyc.* 20.16).
The source here is, again, the *Protagoras* (342a), where Socrates
expounds a line by Simonides and bases his argument on the
premise that Sparta is the oldest home of philosophy in Greece.
Spartans are said to have the knack of condensing wisdom in a

few words. This part of the speech is an urbane and elaborate joke, which counters Protagoras' claim that the sophistic art is very old. But Plutarch seems to have taken Socrates' remarks at face-value. His admiration for Sparta is, undoubtedly, in harmony with Plato's views, but he has used a curious piece of evidence to drive the point home at this stage.

In quoting Plato, Plutarch shows his relish for a striking phrase, which is all the more remarkable because his own prose is deficient in vigour. But the context in which Plato's phrase is set, can be obscured or lost from view. In the *Themistocles* (4.4) we are told how the hero encouraged the Athenians to increase their naval power in order to defend themselves against Persia and come to rule over the Greeks. He made them into marines and sailors in place of 'steadfast hoplites', as Plato puts it,[20] and exposed himself to the charge that 'Themistocles, by depriving the citizens of spear and shield, confined the Athenian people to the rowers' bench and the oar'. In several passages, especially in the *Laws*, Plato comments adversely on the bad political consequences of Athenian sea-power. The political character of a naval democracy is more volatile than that of a state whose main military strength is based on hoplites. The heavy infantry must stay put to fight it out with the enemy, whereas naval forces can take refuge in their ships by a 'shameful act of running away'. In Plato's view Marathon and Plataea made the Greeks better; Salamis and Artemision did not. Plutarch shows that he is familiar with this passage but does not wish to go into the important question 'whether Themistocles harmed the rigour and purity of the state by his actions'. It is said to be a question of a more philosophical kind. But the reader is likely to think that, for a Platonist, this is to dodge the issue. One who knew Plato's thought as well as Plutarch – one who is discussing the functions of the good statesman and, by implication, the criteria of the good state – might well have confronted some of the objections raised against naval power and naval democracy in the Platonic dialogues. These, if we take them seriously, are bound to affect our view of fifth-century Athenian politicians, like Themistocles and Pericles. But Plutarch would probably have felt awkward about going into detail; he wishes to admire, as we have seen, and if he were to accept the criticisms made by Plato he would have to find fault. A basic honesty makes him refer to Plato here; but the consequence of not exploring Plato's thought is to make the phrase 'steadfast hoplites' an ornament rather than a means of insight into the character of the statesman.

The same allusion is treated, though more obscurely, in the *Philopoemen* (14). Plutarch is about to describe an unsuccessful naval attack made by his hero on the Spartan enemy Nabis.[21] The main lesson of the episode is clear enough; Philopoemen, who was a good commander on land, failed to recognize that training is a considerable part of virtue (*arete*). War at sea requires its own preparation, and Philopoemen was therefore presumptuous in expecting that he could turn at a moment to demonstrate his virtue in an unfamiliar element. But the narrative here is introduced by a comparison. 'He seemed to have the same experience as Epameinondas, for his performance at sea was far below his virtue and glory. Yet some say that Epameinondas came back deliberately from Asia and the islands without success, as he was not willing to give his citizens a taste of the advantages to be derived from sea-power, so that they should not gradually turn into sailors and be corrupted, instead of remaining "steadfast hoplites", as Plato puts it.' The discursiveness of this section is baffling and it is difficult to see what started the train of thought. Perhaps it was something like this. Plutarch remembers first that neither of the Thebans succeeded in naval warfare; but he then adds a suggestion that Epameinondas' failure may have been deliberate, as he did not wish to change the nature of Theban power and so cause the corruption mentioned by Plato. The *type* of incident – I mean the sudden switch from war on land to war on sea – *could* have this kind of corruption as a consequence. Yet though we can accept that Philopoemen did not fail deliberately in his naval engagement, we are left wondering whether Plutarch means us to think that he was at fault for embarking on Themistoclean policies for Thebes. As often, his habit of mind is to isolate an event from its particular circumstances and process it through comparison with other events, which have been similarly abstracted. He is indifferent to the question, what were the reasons for this particular naval exercise in the war against Nabis. The use of Plato's remark seems far-fetched until we take into account the fact that Plutarch is surprised and disturbed by the idea that Thebes should have even attempted to become a sea-power.

Our dissatisfaction with these passages is probably caused by the brief allusive manner of quotation. It is fair to add that some quotations are aptly used, and are not just ornamental. Plutarch was much impressed by Plato's note of warning in a letter addressed to Dion.[22] He reminded Dion that the politician must cultivate other men, as this is a medium for his action : 'but stubbornness cohabits with isolation.' Plato was expressing his anxiety about Dion's remoteness; Dion's intentions were pure but his behaviour was ungracious and unpersuasive. Plutarch too is insistent that the statesman should make his virtues credible, which is why he refers to the remark that Aristotle had the gift of persuasiveness. He adapts Plato's warning to two of the heroes, Dion and Coriolanus (*Dion* 8.4 and *Cor.* 15.4). Both men, though in differing ways, are at the opposite pole to flattery, which is of course the vice of demagogues. They seem to have gone to the other extreme, though this is to express the matter in terms of the Aristotelian mean. Dion has too much stiffness and outward arrogance; Coriolanus, through lack of education, is ignorant of the fact that the politician must practise forbearance, a virtue which is popularly scorned. In both cases the quotation seems to be just to the Platonic context and to bring out Plutarch's own demands of the good 'politicus'.

The range of quotations is considerable and shows Plutarch's wide acquaintance with the dialogues. The evidence suggests that Plutarch had a tendency to take memorable phrases from Plato without always assimilating the Platonic context to his own. The quotations may seem ornamental at times; but they usually function as a vehicle for Plutarch's home truths as well. Thus, when we read that Cleopatra 'divided flattery not into four, as Plato says, but into many parts', we should not think of this phrase as a mere sophistic improvement on Plato.[23] Plutarch is reminding us that flattery can be as adverse to the statesman as it is when practised by a demagogue upon his people.

## 6.3 PHILOSOPHERS AND HEROES

It is evident that Plutarch sometimes attaches the label 'philosophy' or 'philosopher' to ideas and men in a way that seems to us to commend rather than describe. We do not feel impelled to call

Solon a political philosopher or to think of Spartan institutions as a kind of philosophy. But Plutarch does this without qualms, since he considers that philosophy aims at the good life and supposes that a good man can be called a philosopher in action, even if he has not been exposed to technical instruction in the narrow sense. Such a person shows by his life that he has done what others advocate or preach. Plutarch's usage is not therefore descriptively rigorous, nor should we expect it to be so. He is reminding his readers that what matters is the example of virtue; and the example or incident, if it comes off, is thought of as implying right ethical theory. We might object that Plutarch is applying to early Greece or distant Rome ethical standards which were invented by Plato. But Plutarch would reply that the standards have always applied; he thinks of Plato as discovering what is there, or formulating that which was implied by action.

This readiness to find philosophy and philosophers where we see none is simply one expression of Plutarch's wish that philosophy should make itself felt in real life. He also draws our attention to relationships between men of power and those who were indisputably philosophical thinkers. In these cases our historical doubts are of a different order. We have no reason to disbelieve that Brutus, for example, consorted with men who were and are called philosophers; but we are inclined to question whether the influence was as Plutarch alleges, or often seems to take for granted. It is a different problem from having to accept that Mnesiphilus was a political philosopher who influenced Themistocles, for here our sense of incredulity is stirred before we ask about the particular influence. In these cases Plutarch is reiterating the principle laid down in his short treatise on the topic that the philosopher should above all converse with leaders or eminent men. He there makes the important point that philosophy which improves a ruler is of more benefit than philosophy which makes the private individual better. Philosophers should not expect men of power to abdicate from their positions of responsibility, but should themselves be in attendance, though not as flatterers. The aim of philosophy is not to enable good citizens to tolerate bad rulers, but to perfect the ruler as a way of improving society as a whole. Philosopher-kings, so to say, are deemed to have precedence over philosopher-citizens. The *Lives* offer several instances of association between philosophers and statesmen; in the following pages I shall explain in what ways the philosopher is alleged to have assisted the statesman.

The discussion is now concerned with those philosophers who had a definite allegiance to a particular school. As we would expect, the school most reverenced by Plutarch was the Academy. The *Dion* and the *Brutus* are put forward as a tribute to Plato's institution, to show that neither Greeks nor Romans should find fault with its services. Dion, who met Plato himself, and Brutus, who was nurtured on his works, were trained in the same establishment and were there prepared for heroic feats. Their careers show that Plato, the high priest of virtue, was right to say that power and good luck must combine with wisdom and justice before political action can be fine. Now it cannot be said that Plutarch is led to make this judgment because Dion and Brutus succeeded in their plans. Indeed, both *Lives* are a story of initial success turning to failure. It seems that Plutarch's admiration for these men, coupled with his zeal to stake a claim for philosophy, has led him to exaggerate their debt to their training.

There is every reason to believe that the living Plato influenced Dion, though it is impossible for us to tell whether his career shows the pupil of Plato more than the Syracusan politician and thwarted kinsman of Dionysius. According to the *Life*, Dion imbibed from Plato a hatred of tyranny. But Plato's concern for his pupil did not stop there. He was perturbed about Dion's character, even when he was satisfied about his principles. He encouraged Dion to be friendly with Speusippus, in order to impart some grace and urbanity to his forbidding stiffness.[24] Plutarch is here anxious to stress the mellowing influence of philosophy on character; it bestows knowledge of right principles and can make political conduct credible. The praise of the Academy recurs towards the end (52.3); while the whole world had turned its gaze on Dion as the liberator of Syracuse, his eyes were fixed on the Academy as the arbiter of his actions. Only the Academy's verdict would count, since that body would not be dazzled by mere success but would only admire the right use of power. At the same time Plutarch wished to make it clear that the Academy could not be blamed for the conspiracy which destroyed Dion. Calippus, the leader of the plot, is portrayed as a false member of the school, a man who had associated with Dion in Athens but was not philosophically educated. This *Life*, therefore, attributes much to Plato's influence, including a realistic preoccupation with making Dion himself more acceptable in Syracusan politics.

It is more difficult to see how the Academy influenced Brutus.[25] We are told that Brutus was acquainted with all the schools but was most enthusiastic about the old Academy (*Brut.* 2.2). His admiration went to Antiochus[26] of Ascalon, whose teaching marked a break with the scepticism of the new Academy. But, as the *Cicero* (4.2) makes plain, Antiochus himself was in some respects a follower of Stoic theory. Like many at this time he was a philosophical eclectic. Plutarch is content to claim Brutus for the Academy without mentioning his own works on philosophy or discussing *how* the Academy influenced him. The comparative pattern, established at the beginning of the *Dion*, is here imposed on Brutus, though it would have been truer to say that he, like Antiochus, was eclectic. In general Plutarch assumes, rather than shows, that the influence of philosophy is detectable in Brutus' life. He does not neglect the descendant of the first Brutus who expelled the Tarquins,[27] but seems to ascribe the hatred of tyranny to the influence of the Academy.

The Academy, then, enjoys pride of place as the school whose philosophy can be of most assistance. Other schools are seldom mentioned in the *Lives*, which are relatively free of those attacks on Stoicism and Epicureanism that are a feature of the *Moralia.* Cassius'[28] Epicureanism is mentioned, but – perhaps surprisingly – there is no explicit comment on his adherence to a philosophy which was thought to condemn man to political quietism. Stoicism, however, is made the subject of a criticism, though it is brief and temperate. 'Stoic philosophy is full of danger for quick, powerful natures; but when it is mixed with a character that is deep and stable, it helps that character to perfect its proper good.' (*Cleom.* 2.6) Plutarch is here saying how the Stoic Sphaerus[29] admired Cleomenes' manliness and stimulated his ambition to act. In this case the influence of Stoicism was not the best for the given character; Cleomenes is described as vehement and fiery, prepared to impose the good on his countrymen by force, if persuasion should fail (*Cleom.* 1.5). Had he been like the younger Cato, with a more settled nature, the observation on Stoicism would not have been made.

Even if we accept the principle that philosophy is useful to men of power, we may well ask for more detail about the actual relationships described by Plutarch. Does he give us instances of how in fact philosophy has helped? Does he illustrate philosophers' influence on particular policies? It seems that Plutarch would cite Dion's political objectives as inspired by Plato, though the case of Brutus is more obscure. Apart from these, there are perhaps only three instances of philosophers exerting an influence on particular policies. Damon is said to have suggested to Pericles the scheme of public payment as a way of bribing the people (*Per.* 9.2–3). But, in the light of the remarks we have made earlier, we can hardly take Damon as a philosopher in the strict sense, even if we accept the tale. Elsewhere, we are told that the Stoic Sphaerus joined Cleomenes as an active participant in his reforms (*Cleom.* 11.4). Yet this is not to say that Sphaerus inspired the reforms; it seems, rather, that he did his part by awakening Cleomenes' urge to action. The Spartan's own patriotism did the rest. The last possibility concerns the relationship between the Stoic Blossius and Tiberius Gracchus. Plutarch admittedly repeats the version of many writers, that Tiberius was prompted to bring in his reforms through the influence of Diophanes the rhetor and Blossius the philosopher. But he gives several other possibilities as well and refuses to commit himself to any of them. In a later passage (*Tib. Gracch.* 20.5) an anecdote stresses the loyalty of Blossius to Tiberius, shown by his attitude to the committee of investigation which was set up after Tiberius' death. It has been argued that Blossius[30] was a philosopher who was politically active, both with Tiberius and with Aristonicus of Pergamum. But it cannot be said that Plutarch makes this point.

My conclusion is that Plutarch does not examine associations between philosophers and heroes in order to show that the former had a direct influence on policies. Perhaps the question would not even have occurred to him in this form. His whole approach to these relationships is more oblique. The use of philosophy to the hero emerges in various ways; and in the rest of this section I shall indicate what is valued by Plutarch in the different paradigms.

We have already noticed in the *Dion* that the philosopher sets out to improve the hero's character. Probably this is a Plutarchan adaptation of the Platonist principle, well described by Taylor as 'the tendance of the soul'. This improvement of character is discerned in the relationship between Anaxagoras and Pericles. According to Plutarch, the philosopher created the statesman who did not need to stoop to demagogic means. Anaxagoras' study of 'things on high' elevated his friend's character and was responsible for his sublime oratory, which was untouched by vulgar buffoonery.[31] The link between the study of cosmology and the effect on character is established through emphasis on words such as 'things on high' and 'making the character lofty'. Anaxagoras also receives the credit for more ordinary traits; Pericles' seriousness, his unhurried walk and restrained voice-delivery. Plutarch gives no evidence for this view. He has accepted the tradition of the dignified Pericles, who was famous for his oratory, and has himself asserted that there was an indebtedness to Anaxagoras. By so doing he shows his sense of what is due to the claims of philosophy rather than his sense of historical judgment.

Even if cosmology does not seem relevant to character, it can assist the 'politicus' by telling the truth about celestial phenomena and so releasing him from superstition (*deisidaimonia*) – the fear that these phenomena are designed for the hurt of mankind. The study of nature replaces this with true piety (*Per.* 6.1). No evidence is here offered for the assertion that Pericles was so liberated by Anaxagoras. But perhaps a later anecdote in this *Life* (35.2) was regarded as evidence by Plutarch. This is a story of how Pericles abated his men's fears of a solar eclipse by a demonstration which suggests that he knew the theory of eclipses, and he could well have learned this from Anaxagoras. Plutarch, in several passages, seems to insist on the point that a knowledge of astronomy can only benefit the 'politicus'. Nicias' anxiety about the lunar eclipse in Sicily would have been less had he known the theory (*Nic.* 23);[32] and Dion, who like Pericles is initiated in philosophy, was not disconcerted by an eclipse of the moon, though his troops needed reassurance from a seer (*Dion* 24).

Philosophy does most for the hero, however, by imparting to him a sense of true values, such as love of freedom and a hatred of flattery. The philosopher appears here as the enemy of the tyrant. Philopoemen, the last of the Greeks, was indebted for his education to two citizens of Megalopolis who had studied with Arcesilaus in the Academy. Plutarch describes these men – Ecdelus and

Demophanes[33] – as 'having brought philosophy into political action, more than any of their contemporaries'. Plutarch knows them as liberators of Megalopolis, and connects their opposition to tyranny with their pursuit of philosophy. He sees their influence on Philopoemen as another tribute to philosophy : 'they included their education of Philopoemen among their other achievements, on the grounds that, with the help of philosophy, they had made him into a benefactor of the whole of Greece.' (*Philop.* 1.5) This freedom implanted by philosophy does not mean autonomy for its own sake or unqualified democracy. It refers to the expulsion of tyrants as a half-way stage on the way to the institution of philosopher-kings. The fact that such figures seldom occur in history matters less than the need to expel tyrants as a necessary pre-condition. But why are tyrants so objectionable, if it is possible to envisage the reform of the tyrant Dionysius? The tyrant, we can say, uses force, where the true leader would employ persuasion. The tyrant's way of life shows that there is a barrier between him and the citizens. With Dionysius it is a barrier consisting of flatterers as well as armed mercenaries. With Aristippus[34] of Argos Plutarch dwells with satisfaction on the timidity and fear which made the tyrant lock himself in every night (*Arat.* 25–26). Tyranny stands for a way of life which will be rejected by anyone who comes in contact with philosophy.

Just as philosophy cures its devotees of tyranny, so too it disposes of the demagogue's vice, flattery. This theme is particularly noticeable in the *Dion*, where it plots a contrast between the philosophical Dion and, on the other hand, the courtier Philistus and the demagogue Heracleides. Plutarch also points out that there is flattery directed at the body as well as at the mind. It is in this context that he first speaks of Socrates' genuine concern for Alcibiades, and differentiates him from the false suitors, dedicated to their own pleasure (*Alc.* 6). Similarly he writes of the profit derived by the elder Cato from the teaching of Nearchus;[35] this Pythagorean reiterated the Platonic doctrine, that pleasure is the greatest incitement to acting wrongly, and so taught Cato to strengthen the attachment to his frugality and self-control.

Philosophy is also a handbook of consolation when events go against one; not only does it provide the spur to action, it is there to provide against withdrawal or disaster. Early on in the *Lucullus*

(1.6), the hero is praised for retiring into philosophy and for 'easing in good time his ambition after his conflict with Pompey'. The judgment is kinder to philosophy than to the facts, for when Plutarch comes to the end of Lucullus' career he writes at length of his hedonistic retirement,[36] though he does give some space to Lucullus the bibliophile, attended by Greek men of learning. The reason for what seems the exaggeration of the first chapter is that Plutarch has in mind a comparison between Lucullus and Marius, a point which is finally made explicit near the end (*Luc.* 38.3). It is better to calm down, away from political strife, than to continue like Marius; and Plutarch thinks he can attribute Lucullus' cure to the influence of philosophy. Philosophers can also act as doctors of the soul in a time of personal grief. Philosophers came from all parts to console Cicero when his daughter died, though they did not succeed (*Cic.* 41.8). And Callisthenes and Anaxarchus (it is noteworthy that Callisthenes is here called philosopher) tried to administer consolation to Alexander after the murder of Cleitus, though Anaxarchus' method is not approved (*Alex.* 52.3).

There are also relationships between philosophers and heroes where no special lesson is to be read; rather, one feels that the connexion is in some way prestigious for both. Plutarch writes at some length about Aristotle[37] as the teacher of Alexander (*Alex.* 7–8); Aristotle ministers to the king's great ambition and is held responsible for his interest in medicine. We are told that Alexander's passion for philosophy never left him, but find it difficult to see that this means much more than a general curiosity. In fact we feel frustrated that Plutarch says nothing about the obvious contrast between the philosopher of the city-state and the creator of the Hellenistic monarchies. But then Plutarch believes that the city-state is the vital, continuing element, present both in the Hellenistic world and in the Roman empire.

Even more obscure is the relationship between Augustus and Areius (*Ant.* 80). Augustus entered Alexandria in the company of the philosopher Areius[38] and honoured him before the people. The reader is meant to take this as a compliment to philosophy, though the political needs of the time suggest that Augustus wished to show his approval of Areius as one who would be useful to him. The story then becomes a pleasing tale of how the emperor pardoned the sophist Philostratus as a way of saving Areius from unpopularity. The sophist is here described as an improper claimant to membership of the Academy, though he may be the same Philostratus[39] as the one who was alleged to have been honoured for his philosophy by the younger Cato (*Cato ii* 57.4).

It is generally true to say that Plutarch claims more for the influence of philosophers than an enquiring reader is prepared to allow. We would like more evidence than is given (or was available) in order to assess the education of a Philopoemen or evaluate the Stoicism of a Cato. We notice too that some relationships are used to illustrate favourite Plutarchan themes, like the moderating of ambition (*Luc.* 1). We can conclude that the emphasis on these relationships was, to a large extent, created by Plutarch himself. But we should next consider why he chose to give this stress to the meagre facts at his disposal.

The reason is, partly, what one might call theoretical. He was attracted to the position which Socrates takes up against Callicles in the *Gorgias*. Philosophy should *not* be just an elegant part of one's education in youth, a suitable employment for young men and an old instructor in a corner.[40] It is concerned with establishing what is right and not right for one's own way of life, and has therefore an influence which can permeate the whole of one's outlook. There is little doubt that Plutarch echoes these sentiments of the *Gorgias*. But to talk of bookish theory is to tell only part of the story. He echoes the book because, in his view, the book happens to be true. Plutarch is throughout concerned to show that philosophy is of service to public life. In an indirect way he is harping on this doctrine in the *Sign of Socrates*, since the preparations for the liberation of Thebes are interspersed with wide-ranging philosophical discussions. Here the dramatic impact is that philosophy is not remote from action, even when it seems to be, for the discussion is always apt to turn to such subjects as the good or the relationship between god and man. Plutarch therefore is far removed from what can be called the traditional Roman view – a view which was clearly no longer that of his Roman friends – that philosophy stands for *otium*, non-involvement in public affairs.

At the same time the effect of the *Lives* is to emphasize that philosophy is respectable, that philosophers are upright men with the same interests as (good) government. The history of the first

219

century AD gives us reason to suppose that philosophy had become divorced from power. The cult of the philosophical Romans, Brutus and Cato, was at times a gesture of defiance against an autocracy.[41] Many so-called philosophers were not socially respectable, and perhaps these were the main targets of imperial edicts of banishment. Thus, among upper-class Romans and among Greek dependants, philosophy had become a form of intellectual protest against the government. Whether deliberately or not, Plutarch takes up a quite different attitude. He might well have done so anyway, as one who was in a sense determined to play the part of Plato to his age. The *fact* that he makes so much of philosophy as beneficial to government, may confirm that the *Lives* were composed under Trajan when philosophers felt free to address and lecture an acceptable monarch. The passages in the *Lives* which describe the heroes' debt to philosophers are so many notes of a factual kind comparable in their way to the more extended dialogues of Dio Chrysostom on kingship – though Diogenes in Dio takes up a position of superiority to Alexander which is foreign to the spirit of Plutarch's paradigms. Here, then, Plutarch was probably in harmony with a new trend, which preached the necessity for philosophers and men of power to act on the same side. Plutarch's view is a world away from the cult of withdrawn philosophy that is advocated by Seneca in a letter to Lucilius (*ep.* 5). Seneca warns against wearing one's philosophy too apparently, as he holds that it is meant to improve the private self without flaunting the signs before others. Plutarch would have agreed about the need to avoid ostentation; but his philosophy is a thing destined to be of value to public men and will therefore benefit political life. Some of the examples show that philosophy is hostile to tyrants, but the implication is always that philosophy can and should cooperate with government. It is not likely that anyone in the Trajanic period would have found in the *Lives* a plotter's inspiration. But their effect in a period of autocratic oppression could well have been very different.

# 7

# *Rhetoric and Oratory*[1]

It is easy to overlook the fact that the author of the *Lives* had received a rhetorical education as well as a training in philosophy. His enthusiasm for Plato makes it seem unlikely that he would have had much respect for the formal training in the rhetorical schools. But he knew the rules, as he shows in some of his essay-speeches, and he also wrote a work on rhetoric which has not survived. Besides, most of the heroes had been distinguished orators – their political careers would have been impossible if they had not wielded the art of persuasion – and the traditions about them included some information about their capacities as speakers both in the law-courts and in political meetings.

Ability as a speaker is not regarded by Plutarch as an end in itself but as a means subordinate to the end of making the statesman more effective in his community. The function of oratory is examined in section 1. In the second place he considers that a man's oratory can be used as a guide to his character. He illustrates oratory not so much by speeches (though some short ones do occur) but by sayings, which are treated as a sufficient index to the oration. Plutarch respects certain qualities in the orator which are not so highly esteemed by rhetorical theorists (section 2).

The rhetoric of the heroes is a manageable subject in a short account such as this; but it would be difficult to include an analysis of Plutarch's own rhetoric in the *Lives*. Though he tends to play down his role in presentation and style, and looks on himself as transmitting moral facts, his own art of comparing and distinguishing is a rhetorical scheme that dominates the comparisons (*sunkriseis*) which end most of the *Parallel Lives* (section 3).

## 7.1 THE FUNCTION OF ORATORY

Plutarch usually makes an allusion to the abilities of the heroes as orators. At a first reading these comments appear to be no more than a complimentary repetition of material found in his sources. Yet, when we look into them more closely, we shall find that his remarks on oratory are conditioned by his requirement that man should be a good statesman or a 'politicus'. He is not interested in the heroes' oratorical talents for their own sake; oratory is only valuable as a support to the good political life. Plutarch's whole approach to this question differs therefore from the attitudes evinced by rhetorical theorists and admirers of oratorical power like Cicero and Quintilian. And we shall see that Plutarch differs from them not merely on the value of oratory as an art. Within the subject he picks out certain qualities and skills as admirable, which would not have the same appeal to a theorist.

It should be remembered, then, that man as a statesman is engaged in a higher form of activity than the orator who has a case to win in the courts or who has to put on an exhibition of his skill. The statesman needs deliberative oratory to present his policies; Plutarch is much less interested in forensic oratory and hardly mentions epideictic oratory in the *Lives*. But he makes it clear that oratory is valued as an instrument; thus we read that 'Fabius' oratory was a means of persuading the people and had the ornament that was appropriate to his way of life. There was no adventitious elegance about it, no insubstantial or popular charm.' (*Fab.* 1.7)[2] He goes on to say that some had compared the depth of meaning to be found in Fabius' maxims with the much-admired *sententiae* of Thucydides. He is not thinking of style only, divorced from content. The discourse of Fabius is supposed to give information about his moral character, which is said to harmonize with what is known about him from other evidence.

The idea that oratory is an instrument is repeated elsewhere. Pericles, who is paired with Fabius, resembles him closely in this respect: 'he had acquired a style of oratory that, like an instrument, fitted his manner of life and the greatness of his conceptions . . .' (*Per.* 8.1) The subordinate nature of oratorical prowess is here emphasized by recording Pericles' debt to Anaxagoras; the latter's study of nature (*phusis*) is described as the dye in which Pericles' oratory was steeped. Thus Pericles the orator gained the qualities for which he was famous – one explanation of his nick-name, the Olympian, ascribed it to his ascendancy as a speaker – from his acquaintance with philosophy. Here Plutarch is taking up the suggestion developed in Plato's *Phaedrus*,[3] that rhetoric can only become an art if it comprises knowledge of the nature of the soul; and it is not possible to acquire this 'psychology' unless one first inquires into the nature of the universe. Plato was prepared to make some concessions to the supporters of rhetoric, but only by altering the very nature of the subject which they professed. Plutarch, similarly, wishes to emphasize that a man's rhetoric gets its colour from more worthy things. Pericles had some considerable reputation as an orator, and Plutarch is ready to interpret this not as a testimony to the power of oratory, but as evidence that Pericles was influenced for good by a philosopher.

In both cases Plutarch thought he had some record of the heroes' discourse. He refers to an encomium delivered by Fabius on his son (though it is not clear that he is claiming to have read this alleged speech himself) and he quotes one or two of the famous sayings attributed to Pericles. These were common knowledge in antiquity, though it is interesting to note that Quintilian[4] is reserved about the claims made for Periclean oratory on the strength of the fragments. Plutarch, however, is more confident and assertive. Evidence of this sort was, of course, very acceptable to Plutarch, as it enabled him to deploy a saying effectively. The saying is to the full speech as the incident is to the campaign, and this is one reason why it is mentioned in the programme-statement in the *Alexander*. Yet though Plutarch had evidence for the oratory of Fabius and Pericles, he did not approach the question of a hero's oratory in a careful way, by looking up their speeches and asking if they were genuine. He even comments on the oratory of early figures like Publicola and Coriolanus and says that they were powerful speakers. It is possible that he thought he could base his judgment on the speeches attributed to them by Dionysius of Halicarnassus (though this is not to say that he believed them to be a faithful record).[5] But one begins to think that the early Romans are given credit for their oratory simply because it is a Plutarchan tenet that the statesman must be able to speak well.

The main function of this oratory is 'to inform and persuade'.

Fabius tries to cure the Romans' anxiety after their defeat at Trasimene by telling the people that the disaster happened because their general had neglected the gods (*Fab.* 4.4). Pericles tells the Athenians that they can do as they wish with their allies' financial contributions, since Athens guarantees their military defence (*Per.* 12.3). The statesman uses oratory to point out 'facts' about the situation, which are either forgotten or not noticed by the people. Plutarch, then, is prone to think of his statesman-heroes as men who know the better and have mainly to expound it; they are, or tend to be, paternalists, administering truths. Now it is certainly the case that rhetorical theory acknowledged 'teaching' as one of the orator's functions. But the theorists think that the art of moving the emotions is an even clearer index to oratorical ability.[6] The ability to sway an audience was a quality admired in Cicero, which he also admires in his theoretical works. Though Plutarch does mention this quality, his preferred model of political behaviour is not that of men competing for influence, but of one man imposing his certainty on the ignorant many. Aemilius' speeches to the Romans are good examples of Plutarch's preferences in political oratory. When elected consul, he tells the people that he did not seek power; if they wanted him to rule they should accept his decisions and methods. He makes a point of not flattering the people (*Aem.* 11). His later discourses on the subject of fortune and its mutability are a sort of moral instruction delivered by the expert to the uneducated (*Aem.* 17 and 36). The oratory admired here resembles deliberative oratory, for the speaker is dealing with the topic, what is best for his audience. But since he is deemed to *know* the answer, his discourse is a lecture rather than a speech to which assent or dissent can be the proper reaction.

Plutarch writes with approval of Aemilius' abstention from forensic oratory. It would be wrong to divert one's potential for virtue into a smaller field than the opportunities provided by war and politics. He recognizes (*Luc.* 1) that Romans were litigious but prefers to interpret the fact as a way of teaching the young to admire virtue, not as a way of engaging in politics through prosecutions in the courts. But though he dislikes the idea that oratory can be used to promote oneself, he admits that it can and should be used as a defensive weapon. The statesman must know how to defend himself against unjust attacks, as Marcellus does when slandered by the tribune Bibulus or accused by the Syracusans (*Marc.* 27 and 23). Self-defence through oratory is legitimate just as talking about one's exploits can be legitimate, when one is unjustly attacked.[7] He dwells therefore on the idea that oratory is a means of defence; the assaults mounted by demagogues and bad statesmen are instances of a misuse of oratory.

Plutarch's whole attitude to the function of oratory is well summarized by his comment on the younger Cato. 'He also practised the oratory which is an instrument for dealing with assemblies; he thought it right that political philosophy, as in a large city, should have a bodyguard alongside.' (*Cato ii* 4.3) Oratory, that is, stands to political virtue, as the soldiers in Plato's *Republic* stand to the guardians. Oratory does not know about political ends, but it is indispensable; and the principal uses are to expound truths or defend against injustice.

The phrasing of some comments on oratory suggests that good character is more important in Plutarch's eyes than skill with words; and this principle is one way of distinguishing between the statesman and the demagogue. The point is made in an anecdote in the *Precepts on Public Life* about a meeting of the Spartan assembly, during which a course of action was persuasively advocated by a person notorious for bad conduct. Although the proposal seemed attractive, it was not accepted until the same case had been presented by a less adroit but more upright citizen (801B). The Athenians did not even need to hear a proposal advocated by Themistocles; it was enough for them that Aristeides had rejected it, on the grounds that, though expedient, it was unjust (*Them.* 20.1–2). The primacy of good character is clearly illustrated in Plutarch's description of the Catos. The elder Cato was a powerful advocate, but Plutarch attaches most importance to his imitation of the ancient virtues, frugality and austerity. The Romans applied a special name to those who lived immorally but uttered solemn warnings about the need to maintain moral standards. They called them 'Catos', not because the younger Cato was himself like this, but because he was so obviously *not* an instance of conflict between way of life and way of speaking (*Cato ii* 19.9).[8]

Here Plutarch's ideas are more in accord with those of rhetorical theorists. Rhetorical theory had safeguarded oratory against the charge that it can be used for bad ends, by introducing the notion that the perfect orator is a good man skilled in speaking. That once said, however, rhetorical theory was of course free to discuss how to perfect the technical ways of improving skill. Though Plutarch puts most emphasis on the need for good character, he does not overlook presentation entirely. He quotes Menander, 'It is the character of the speaker that persuades, not his oratory,' but modifies the doctrine, one might call it, by saying that persuasion is achieved by both character and oratorical skill.[9]

Throughout the *Lives*, there is the assumption that oratory *per se* is not a sufficient objective for the good man. This leads Plutarch to ignore (on the whole) the importance of forensic oratory in the political life of Greece and Rome, and to dwell on one or two aspects only of deliberative oratory. Within these limits he sees that oratory has a place, rather as slaves have a place in Aristotle's political theory; they are instruments whose function is to assist the exercise of political virtue. Several heroes would have excelled in oratory had they not been called to higher things; perhaps Caesar and Sertorius are the outstanding examples.[10] On the other hand, it is plain that Marius was lacking in oratorical persuasiveness; he owed his success to his achievements, and did not have that 'persuasiveness of language' which is ascribed to Pompey (*Pomp.* 1.4). Plutarch might have portrayed Marius as a blunt, no-nonsense Roman. Instead he assimilates the defects of the speaker to the defects of the man. He objects to the over-confidence of Marius' speeches (*Mar.* 9.2), and disapproves of his boastfulness before the people, as this offends against the Plutarchan canon that one is allowed to mention oneself by way of defence but not as a means of seeking power.

## 7.2 STYLE AND THE MAN

I have already alluded to certain differences between Plutarch's attitude to oratory and the value placed on it by rhetorical theorists. Plutarch would never have admitted the claims made by Cicero, that the orator is the founder and bringer of civilization.[11] Rather similarly, he differs from the theorists about the virtues of style, and he tends to consider these not in the context of the speech or the occasion but in relation to the whole man.

Brevity is the quality of style that appeals most to Plutarch and is the subject of fairly extensive illustration. By brevity is meant the art of conveying much in a few words, through such forms as the maxim or epigram. Plutarch holds that this quality was culti-vated by the Spartans more than others, and he finds evidence that laconic brevity was not merely displayed by Spartan statesmen, but was a feature of the whole society. The Spartan relish for apophthegms shows the disrepute of long-winded speeches at Sparta. All the Spartan *Lives* illustrate this liking for brevity, but the *Lycurgus* (especially 20) is particularly rich in examples. It is not easy for us to accept that sayings and apophthegms[12] are sufficient evidence of oratorical skill. But Plutarch, as we have seen, is only too ready to make this very assumption, since it suits his method to see the saying as an illustration of the speech; many of the sayings which he incorporates in the *Lives* have a tart brevity about them, which would be intolerable if affected throughout a speech. But then Plutarch is not really interested in speeches except in so far as he regards them as a guide to character. The brevity he admires is the outward sign of a deep seriousness imbued with oracular pungency. Perhaps the admiration of brevity is most apparent in the *Phocion*, in which there are more than fifty laconic utterances attributed to the hero. Demosthenes referred to Phocion as the 'chopper of his speeches', though Plutarch here adds that this may refer to the character rather than the discourse of Phocion (*Phoc.* 5.10). But there is a sense in which Phocion's oratory is made to disclose the same characteristics as the rest of his life. His discourse was marked by a 'stern and imperious brevity unadorned with pleasing devices' (*Phoc.* 5.3). This utterance, there-fore, is appropriate to one who is used to giving commands. As we have seen, laconic brevity is not a monopoly of the Spartan system; Pelopidas, for example, achieved a greater 'simplicity' than they did (*Pel.* 30.5).

Rhetorical theorists, however, admit brevity[13] as an excellence, a grace of discourse, though not in the same way. They are aware that a predilection for brevity can ruin a case, since the exposition of facts must not be skimped. Theorists would probably not have been as well-disposed to Brutus as Plutarch was, since Brutus seems to have been brief to the point of obscurity (*Brut.* 6.7).[14] But for Plutarch this points to moral seriousness and depth of conviction rather than to an oratorical defect. Similarly, the enthusiasm for Spartan brevity would have struck a rhetorical theorist as perverse. Cicero[15] declares that no Spartan had achieved fame as an orator; and even though Menelaus is cited by theorists as an instance of good oratory, he is clearly less of an orator in their eyes than speakers like Ulysses and Nestor.[16] He can be held to represent the virtues of the plain style; but this is only one kind of oratorical excellence and is not as difficult to achieve as, for instance, the ornament demanded by the grand style. In short, Plutarch's admiration for brevity is a sign that he does not care for speeches in themselves; he values it because he respects the voice of sententious command, which is an appropriate mode of utterance for his ideal statesman.

I should mention, in passing, that Plutarch puts a high value on silence, as a kind of mystic preparation for speaking. Knowing when to speak means also knowing when to be silent. This seems to be the point of a curious remark attributed to the younger Cato, who was criticized by his friends for not speaking out. He replied: 'I shall start speaking when I have something to say that I should not be silent about.' (*Cato ii* 4.4) Evidently Plutarch takes this remark as evidence of Cato's moral preparation. The value of silence[17] is derived partly from the mysteries, where men are forbidden to divulge secrets, partly from those societies in which the young have to be silent as a mark of respect to their elders. Plutarch also gives a semi-humorous justification from anatomy; we have been given two ears and one tongue, which is taken to mean that we should listen more than we speak (502C).

Another topic, which provides the opportunity to compare Plutarch with the rhetoricians, is the use of wit, which is mentioned at some length in the *Lycurgus*, *Cato i* and the *Cicero*. It appears from the *Lycurgus* that Spartans were famous for their wit as well as for their brevity. The Spartan educational system encouraged the ability to put up with badinage, which is seen therefore to have a moral value. Wit, in this sense, is a pungent adjunct to brevity, adding to the truth delivered in the maxim. The Spartan who was invited to hear a man doing an imitation of a nightingale, replied, 'I have heard the bird itself' (*Lyc.* 20.12). We have to distinguish this kind of wit – the unprovoked response by way of jest – from what Plutarch calls buffoonery. Some of Antony's diversions are to be rated as childish, not serious, amusement, whereas Cleomenes' army was unspoilt by this buffoonery, though it enjoyed the advantages of witty, laconic speech (*Cleom.* 12.4). Wit enhances the serious purpose, it is not valued just as a joke; thus the elder Cato is described as both 'fond of jokes and severe' (*Cato i* 7.1). Some of his sayings illustrate both brevity and a caustic wit approximating to rudeness. As we saw above, jests, like sayings and minor incidents, are a convenience for the biographer in his attempt to give a succinct rendering of character; they are also valued for the moral quality they are supposed to reveal.

The fullest account of the subject is in the *Life* of Cicero, who in antiquity was noted for his jokes.[18] Plutarch comments that over-addiction to witticisms is a typical lawyer's fault, a habit created by the sharp exchanges in courts of law. Cicero is said to have erred because he used witticisms when there was no need; his jesting was unprovoked, and made him unpopular because it often seemed a deliberate and unnecessary humiliation of another person. People felt that his jokes had been elaborated at home and were carried round like so many barbs waiting to be delivered. Essentially, the joke should be an uncalculated response, with some resemblance therefore to the defensive function of talking about one's own exploits.[19] The jokes ascribed to Cicero may not strike a modern reader as funny, but that is not the point. The point is that he overdid them and therefore seemed to offend against persons gratuitously. More general statements about wit are to be found in the *Precepts on Public Life*; wit is there disallowed when it serves to lower the reputation of others or is wit for wit's sake (803B).

In his comments on wit Plutarch is closer to the rhetorical theorists than in his discussion of brevity, though there are some differences. Both Plutarch and the theorists agree, for example, that Cicero abused his talents in this respect; and both give the same reason, that it constitutes a breach of decorum, though perhaps the orator's idea of decorum should not be assumed to be the same as that of Plutarch's statesman. They agree, too, that the joke serves best when it is an immediate response. But Plutarch seems to be interested in one only of the two main kinds of humour analysed by the theorists. They distinguish between the witty saying and the graceful humour which plays around a whole discourse.[20] Plutarch seems to care only for aphoristic wit, because a truth is thereby seasoned. The theorists find that wit is effective as a forensic weapon, which would be of little interest to Plutarch. Finally, it seems doubtful whether Plutarch values wit for those qualities which are praised by Cicero and Quintilian, *humanitas* and *urbanitas*. It is true that wit, for Plutarch, does have a certain binding force, as it clearly promotes fellow-feeling in the army of Cleomenes (*Cleom.* 12.4). But it is doubtful whether Plutarch respects it as a polite elegance.

This account has so far been restricted to the topics of brevity and wit, which have, nevertheless, illuminated Plutarch's taste in the spoken word. He also makes more general observations on the style of some heroes, though these are few in number compared with those of whom he says in passing that they were powerful speakers. As often, we should remember that he is not interested in style for its own sake but as a guide to character. He explicitly rejects any idea of comparing the speeches of Cicero and Demosthenes (*Dem.* 3.2) and thinks that it was folly of Caecilius[21] to attempt this. He is thinking here of *stylistic* comparison in the narrow sense, to decide which of the two was more pleasing or powerful. His own Latin, acquired late, was inadequate for such a task, even if his inclination and values had allowed him to settle to the kind of dissection practised by a Dionysius.[22] Thus, when he does comment on qualities of style, these tend to be moral characteristics, as the discourse is assumed to be a window on to the soul.

Plutarch's account of the elder Cato's oratory follows closely on his characterization of this hero. He records how Cato behaved as a governor in dependent cities; his frugal, economic ways gave the impression that he was demeaning his office. Yet this was offset by his rigour in deciding cases, as a result of which he restored dignity to the position he held. His virtues are therefore felt to be opposites, or to give that impression, but both sorts of virtue are essential to the man. This compound of opposites is said to appear in his oratory. 'He was both graceful and powerful, able to charm and to stir the emotions, fond of jokes yet stern, epigrammatic yet capable of sustained argument. As Plato says of Socrates, he appeared to those who sampled the externals, an odd man, like a satyr, offensive to others; but to those who peered within he was full of serious matter and could move his audience to tears. Hence I do not understand why some people say that Cato's oratory is very like that of Lysias.' (*Cato i* 7.1) He then goes on, rather contemptuously, to leave this topic for those who can decide on the various kinds of Roman oratory.

This allusive refusal to equate Lysias and Cato is of great interest. Lysias was admired by Atticists for many qualities, such as simple language, clarity and vividness, to say nothing of his brevity. His command of fairly limited oratorical resources creates the impression that a speaker's character is the mirror-image of his speech. Plutarch considers that Cato's oratory is not translucent in this way; in his case the complexities of the speech correspond to a complexity of character, indicated by the description in pairs of adjectives. One cannot therefore understand Cato's character from his speech in the direct way that one infers character from a speech by Lysias. It is obvious that Plutarch prefers Cato, for the comparison with Socrates must be decisive. Here again he diverges from the judgment of the rhetorical theorist, for Cicero himself discusses the alleged parallel between Cato and Lysias.[23] He decides in favour of Lysias, saying that he is more successful in every praiseworthy quality. Cicero's standards and presuppositions are of course different from those of Plutarch, since Cicero is considering oratory as an art capable of development and perfection. He regards Lysias as one example of perfected Attic oratory, whereas Cato seems to him a worthy but archaic precursor of the excellence that is still to come in Latin oratory. Any idea of development and perfection within the genre seems foreign to Plutarch's approach here. He is extracting (or thinks he is) the moral qualities from the speech, and his preference goes to the Roman because his character seems to combine opposite virtues; it offers more of the good.

A passage on the younger Cato's first major speech shows a similar aversion from the polished oratorical product. Cato was admired for his opposition to the tribunes' proposal to remove a pillar in the basilica erected by the elder Cato. 'There was nothing juvenile or fanciful about his speech; it was high-pitched, moving and rough. However, there was a charm, compelling attention, that played over the roughness of the ideas; the speech was imbued with his character, which gave to his note of dignity a certain delightful grace.' (*Cato ii* 5.3) Plutarch goes on to mention that Cato had a powerful voice, a fact which is relevant to the filibustering activities mentioned elsewhere.

231

Plutarch is attracted by what he calls the roughness[24] of Cato's oratory; as usual, we cannot be sure if he read some of Cato's extant remains or whether he took the judgment ready-made from a Roman friend or source. The former cannot be excluded but seems unlikely. The praise of Cato's oratory is expressed in what is almost a paradox, for one does not expect the 'rough' to exert this persuasive charm upon the audience. Plutarch holds that the speech, in an odd way, aptly portrayed the genuine character of the man; as with Fabius, there is a hint that the speech was pregnant with Thucydidean thoughts. Here too Plutarch differs from rhetorical theorists. In the first place, while they do admit that roughness can be a grace and devote some attention to it, it is only one grace among many. Secondly, Plutarch's judgment on Cato differs from that of Cicero, who at any rate professes to admire Cato because he can discourse on Stoic themes before a popular audience.[25] Cicero argues that he is able to do this, in spite of the fact that Stoicism is not a good training for orators, because he has the skills and ornaments of the accomplished speaker. Thus Cicero (though perhaps there is special pleading here) admires in Cato oratorical mastery of a more conventional kind than is suggested in Plutarch's brief outline. This is not to say that we should ask which of the two is right, as though that were possible to decide. It is sufficient to note that Plutarch approves of Cato's oratory for reasons which would seem less cogent to a theorist or historian of rhetoric as an art.

The Gracchi gave Plutarch further scope for elaborating on the different moral characters as revealed in their speeches and delivery. Tiberius appears as the calmer brother, while Gaius[26] is more vehement; for Plutarch these facts are confirmed by their different modes of delivery, for Tiberius did not alter his expression or move about, whereas Gaius initiated a change in the way of addressing the people. He did not stay still in one place, and, furthermore, used his *toga* for effect, rather as Cleon had behaved at Athens. (The comparison with Cleon is not meant to depreciate Gaius by equating him with a demagogue, since his purpose is clearly a good one, unlike that of Cleon. It is, rather, a parallelism which occurs to Plutarch as he writes, and is probably void of moral reflexion as regards Gaius.) Their speeches too are compared; Gaius is the more forceful and effective, whereas Tiberius is said to have had more charm and to have succeeded in stirring pity among his hearers (*Tib. Gracch.* 2.3).

At this point in his narrative, Plutarch is expressly concerned with differentiating the brothers' characters and uses what he knows of their oratory to that end. Once again, it is easy to see that his judgment is of a different order from that invoked by students of rhetoric. Gellius' account of a passage from a speech by Gaius is designed to show how relatively undeveloped and imperfect it is as a piece of discourse.[27] This view will certainly commend itself to anyone who can imagine the more effective composition with which Cicero would have treated the atrocities related by Gaius. But Plutarch, as we have seen, is not concerned with the idea of oratorical perfection, but works with a straightforward assumption that moral character is revealed through one's speeches.

In this brief account I have sought to point out what is most characteristic of Plutarch's approach to what he knows of a hero's oratory. He thinks that a few brief sayings can do service for a whole speech or number of speeches. He is not interested in speeches as evidence of oratorical perfection but evaluates them by other standards. He prefers the unclear urgency of a Brutus, because it registers his conviction and sincerity, to a facile, superficially polished discourse. He believes that oratory does disclose character and analyses speeches in order to bring out qualities that are known from other evidence; thus the fact that Gaius Gracchus sometimes became shrill with anger and employed a slave to stand near and strike a warning note on an instrument,[28] confirms the vehemence and impetuosity of this particular character (*C. Gracch.* 3.7).

He seems at times to draw large conclusions from slender evidence (quite apart from the uncomfortable doubts that come to mind as we review his enthusiasm for the alien oratory of the Catos and the Gracchi). *We* are bound to feel that a saying cannot stand in for a speech. But this difference is a consequence of Plutarch's enthusiasm for his method, his belief that 'sayings and jests' are reliable guides to character. He is sometimes ready to go to extreme lengths in this respect, as is shown by two particular incidents. He mentions the fact that in Athens the platform on the Pnyx, from which the orators spoke, faced the sea in Themistocles' time, and had its aspect changed by the Thirty Tyrants, since they objected to the cult of naval power as the source of democracy (*Them.* 19). The seaward aspect of the platform is regarded as a convenient index to the fact that Athens grew as a sea-power in the fifth century. Archaeological enquiry does not entirely deny the fact into which Plutarch reads so much moral significance; it admits that a change was made, but gives, so to say, the archaeological reason, namely that the retaining wall had collapsed.[29] Rather in the same way, Plutarch mentions that Gaius Gracchus started the practice of looking in the direction of the forum while making a speech from the rostra. The change is held to symbolize the shift in power from the aristocracy to the democracy; 'by a small change and alteration he set great events in motion and in a way transferred political emphasis in that speakers must now set their sights upon the many, not the senate.' (*C. Gracch.* 5.4) Again, too much moral and political significance is read into this fragment. It has been suggested in modern times that the change was connected with a change in the voting at public assemblies. Even in antiquity there were other views about the innovator – thus Cicero says that the practice was started by C. Licinius Crassus.[30]

To point out such discrepancies is not intended to make this form of biography look foolish or inept. It is only by noticing how Plutarch applies his principles, especially his theory about the value of 'minor incidents' and so on, that we can appreciate how far he is prepared to go. The incidents described in these two cases have a certain aptness to Plutarch's picture of fifth-century Athenian democracy and the increasing power of the many in Gracchan Rome. But his comments on style are coloured by his own preconception about the role of oratory in the statesman's life. Perfection as an orator is a lesser good than the perfection as leader and citizen which is demanded of the 'politicus'.

### 7.3 THE COMPARISONS

Most of the *Parallel Lives* are terminated by a comparison (*sunkrisis*) in which Plutarch sums up the likenesses and differences between the two heroes. These comparisons were once admired, as by Montaigne;[31] but in modern times they have been made the subject of derisive comment.[32] They have, for instance, been labelled artificial and rhetorical, with the implication that they exist only as a framework imposed by the writer's skill. But provided we can take the first step of accepting that figures from different periods are comparable, it will not be difficult to see that these final exercises are integral to the pair of *Lives* they follow. The comparative note is struck at the beginning of many *Lives*, which shows that Plutarch did not wait until he had finished a particular pair before starting to pit one man against the other. Furthermore, though the stricture 'rhetorical' was meant adversely (as a reflexion on literature that is said to have no genuine content, only style), it is a useful starting-point for an analysis of the comparisons. The comparison was much used by orators and rhetoricians in antiquity, and it will be helpful to see how a Plutarchan comparison differs.

It is easy to see why the comparisons have been criticized, since most of them contain at least one assertion that will seem extraordinary to a modern reader. The comparison of *Agesilaus-Pompey* criticizes the Roman general for leaving Rome at the start of the civil war with Caesar, and contrasts him in this respect with Agesilaus, who did not abandon Sparta when she was threatened by the Greek armies under Epameinondas. The comment will seem unfounded if we bear in mind the point (which is obvious to a historian) that Pompey's retreat to the east was designed to give him time to assemble an army; his troops in Italy would have been no match for the experienced armies under Caesar. But this is to repeat once more that Plutarch's reflexions on events do not satisfy *our* sensitivity to historical details. We ask the question, why did the general behave in this way? Plutarch, however, ignoring such items as the propaganda-effect of Caesar's clemency, concentrates on the failure of Pompey as a statesman to make terms with a relative by marriage and so spare Rome a civil war. The bare fact of Pompey's departure from Rome is therefore measured by standards which apply to the 'politicus' as the harmonizer of his people. Other cases of apparent absurdity are also to be explained in this way. Thus the sexual affairs of Theseus are made to count against him whereas Romulus' rape of the Sabines is put down to his credit, because it was intended to benefit his community as a whole.[33] I do not mean that all the statements which stir a historian's amusement can be accounted for in this way, by bearing in mind Plutarch's criteria for statesmen, but many of them seem less strange after some such reflexion.

Another point to notice, before examining the comparisons in detail, is that they were not intended to make the Greeks seem preferable to the Romans just because they were Greeks. It has been said, for example, that 'there is very little evidence in his *Parallel Lives* that he really admired the Romans. In each pair the Greek worthy is generally more attractively drawn than the Roman;[34] and it might be thought that the comparisons are there to underline this aim. Now it might be possible to argue, if we could agree on a quantifying method, that the Greek members of the pairs have in fact more to their credit than their Roman partners. Even if this is so, it is not because they are Greeks but because their careers satisfy what Plutarch expects of his statesman or leader. One of his highest terms of praise is 'Hellenic',[35] and it is sometimes bestowed on Romans, as on Numa, not as a piece of condescension but as the proper title for his conduct. It is noticeable, too, from his vague remarks on language,[36] that he thinks of the two peoples as connected, because Latin has in some way developed out of Greek. In short, though he is a patriot in the narrow sense, he does not write with a nationalistic bias. Both Greeks and Romans are envisaged as partners in a Hellenic whole, and whether his preference goes to one or the other is, in a sense, a minor matter.

Comparisons are missing from four pairs of *Lives*, the *Cato ii-Phocion*, the *Themistocles-Camillus*, the *Pyrrhus-Marius* and the *Alexander-Caesar*. It is not certain whether these were written but have not been transmitted, or whether they were never composed in the first place. It has recently been argued[37] that these comparisons were not attempted by Plutarch, on the grounds that, in differing ways, they represent extreme cases of difficulty for the comparative method. An early passage in the *Phocion* (3.8) states that Phocion and his Roman partner were alike in the details of their virtues, not merely because both displayed a particular virtue such as justice, the mode of which is subject to variation. Plutarch adds that one needs a refined theory to separate and discover the differences between these two men. Hence, on the basis of this passage, the suggestion has been made that a concluding comparison was too difficult an exercise, because the differences were insufficiently startling. On the other hand, the other three pairs of *Lives* are said to represent the opposite case, where the heroes are too unlike each other. Thus, in the one case we have no difference at all, in the other three too much. The view is well argued but is not persuasive. Plutarch says of Cicero and Demosthenes (*Dem.* 3.3) that there are so many similarities that one might think that the god was trying to make the same man; but this did not stop him from attempting a comparison. Again, there are other *Lives*, where the heroes seem (to a modern) not very comparable; Sertorius and Eumenes are yoked, it seems, because both were rulers over peoples not their own. Though Plutarch himself found little to say on this occasion, there is nevertheless a formal comparison. Thirdly, it is not difficult to imagine the feasibility of a Plutarchan comparison to finish off the *Lives* from which it is missing. This is not to say that all existing comparisons employ the same formula; rather, they employ a variety of formulas, some of which could be used as the framework for a plausible invention. All in all, it seems best to say that we do not know why these comparisons are not there, instead of relying on argument from internal evidence which is bound to be partial.

The main purpose of the comparisons is to point out the differences between men of similar achievement and similar virtue (*aretē*). In some cases the material does not seem promising; thus the comparison of Aemilius and Timoleon begins with the remark '. . . it is clear that the comparison does not have many differences or unlikenesses' (*Comp.* 1.1) and this account is relatively brief. The discussion of Aristeides and Cato i begins in much the same way – 'the difference is not easy to see, as it appears only among many, great likenesses' – but develops into a longer discussion, as Plutarch finds himself caught up in a general survey of an important question, whether the statesman should (within the law) benefit himself as well as the state by his activity. The end of the comparison between Agis, Cleomenes and the Gracchi exhibits the same preoccupation with difference: 'you can yourself see the difference on the basis of what we have said; but if we must describe it individually, I say that Tiberius was the first in virtue, that Agis the young king made fewest mistakes, whereas Gaius was not a little behind Cleomenes in action and daring.' (*Comp.* 5.7)

The search for difference sometimes leads to what looks like mannered antithesis, as with Agesilaus and Pompey. 'The very charges we make against the Egyptians because of [their treatment of] Pompey, are made by the Egyptians against Agesilaus. Pompey trusted the Egyptians but was avenged by them, whereas Agesilaus, who was trusted by them, deserted them and went over to those who were at war with the people he came to help.' (*Comp.* 5) This looks at first like mere artifice, but this would be a misinterpretation; the antithesis is not sought for its own sake but as a means of sharpening our awareness of character as shown by particular actions. It does not work for a modern reader as it was intended, because the important term 'Egyptians' is clearly not the same in both cases, though Plutarch seems to assume it is. And in the *Lysander-Sulla* (*Comp.* 3.8) antithesis is assisted by paradox; 'Sulla was licentious and extravagant but sought to control the citizens, while Lysander filled his city with defects from which he was himself free.'[38] This is sharper, more ingenious writing than is usual with Plutarch, but it is meant to alert us to the moral difference, not to evoke admiration for an epigram.

The general form of the comparisons is varied. In several the reader can detect little more than a point-by-point treatment of the salient features, and the composition moves forward, if at all, by means of disconnected additions. But in a few cases the writing is more developed and sustained, and there is a unity of thought about the whole piece which is imparted by persuasion and advocacy. The *Theseus-Romulus* begins with an enumeration of points which can be made in favour of the superiority of Theseus; thus we read that Theseus acted from free choice (he might have stayed at home in Troezen but elected not to do so) whereas Romulus had no option but to attack and destroy his tyrannical oppressor. It seems as though we are asked to see that the facts will make us prefer Theseus, especially when it is said that Theseus' change toward demagogy is less objectionable than Romulus' decline towards arbitrary rule. But the accent changes, and Plutarch proceeds to draw attention to several matters in which Romulus was better or less culpable. Though the argument is not assessed at the end, there is a clear inference that the game is drawn; the advocacy is modelled on the impartial judge, who decides to acquit or accept both, rather than the practice of the barrister seeking to make a case for one alone. The *Dion-Brutus* is developed along similar lines. Plutarch begins with several items that plead, so to say, for the victory of Dion; and this seems to reach its peak when he mentions the accusation brought against Brutus, that he showed ingratitude to his saviour Caesar. Yet this very point, which appears to damn Brutus, is made the turning point of the exercise, since Plutarch exploits it to argue that Brutus did not act against Caesar for personal reasons but from principle (3.4–6), whereas Dion acted not as a rebel but because he was expelled. There is a contest in appearance only; it is true that the reader is expected to note details which provide him with good examples, but he is not asked to make an exclusive choice between the two heroes. Or, to put it another way, the preferences within the company of heroes are minor compared with the striking differences between hero and demagogue or hero and tyrant.

The ideas through which the comparisons are made reiterate, though in a condensed way, Plutarch's concern with the ideal statesman. One of the most obvious divisions to be noticed in the comparisons is that between a hero's political activity (*politeia*) and his performance as a general. The *Pericles-Fabius* begins with the comment that both men have left behind them many fine examples of their 'political and military virtue' (1.1). Plutarch then treats first of their military achievements and does not pass on to a comparison of their politics until near the end (3.1). In a sense the division matters less than the idea that both parts are needed to make a full political life in Plutarch's view; Demosthenes, like others in the Athens of his time, is a lesser figure than the great men in the fifth century, when the same man was politician and general. The division is therefore a reminder that most of the heroes have displayed virtue in both fields. Plutarch does at times analyse the military achievement in a narrow way, by assessing a hero for his technical competence at deception or by counting up the number of victories. But his interests are seldom technical in this sense for long; if he had had more enthusiasm for the general's art as such, he would surely have given Marcellus more credit for his capture of Syracuse (*Pel.-Marc. comp.* 2). Instead, he prefers to dwell on the political character that can be extracted from the hero's activity as commander or soldier; thus Fabius' rescue of

Minucius exhibits his courage, prudence and kindness (*Per.-Fab. comp.* 2.2). Generalship and politics are different spheres in which it is possible to display the same art, the art of command; Lucullus' failure to retain the loyalty of his troops is a reflexion on his general political ability in the widest sense (*Cim.-Luc. comp.* 2.3). Hence the common reference to political and military achievement gives a convenient framework; but both parts are complementary to each other in the full political life.

Inside this broad frame of war and politics, there is an attempt to distinguish between 'common' features and those features which are 'peculiar' to one or the other (*koinon* and *idion*). I use the term features advisedly, rather than qualities of character, since the latter are not always as prominent as we should expect. Thus what is most 'common' to Lucullus and Cimon is the fact that both men died before their countries were affected by catastrophic political change. The Roman civil wars are (somewhat daringly) equated with the confusion in Greece (by which Plutarch means above all the Peloponnesian War that broke out in 431 BC). Thus the two heroes are felicitated for dying at the right time, a theme which would appear to be more germane to encomium proper. As used here (*Cim.-Luc. comp* 1.1–2) it is not so much encomiastic as an attempt to set the men against their changing historical background. The start to the *Eumenes-Sertorius* is also unpromising and seems to labour the adventitious; here the 'common' feature is that both were exiles and ruled over foreign peoples. What is 'peculiar' to Sertorius is that he received power from subjects who wished to be governed, whereas the subjects of Eumenes obeyed him because they could not rule themselves. Hence the distinction here, while it does not serve to show character directly, does throw light on the particular kind of political career. In Plutarch's eyes, the holding of office is more creditable when the governed consent to the ruler and freely admit that his virtue deserves power.

Even when this distinction is not made explicit, it can usually be found to operate throughout a comparison. There are two subsidiary ideas about 'common' and 'peculiar' which should be noticed. In the first place, Plutarch is sometimes at pains to work out how far a hero's achievement is his own or shared with others of his time. Thus he comments that Pericles' success as a general occurred at a time of 'common good fortune' when other Athenian generals were also winning, while Fabius' victories were gained during a period of national disaster. This makes the latter's achievement more prestigious. The conduct of Timoleon in Sicily is the more remarkable in that other Greeks who had to do with Sicilian affairs, behaved corruptly (*Aem.-Tim. comp.* 2). Sulla's grand titles and offices cannot be accepted uncritically as evidence that he deserved power, since he lived in a corrupt age when power was often held by unworthy men (*Lys.-Sulla comp.* 1). Thus we have a secondary use of 'common', by means of which Plutarch, in his way, tries to set the heroes against their contemporary background and to isolate what is their own doing. Secondly, there are times when 'peculiar' (*idion*) is used, not to denote what is distinctive of one of a pair, but to describe an oddity or paradox. Lysander was good but corrupted Sparta by wealth; whereas Sulla the self-indulgent passed laws to curb luxury (*Lys.-Sulla comp.* 3.4). Camillus, who held so many offices, was never once consul (*Cam.* 1.1). The author of the *Lives* was a collector of such curiosities as well as a student of character.

Within the body of the comparisons we meet many ideas in summary form which have already been discussed in the text. The contrast between choice (*proairesis*) and necessity recurs, and there are numerous references to the right use of wealth. Both these subjects are central to Plutarch's conception of the good political life. Another idea, which is perhaps less emphasized in the narratives, is that of the 'starting-point' (*aphormē*), since an obvious way of assessing achievement is to measure the gap between beginning and end. The elder Cato is admired because it was difficult for him as a citizen of a small town to compete in politics with wealthy Romans (*Arist.-Cato i comp.* 1.3). The notion of 'starting-point' can refer, as here, to the material means at the hero's disposal when he begins his career. But it is extended to the whole way of achieving greatness; in this respect Pompey comes off better than Agesilaus, who became king at Sparta because of the special reading put on an oracle, not by his own merits (*Ages.-Pomp. comp.* 1.2). In this context of thought Plutarch probably has in mind the adage that 'fine things are difficult', and the overcoming of obstacles is therefore put down to the hero's credit.

The comparisons also include more by way of explicit comments on the hero's death than is usually found in the narratives. In general Plutarch seems to apply a fairly obvious heroic standard. Crassus' death is less discreditable than that of Nicias, since he did not surrender and was not imprisoned or deceived (*Nic.-Crass. comp.* 5.4). Sertorius' death did no dishonour to his life, whereas Eumenes, by continuing to live as a prisoner, gave his enemies control of his soul as well as of his body (*Sert.-Eum. comp.* 2.8). The suicide of Demosthenes is praised as the retreat to a 'higher altar', a refuge from the cruelty of Antipater (*Dem.-Cic. comp.* 5). Antony too is given credit for not letting his enemy have the power to do as he wished with his person (*Demetr.-Ant. comp.* 6.3). These examples suggest that life is not regarded as a good, to be held on to at any cost. But the 'politicus' must not give up too readily, or he will make the same mistake as Brutus (*Dion-Brut. comp.* 3.2). Nor should a leader of men die like a common soldier; Plutarch cannot praise the deaths of Pelopidas and Marcellus, who met their end impetuously. He praises instead the discipline of the soldier, who can let go the enemy he is about to strike when he hears the retreat sounded (*Pel.-Marc. comp.* 3.2). It is not far-fetched to infer that there is a discipline to be observed by the hero-leader himself.

Several ideas used in making the comparisons suggest an affinity with encomium. The encomiast would exploit the idea of the 'starting-point' in order to magnify the achievement, and would, if possible, incorporate the manner or time of dying into his feats of praise. Yet the effect of such items, in Plutarch's comparisons, is not the same as in encomium. The intellectual equipment is not much different, but one always has the impression of a mind struggling to establish a moral truth and not seeking to dazzle or sway an audience. The same point applies if we turn from Plutarch's comparisons to the comparisons employed by Greek and Roman orators. The extant speeches provide us with numerous instances in which a contemporary figure is vilified or praised by comparison with *exempla* from the past. In the orators the details of these *exempla* are relatively lacking compared with the greater documentation offered in a Plutarchan comparison. And secondly, (which is more important), we can never forget that the forensic or deliberative orator's aim is to get his own way, not to ascertain and present the moral truth.

I have suggested that Plutarch's comparisons are related – in some details of presentation rather than purpose – to the comparison as practised in various branches of ancient oratory. Yet the fact is that Plutarch compares Greeks and Romans as equals, and it is worth considering whether this was a novelty. Although much ancient literature has been lost, we can place his general attitude by comparison with some Greek and Roman writers. He does not, like Polybius,[39] hold up the Romans as masters of statecraft at the expense of Greeks; or anxiously explain, like Dionysius, that the Romans are not really barbarians. On the other hand, Roman literature is full of comparisons between Greeks and Romans from which the note of condescension is seldom absent. Cicero's discussion of rhetoric is directed by a contrast between Roman achievement and Greek theory;[40] Livy had written against those who ventured to say that Alexander was a better general than any Roman.[41] The examples of virtue and wrong conduct collected by Valerius Maximus are largely Roman, though he adds a number of Greek and other instances. But his attitude is plainly patriotic – the Romans are the preferred models – and his Greeks and others are so many honest afterthoughts, a way of varying the content. For him Roman examples would by themselves suffice to teach the world, but it will not be wearisome to the reader to give briefly some foreign instances. As Valerius says : 'my mind dwells on our own examples, but the fair play of Rome urges me to relate instances from the history of other peoples.'[42] The Roman sense of superiority makes itself heard in all these writers.

By comparison with these, Nepos[43] seems fairer and more objective. He protests against those who are ignorant of Greek literature and who adopt the line that only Roman precedents are worth having. His book on the *Generals of other Peoples* is prefaced by a reminder that different countries have different standards. Romans should not look down their noses if the biographer tells them who taught Epameinondas music; they must instead accept that custom differs and that what is trivial in Rome has not been so regarded elsewhere. The biographer, in writing about the Greeks, must 'follow their customs'. But we are not in a position to see how Nepos made use of this apparent moral relativism, as his work on Romans has not survived. We can say this much, that he has hit on an idea which would have lead to a different form of biography from that written by Plutarch, since the latter assumes that political conduct can always be evaluated by the same criteria.

The striking fact about Plutarch's comparing is that he is on the whole indifferent to this question of parity or otherwise between Greeks and Romans. He is interested in deciding on his preference for the better statesman, not in picking and choosing among Greeks and Romans; but it is difficult for us to say whether his attitude would have struck his Greek friends as 'establishment' or his Roman contemporaries as impertinent. It seems that the comparison was an orator's device and that the idea was perhaps suggested to Plutarch by the school-practice of comparing *exempla*. He modified the scheme by analysing the details of action more closely and by emphasizing such ideas as the function of choice. He is at the furthest remove from the orator and rhetorician in his strenuous pursuit of moral truth.

# Conclusion

The *Lives* are so varied in subject-matter that there is bound to be some difference of opinion about what is most important in them, and what is most characteristic of their author's thought. As Montaigne[1] observed, Plutarch has the habit of starting countless trains of thought, which he treats suggestively rather than in exhaustive detail. Though I am bound to concede that there are as many Plutarchs as there are readers, I venture to hope that the foregoing analyses will give a picture that is neither misleading nor unfair. I have tried throughout this book to let Plutarch speak with his own voice, so that the reader who is perhaps concerned with one *Life* only, can see how aspects of character are treated in other *Lives*. By way of conclusion I will return briefly to some of the topics which seem to me to be most significant.

The central portion of this book (Chapters 2–4) describes what Plutarch expects of his ideal statesman, the 'politicus', and differentiates him from those false politicians, the tyrant and the demagogue. Plutarch is concerned above all with looking for examples of men who embarked on a political career with a fixed purpose (*proairesis*) in order to accomplish a good end. It seems to me that his requirements of the ideal statesman are derived from his admiration of Platonist views about the good ruler, as expressed (above all) in the *Republic* and the *Laws*. The city-state in Plutarch's time was no longer the independent political force in foreign policy that it had been in Plato's time. But its institutions were still the framework of political activity, and Plutarch can be regarded as a *moral* legislator for office-holders in such a society. In this way the *Lives* are an extended meditation on Platonist themes, and, other things apart, deserve a niche in the history of

Plato's influence on later thought. The political life, in Plutarch's view, is a form of philosophy in action (cf. Chapter 6).

As a biographer Plutarch seems to me to be (in some ways) more dependent on historians proper than his remarks in the *Alexander* (1) would at first suggest. In that passage he adumbrates ideas about method which could be used in the composition of a different kind of biography from that which he has left. Boswell[2] used this passage, together with Johnson's thoughts on biography, as part of his justification for writing the life of one who was not concerned with politics. This is not to say that Boswell was in error, since his views seem to be an allowable development of Plutarch's ideas in a different culture and society. But Plutarch's main interest, as we have seen, was in the conduct of man while holding political office. It had not occurred to him that the career of a private citizen, not involved in politics, was a feasible or profitable area of study. Because of this he often follows what I have called the historian's emphasis (cf. p. 8f. above) and often therefore produces what a critic might reasonably call a compendious history rather than autonomous biography.

# Notes

## PRINCIPAL ABBREVIATIONS

| | |
|---|---|
| CQ | Classical Quarterly |
| HSCPh | Harvard Studies in Classical Philology |
| JRS | Journal of Roman Studies |
| LEC | Les Études Classiques |
| REG | Revue des Études Grecques |
| TAPhA | Transactions of the American Philological Association |
| F.Gr.Hist | Die Fragmente der Griechischen Historiker, ed. F. Jacoby |
| ORF | Oratorum Romanorum Fragmenta, ed. H. Malcovati |
| RE | Real Encyclopädie für Altertumswissenschaft |

## CHAPTER 1

1. For more detailed discussion see A. E. Wardman, *CQ*, xxi (1971), p. 254f; and J. R. Hamilton, *Plutarch, Alexander* (1969), p. xxxviii and pp. 1–2 of commentary.
2. I have preferred 'badness', not 'vice', as the equivalent to *kakia* for this reason. 'Vice' seems too extreme a term to cover the cases of men like Demetrius and Antony, who have many lesser virtues but misuse their natural gifts and (to some extent) such virtues as they have. *Kakia* is defined as an 'unevenness of character', an 'inconsistency' (*Nic.-Crass. comp.* 1.4); hence men who are *kakoi* are, so to say, bad at living, but their badness is only noticeable because they have some good features. Finally, Demetrius and Antony are not as villainous as men like Pausanias the Spartan or some demagogues and tyrants. See also below, pp. 32, 34 and 65.
3. See below, chapter 5, pp. 154–161.
4. See H. D. Westlake, *Individuals in Thucydides* (1968).
5. Xen. *Hellenica* ii 3.56; *Anab.* ii 6.
6. See e.g. Polybius ix 22 (Hannibal) and v 39 (Cleomenes).
7. *Ant.Rom.* v 48 (Publicola); see also his remarks on Coriolanus at viii 60–62.
8. Thus Livy xxx 26.7 gives a brief sketch of Fabius, and raises the question whether he was cautious by nature or policy. Livy xli 28 alludes to Titus' death but gives no character.
9. Cf. on this subject in general P. Kirn, *Das Bild des Menschen in der Geschichtsschreibung von Polybius bis Ranke* (1956).

10. For Timocleia see P. A. Stadter, *Plutarch's Historical Methods* (1965), pp. 112–114.
11. See especially *Laws* i 637Af. and cf. ii 652A.
12. The fullest discussion is in the *Cic.* 25–27; cf. below, p. 229.
13. Plataea and connected events take up chapters 10–22 of this relatively short *Life* (27 chapters in all).
14. On digressions in historical writing see A. E. Wardman, *Historia*, ix (1960), p. 406.
15. For other passages on names see especially *Marc.* 8; *Rom.* 15; *Numa* 7; *Publ.* 10.9, 16.7 and 17.5. There are many brief comments, as at *Cic.* 1.
16. Livy xxv 24.11 (Syracuse) and xxii 7.6 (news of Trasimene).
17. See G. B. Townend in *Latin Biography* (1967) (ed. Dorey), 'Suetonius and his Influence', p. 81.
18. Polybius x 21.5; for comment cf. R. M. Errington, *Philopoemen* (1969), p. 232f., and F. W. Walbank, *Commentary*, ii (1967), p. 221. For comments on G. Uxkull-Gyllenband's theory about encomium and Plutarchan biography (*Plutarch und die Griechische Biographie*, 1927), see e.g. A. Dihle, *Studien zur Griechischen Biographie* (1956), p. 9, n. 1.
19. Cf. Plut. *Dem.* 1.3.
20. See below, ch. 5.4, p. 179f.
21. Xen. *Ages.* 11.1.
22. Isocrates, *Evag.*, especially 5–6 and 8.
23. Polybius ix 22.9–10. There is a trace of this idea in Plut. *Cim.* 2.5, where Plutarch speaks of faults and blemishes caused by 'political necessity'.
24. Aeschines i, especially 28f. and 40f.
25. Plut. *Phoc.* 1, cf. *ibid.* 37–38.
26. See Plut. *Dem.* 31.4 (Demades); *Arat.* 54.4 (Philip); *Crass.* 33.7 (Orodes).
27. On the dating see C. P. Jones, *JRS*, lvi (1966), p. 61f.
28. I mean because of insufficient evidence.
29. I have in mind Aristotle's treatment of *megaloprepeia* and *megalopsuchia* in *EN* iv.
30. Freedom appears among the list of 'goods' cited at *Mor.* 826C. But Plutarch seems to value the freedom of city-state institutions to operate as the law-giver intended, unhampered by external interference, rather than the freedom of individuals or groups. He approves of Pericles for restraining the people at Athens; cf. *Per.* 7.8 and 15.
31. For interesting reflexions on this whole subject see G. T. Griffith in *Fifty Years (And Twelve) of Classical Scholarship* (1968), p. 186.
32. Cf. *Quaest. conviv.* viii 10, especially 735A.
33. See below, ch. 4.4, pp. 107–15.
34. On art and imitation see D. W. Lucas, *Aristotle, Poetics* (1968), Appendix i; also T. B. L. Webster, *CQ*, xxxiii (1939), p. 166f.
35. Plut. *Mor.* (Loeb), iv, p. 490f.
36. For the famous quotation from Simonides, see *Mor.* 17F; 346F; 58B; 748A; also D. W. Lucas, *op. cit.*, p. 270f.
37. Cic. *pro Archia* 30. For an earlier reflexion on this theme see Isocrates, *Evag.* 73f.
38. The famous example of the Spartans making the Helots drunk is not approved at *Demetr.* 1.5 since it means treating part of the state (the Helots) in an inhumane fashion. But see *Mor.* 455E.
39. On this see F. W. Walbank, *Aratos of Sicyon* (1933), p. 165.
40. *F.Gr.Hist.* 87 F 42.

41. See *Pel.-Marc. comp.* 3.6.
42. For the poverty of Epameinondas see *Fab.* 27; *Lyc.* 13; *Arist.* 1; *Arat.* 19 (refusing bribes); and for critical comment see *RE* v 2. 2676.
43. But the fifth-century Athenians are highly commended at *Dem.* 13.6, where there is emphasis on their outstanding virtue as individuals.
44. For Cleomenes in Plutarch see A. Dihle, *Studien zur Griechischen Biographie* (1956), ch. v; also M. Hadas and M. Smith, *Heroes and Gods* (1965), ch. ix.
45. But see *Per.* 7.6 and cf. A. W. Gomme, *A Historical Commentary on Thucydides,* i (1945), p. 69.
46. For an account of this term see below, ch. 2, especially pp. 49–58.
47. Q. Caecilius Metellus Numidicus; see J. van Ooteghem, *Les Caecilii Metelli de la République* (1967), p. 124f.
48. See especially Plut. *Pomp.* 53 and cf. *Crass.* 14.5.
49. I am here extending the phrase used by Plutarch to describe Demetrius and Antony (and perhaps others), to cover those who have much less *aretē*.
50. Cf. Plutarch's remarks at *Phoc.* 1.
51. For the political character of Aemilius see H. H. Scullard, *Roman Politics* (1951), p. 223.
52. Cf. *Phoc.* 37–38 and note the comparison with Socrates.
53. For Heracleides see *Dion* 33.2, 47f. and 53; for Callippus, as another variant of the false statesman, see *Dion* 54f. and cf. Plato *epist.* vii 333E.
54. *Dion* 52.5 and cf. *Cor.* 1.4.
55. See especially *Ant.* 17.4–6.
56. See below, ch. 2.3, p. 68f. on the term *dēmotikos*.
57. *Demetr.* 18; cf. *Arist.* 6.
58. Cf. *Ant.* 62.1 and 66.7 and *Pomp.* 63–65.
59. See D. A. Russell, *JRS,* liii (1963), pp. 21–28.
60. One might say that modern emphasis on the popularity of the *Lives* is a consequence of the various proofs that they do not satisfy academic standards of criticism. Niebuhr's remarks are of great interest; see *Lectures on Ancient History,* ii (1852), pp. 298–299 (translation by Dr Schmitz).
61. For a full account of the Roman friends see C. P. Jones, *Plutarch and Rome* (1971), ch. vi, 'Plutarch's Society: Rome and the West'.
62. For Sosius' origin see C. P. Jones, *JRS,* lx (1970), p. 103, as well as his remarks in *Plutarch and Rome* (1971), p. 55. For Sosius in the *Lives* see *Thes.* 1; *Dem.* 1 and 31; *Dion* 1.
63. *Quomodo adulator ab amico internoscatur,* especially 52A. See also the interesting study of Alcibiades in D. A. Russell, *Plutarch* (1973), ch. 7, p. 117f.
64. Cf. Cic. *ad Att.* xiii 12.2 and n.b. the word 'intexere'.
65. Mestrius Florus obtained the Roman citizenship for Plutarch, (*Sylloge*[3], ed. Dittenberger, 829A), and visited Bedriacum with him (*Otho* 14.2). For Rusticus at one of Plutarch's lectures in Rome see *De curiositate* 522D–E.
66. Simonides fr. 36D.
67. Tac. *Agricola* 4.3. For the idea cf. Suet. *Nero* 52.
68. *Ant.Rom.* i 4–5.
69. See Th. Renoirte, *Les 'Conseils Politiques' de Plutarque* (1951).
70. See *De cohibenda ira,* especially 456D.
71. See below, ch. 4, p. 107f.

72.  See D. Stockton, *Cicero, A Political Biography* (1971), p. 190.
73.  Theophrastus, fr. 146 (Wimmer). It is worth comparing Aulus Gellius, *NA* i 3.
74.  For a study of this see E. Auerbach, *Mimesis* (1968), p. 33f.
75.  Cf. R. G. Ussher, *The Characters of Theophrastus* (1960), p. 1, 'a moral is pointed only twice'.
76.  Cic. *De fato* v 10, on Zopyrus.


CHAPTER 2

1.  *Lyc.-Numa comp.* 4.13. But Plutarch then goes on to say that Rome increased in power after abandoning Numa's constitution. Rome's attitude to defeated peoples is praised at *Rom.* 16.3.
2.  *Ages.* 1 and *Dion* 4.4–7.
3.  See D. A. Russell, *Greece and Rome*, xiii (1966), p. 143.
4.  For an analysis of this term see C. Brandstätter, *De notionum* πολιτικός *et* σοφιστης *usu rhetorico*: (*Leipzig. Stud. zur class. Phil.*, xv [1894], p. 129f.).
5.  The term is usually unfriendly; cf. A. Andrewes, *Greek Society* (1971), p. 203. But see W. Connor, *The New Politicians of Fifth-Century Athens* (1971), p. 3f.
6.  In Theophrastus, *Characters* 26, the oligarchical man complains of Theseus as the source of trouble for Athens by the synoecism. For Theseus and Menestheus see W. den Boer, *Greece and Rome*, xvi (1969), p. 1f.
7.  For the thought cf. *Lys.-Sulla comp.* 2 and note the Platonist comparison with the dog-trainer and horse-trainer.
8.  Peisistratus is obviously one of the better autocrats; for a wicked tyrant see *Arat.* 26 – Aristippus of Argos.
9.  Cf. Arist. *EN* 1094ª9f.
10.  Cf. *Marc* 9.7 = *F.Gr.Hist.* 87 F42 (Poseidonius).
11.  *Pel.* 18–19; Homer, *Iliad* ii 363.
12.  Cf. *Mor.* 313E and 750B.
13.  Plato, *Phaedrus* 255b. For the divine parentage and character of Harmony see *Mor.* 370C–371A.
14.  Cf. *Them.* 3.2 and *Arist.* 2.3 (from Ariston).
15.  *Thes.-Rom. comp.* 1.6: cf. *Mor* 780D. R. Flacelière, *REG*, lxi (1948), p. 101, argues that the definition is ambiguous; but it is surely man who serves the gods. I take Plutarch to mean that god may inspire *erōs*, the content of which is care for the young as a kind of tribute to the gods. See below, p. 164.
16.  On Caesar see below, p. 148.
17.  *Dion* 11.4–12; *Fab.* 1.5–6.
18.  See also *Publ.* 25.1; *Cim.* 6.2; *Per.* 4.6 and 39.3; *Cor.* 21.2; *Ant.* 62.2.
19.  On self-praise see below, p. 224–5.
20.  *Per.* 5.3 = *F.Gr.Hist.* 392 F15.
21.  Eur. *Iph. Aul.* 449.
22.  Cf. *Nic.* 2.6; 11.2; *Crass.* 3.2; *Cato i* 4.2.
23.  *Aesch.* iii 169.
24.  Cf. *Mor.* 537 and von Arnim, *Stoicorum Veterum Fragmenta* iii 415.

# Notes

25. See D. C. Earl, *The Moral and Political Traditions of Rome* (1967), pp. 30–31.
26. For the political context see C. Hignett, *A History of the Athenian Constitution* (1952), pp. 159–166.
27. See G. Soury, *La Démonologie de Plutarque* (1942).
28. Homer, *Iliad* xxiv 525–533.
29. See also *Arist.* 7.8; Homer, *Iliad* i 240.

## CHAPTER 3

1. See especially *Mor.* 523C and cf. the useful remarks in Plut. *Mor.* (Loeb) vii p. 2f.
2. For the idea that oratory is an instrument for the performance of fine actions see below, ch. 7.1, p. 222f.
3. For an example cf. Livy xxxiv 2f. (on the *lex Oppia*).
4. On Cato's activity here see H. H. Scullard, *Roman Politics* (1951), p. 14.
5. See F. Wehrli, *Die Schule des Aristoteles, Demetrios von Phaleron²* (1968), fr. 95, and cf. *Kommentar*, p. 64.
6. Arist. *Ath.Pol.* 27.3; see C. Hignett, *A History of the Athenian Constitution* (1952), p. 191.
7. D. A. Russell, *JRS*, liii (1963), p. 24, points out the contrast between Plutarch's account and the version of Dionysius in *Ant.Rom.* vi 94.
8. Cf. Aristoph. *Plutus* 90 and see Leutsch, *Corpus Paroemiographorum Graecorum* ii, p. 223 = Macarii, Centuria 8.60.
9. See H. A. Moellering, *Plutarch's 'De Superstitione' in the Context of his Theological Writings* (1962).
10. For this character in Theophrastus see R. G. Ussher, *The Characters of Theophrastus* (1960), p. 135f.
11. See Polybius vi 56 and F. W. Walbank, *Commentary* i (1957), p. 741f.
12. See A. D. Simpson, *TAPhA*, lxix (1938), p. 532f.; and J. van Ooteghem, *LEC*, xxi (1953), p. 396.
13. Diels-Kranz, *FVS* ii 59 A16. Ostracism of Thucydides in 442 BC.
14. Livy ii 40. See R. M. Ogilvie, *A Commentary on Livy 1–5* (1965), p. 336; also the discussion in R. Flacelière, *Plutarque, Vies* iii (1964), p. 175.
15. *Them.* 13.2; cf. *Arist.* 9.2; also *Marc.* 3.6.
16. Cf. *Praec. ger. reip.* 824C.
17. The antithesis is used to exaggerated effect in the epideictic speeches *De Alexandri Magni virtute aut fortuna*, and more soberly in the *Lives*, as at *Lyc.* 31.2.
18. Plutarch mentions two Maximi, Valerius (494 BC) and Fabius Rullus, for whom cf. *Fab.* 1.3.
19. Cf. above, ch. 2.1, p. 57.
20. For Clodius see e.g. *Pomp.* 49.2; *Cato ii* 31.2.
21. For Marius in politics see T. Carney, *Wiener Studien*, lxiii (1960), p. 83f. ('Cicero's Picture of Marius'); and especially E. Badian, *Historia*, xi (1962), p. 197f.
22. See above, ch. 1.4, p. 31 and n. 47.
23. Coriolanus; see D. A. Russell, *JRS*, liii (1963), p. 21f., and R. A. Brower, *Hero and Saint: Shakespeare and the Graeco-Roman Heroic Tradition* (1971), p. 354f.

251

24. On cultural conditions in general see especially G. W. Bowersock, *Augustus and the Greek World* (1965), and *Greek Sophists in the Roman Empire* (1969).
25. See A. H. M. Jones, *The Greek City* (1940), especially p. 170f.
26. Dio Chrys. *or.* i–iv especially.
27. Sen. *ep.* 5.
28. G. W. Bowersock, *Greek Sophists in the Roman Empire* (1969), p. 43f.
29. On his glorious death see Val.Max. 3.2 *Ext.* 5.
30. See R. MacMullen, *Enemies of the Roman Order* (1967), especially chs. i and ii.

CHAPTER 4

1. See R. Joly, *Le Thème Philosophique des Genres de Vie* (1955), especially
2. See D. Babut, *Plutarque et le Stoicisme* (1969), p. 318f. and especially chs. iv and v.
   p. 333.
3. The term had been long established in philosophical and in ordinary literary usage; for instances cf. Arist. *EN* 1111$^{b}$ and Aeschines, *contra Timarchum* 74f. Plutarch was adapting a traditional idea to his own views of what was important in character.
4. Known for his striking phrases – cf. *Sol.* 17.3; *Phoc.* 1.1 and 22.5 – but a contrast to Phocion and Demosthenes.
5. M. I. Finley, *Ancient Sicily to the Arab Conquest* (1968), pp. 95–97; n.b. the remark on p. 97 – 'Were it not for the myth which has been created about him, he would be called a tyrant.'
6. See H. D. Westlake, *Timoleon and his Relations with Tyrants* (1952), especially p. 7f.
7. *F.Gr.Hist.* 115 F326.
8. Cf. above, p. 62.
9. With Pausanias, for example (cf. p. 65 above), the decline from success at Plataea to his disgrace and death would have been shocking; see below, p. 132f., on change. Themistocles' exile *might* have posed similar problems, except that there were numerous tales of his prestige among the Persians.
10. See below, ch. 5.4, p. 179f.
11. Arist. *EN* 1125$^{b}$ 1–25; the mean has no name in this case, hence the extreme terms, *philotimia* and *aphilotimia*, are applied to the middle position, depending on the point of view.
12. See H. Bolkestein, *Wohltätigkeit und Armenpflege in vorchristlichem Altertum* (1959), p. 152f.; and L. Robert, *Les Gladiateurs dans l'Orient Grec* (1940), pp. 276–280.
13. For *philonikia* (love of victory) and *philoneikia* (love of strife) cf. below. p. 120.
14. For Ixion see further Dio Chrys. *or.* iv *de regno* 123f. and 130, and see below, p. 124.
15. Cf. *Mor.* 787C–D.
16. Cf. above, ch. 2.1, especially p. 57.
17. Eur. *Phoen.* 531f.
18. For his political role see H. H. Scullard, *Roman Politics* (1951), pp. 108 and 115f.

19. Cf. *Cor.* 1.6 where Plutarch says that the common name (*aretē-virtus*) was applied to the particular virtue courage.
20. Cf. *Cor.* 1.5 and see Plutarch's comments on the Spartans as both 'musical and warlike' – *Lyc.* 21.5–7.
21. For Thucydides' treatment of Alcibiades see A. W. Gomme, A. Andrewes, K. J. Dover, *Commentary on Thucydides* iv (1970), note on Thuc. v 43, p. 48f.
22. Plato, *Rep.* 548c f.
23. Cf. the comments on the effect of the honours granted to Demetrius, *Demetr.* 13.
24. Homer, *Odyssey* xix 179.
25. It is worth noticing that Agesilaus receives particular commendation for his 'political *aretē*' in obeying at once the order for his recall from Asia; *Ages.* 15.
26. The versions in Livy xxvi 26–32 and Val. Max. 4.1.7 lay stress on *moderatio animi*. Note that at *Marc.* 20.1 there is a variant reading, *dikaioterous* (more just) instead of the superlative.
27. Cf. the remarks of D. A. Russell, *Greece and Rome* xiii (1966), p. 145f.; A. W. Gomme, *Commentary on Thucydides* i (1945), p. 66 n. 2; R. Syme, *Tacitus* i (1958), p. 421 and n. 8.
28. See F. W. Walbank, *Philip V of Macedon* (1940), pp. 260–264.
29. Cf. Plato, *Gorgias* 476a f.
30. A list of melancholics is given in Arist. *Problemata* xxx 1. See R. Klibansky, E. Panofsky and F. Saxl, *Saturn and Melancholy* (1964), Part I, ch. 1.
31. *Alex.* 4.5. See J. R. Hamilton, *Plutarch, Alexander*, pp. lxiv and 12.
32. For Pericles see A. W. Gomme, *Commentary on Thucydides* i (1945), p. 66f.; W. Connor, *Theopompus and Fifth-Century Athens* (1968), especially pp. 33–37; for Pericles in Attic comedy see J. Schwarze, *Die Beurteilung des Perikles durch die Attische Komödie* (1971) = Zetemata 51.
33. See *Tim.* 14–15.
34. See especially E. C. Evans, 'Roman Descriptions of Personal Appearance in History and Biography', *HSCPh*, xlvi (1935), pp. 43–85; A. E. Wardman, *CQ*, xvii (1967), pp. 414–420.
35. Dio Chrys. *or.* xxxi and xxxvii. Cf. H. Blanck, *Wiederverwendung alter Statuen als Ehrendenkmäler bei Griechen und Römern* (1963), p. 23f.
36. For other statues of him cf. Polybius xxxix 16.10; Paus. ii 7.5 and vi 12.5.
37. Plato, *Rep.* 404a.
38. Cf. *Per.* 5.3, which criticizes Ion.
39. On the subject of physiognomy, see E. C. Evans, *TAPhA*, lxxii (1941), p. 96f.; and R. A. Pack, *ibid.*, p. 321.
40. Cf. Suet. *Nero* 19.3.
41. See G. B. Townend, *Latin Biography* (1967), ed. Dorey, p. 85.
42. Cf. A. Garzetti, *Plutarchi, Vita Caesaris* (1954), p. xlvii.
43. See *Jul.* 75.5; *Aug.* 51.1; *Tib.* 11.1; *Cal.* 3.2 and 52; *Claud.* 12.1.
44. See especially D. M. Pippidi, *Autour de Tibère* (1944), p. 11f.; on Tacitus' presentation of Tiberius see R. Seager, *Tiberius* (1972), p. 262.

CHAPTER 5

1. This account is based on my paper in *CQ*, xxi (1972), p. 254f.
2. On Timaeus (*F.Gr.Hist.* 566) see especially T. S. Brown, *Timaeus of*

*Tauromenium* (1958). One is rather at a loss to see why Philistus should have been put on a par with Thucydides, but his work was admired and used.

3. Nicias' *eulabeia*; see especially *Nic.* 2.2–4 where it is contrasted with the over-boldness and over-confidence of Cleon.

4. Near Babylon, in the autumn of 401 BC.

5. Xen. *Anab.* ii 6.1–15 (Clearchus).

6. Ctesias changed the order of Plataea and Salamis; cf. A. D. Momigliano, *History*, xliii (1958), p. 4.

7. On Plutarch's knowledge of Latin see in particular C. P. Jones, *Plutarch and Rome* (1971), especially pp. 81–87.

8. J. van Ooteghem, *Les Caecilii Metelli de la République* (1967), pp. 182–3, calls Plutarch's comments 'des phrases de rhétorique'; but *RE* Pompeius 206–9 finds Plutarch more credible.

9. The phrase is more familiar from Polybius; see e.g. F. W. Walbank, *Commentary* i, note on Bk. i 2.8.

10. There is a useful essay in N. Barbu, *Les procédés de la peinture des caractères et la vérité historique dans les biographies de Plutarque* (1934), ch. iv 2b.

11. Cf. Agathon in Arist. *Rhet.* ii 24 = 1402$^b$ 11.

12. According to Plutarch, Fabius followed Diocles' account. For Fabius Pictor see Peter, *Historicorum Romanorum Reliquiae* i, p. lxixf.

13. Cf. the terser account in Livy i 3.10f.

14. Bacchylides fr. 27 (Snell).

15. See Livy i 16 and cf. R. M. Ogilvie, *A Commentary on Livy 1–5*, p. 84.

16. For the Spartan attitude to the Helots cf. Thuc. iv 80.

17. See especially *Laws* i 628c f.

18. *F.Gr.Hist.* 338 F8.

19. For the political background, see C. Hignett, *A History of the Athenian Constitution* (1952), p. 193.

20. *F.Gr.Hist.* 76 F70.

21. See especially B. L. Ullman, *TAPhA*, lxxiii (1942), p. 23f.; P. de Lacy, *AJPh*, lxxiii (1952), p. 159f.; F. W. Walbank, *BICS*, ii (1955), p. 4f. On the allied topic of Plutarch's attitude to the poets see H. Schläpfer, *Plutarch und die Klassischen Dichter* (1950).

22. For the facts see M. W. MacCallum, *Shakespeare's Roman Plays* (1910), and, for a critical study, R. A. Brower, *Hero and Saint* (1971).

23. See e.g. *Quomodo adolescens poetas audire debeat 15D*.

24. See *Rom.* 16.5; *Cam.* 7; *Publ.* 9.9; and cf. above, p. 72.

25. See above, ch. 2.4, p. 73.

26. Arist. *Poet.* 1451$^b$8; cf. D. W. Lucas, *Aristotle's Poetics* (1968), p. 119.

27. At *Mor.* 20B–C Plutarch states that philosophers use historical events as examples, while poets 'do the same thing by making stories up'.

28. Homer, *Iliad* xxiv 525; quoted at *Mor.* 20F and 22B.

29. *F.Gr.Hist.* 81 F76.

30. See *F.Gr.Hist.* 115 F85f. for Theopompus' remarks on the *dēmagōgoi*.

31. Plutarch here argues from the silence of Thucydides, Ephorus and Aristotle (*fr.* 536).

32. *Phoc.* 37.1 mentions that the execution coincided with a procession to Zeus; Plutarch writes with restrained emotion.

33. See especially *Brut.* 7.1–5; 9; 29–30; 34; 40.

34. The case is put by P. de Lacy; see n. 21 above.

# Notes

35. Livy xxv 24.11–25. 9.
36. See *Marc.* 21 and *Fab.* 22; Livy xxvii 16. (It is fair to note that D. A. Russell, *Plutarch* (1973), e.g. p. 160, is much more sympathetic to Plutarch's style.)
37. See F. W. Walbank, *Commentary on Polybius* i (1957), p. 16f.; also A. Passerini, *Il Concetto antico di fortuna, Phil.*, xl (1935), pp. 90–97.
38. There is a more sympathetic approach to Philistus in M. I. Finley, *Ancient Sicily to the Arab Conquest* (1968), p. 85f.
39. Actaeon the Boeotian hero (with a cult at Plataea); and the Corinthian, son of Melissus.
40. As at *Odyssey* ix 339, quoted at *Cor.* 32.5.
41. There is a balanced account in J. R. Hamilton, *Plutarch, Alexander* (1969), p. xxiiif. Though I accept many of his comments on my paper in *CQ*, v (1955), p. 96f., I doubt whether Plutarch was ever the kind of rhetorician to be concerned only with the manner of his performance.
42. Cf. ch. 4, n. 6 above.
43. Cic. *de imp. Cn. Pompeii* 47–48.
44. See J. van Ooteghem, *L. Licinius Lucullus* (1959), p. 159.
45. See especially J. P. V. D. Balsdon, *JRS*, xli (1951), p. 2f.
46. On the memoirs see Ida Calabi, *Atti della Accademia Nazionale dei Lincei*, ser. viii (1950), p. 242f.; and contrast E. Valgiglio, *Plutarco, Vita di Mario* (1956), p. vi.
47. In general see P. E. Legrand, *Mélanges Glotz* (1932), ii p. 535f.; and L. Pearson, *Plutarch's Moralia* (Loeb), xi p. 2f.
48. Plutarch is probably playing on the idea expressed in Arist. *EN* 1096.ᵃ 16.
49. The word is *theolēptos*; it is interesting to note that at 1117A Plutarch refers to Socrates as one who was *theolēptos* as regards *aretē*. Hence the term was not pejorative only.
50. On Cleon in the *Lives* see e.g. *Per.* 33; *Nic.* 2.2–4. He is used as a contrast to both Pericles and Nicias.
51. On the belittling of Cato's suicide see App. *B.C.* ii 101; contrast Cic. *Tusc.* i 30.74; cf. R. MacMullen, *Enemies of the Roman Order* (1967), ch. i, n. 3.
52. See A. D. Momigliano, *History*, xliii (1958), pp. 1–13, or in *Secondo Contributo alla Storia degli Studi Classici* (1960), Parte prima no ii.
53. Herodotus vii 152.3.
54. Most clearly at *Brut.* 9 which corrects the hostile version of 8.6.
55. Plutarch here uses the term *blasphēmia* which occurs several times in the *De Herodoti malignitate*, e.g. 855D.
56. See above, ch. 1, n. 39.
57. They are admired by Polybius at ii 20.4. Cf. the discussion in W. H. Porter, *Plutarch's Life of Aratus* (1937), p. xvf.
58. See R. M. Errington, *Philopoemen* (1969), p. 216f.
59. *Cato* ii 6.4; 11.7; 52.6.
60. *Cato* ii 30.9 and 44.1. In the latter passage the criticism of Cato's manner of dressing is followed by a report of his drinking which is flatly denied.

CHAPTER 6

1. *De animae procreatione in Timaeo.* In general see R. M. Jones, *The Platonism of Plutarch* (1916).

2. Cic. *Tusc.* V.10.
3. On *sophos* as applied to Solon and others see W. K. C. Guthrie, *A History of Greek Philosophy*, i (1962), p. 51.
4. See J. Defradas, *Plutarque, Le Banquet des Sept Sages* (1954).
5. Plutarch excludes Periander from the Seven Sages (probably because he was a tyrant) and makes Anacharsis a dominant figure in the *Septem sapientium convivium*; see Defradas, *op. cit.* pp. 18–20.
6. Accredited with wise maxims; cf. *Schol. Euripid. in Hippolytum* 264.
7. Plutarch wrote a commentary on the *Works and Days*, admiring Hesiod as a compatriot and a repository of truths: see e.g. Plut. *Mor.* vii (1967), ed. Sandbach, p. 43, no. 62.
8. *Mor.* 154C–D.
9. Herodotus viii 57–58.
10. Cf. Diog. Laert. i 38.
11. Plutarch's own concern with Homer is well illustrated by the range of quotations; cf. W. C. Helmbold and E. N. O'Neil, *Plutarch's Quotations* (1959), p. 40f.
12. Plato, *Protagoras* 316c f.
13. Cf. *Alc.* 1 and 4.
14. The word *kathēgemōn* is used as a title of divinities; cf. Liddell & Scott, Jones, *Greek Lexicon*, s.v.
15. Cf. *Dion* 13; 16 and 20.3.
16. For Plato's remark, see *Dion* 11.3. For examples of Plutarch's use of this antithesis see *Lyc.* 8.5; and 31; *Philop.* 4.8; cf. above, ch. 3, n. 17.
17. Cf. *Rep.* 501e; 487e; and *Laws* 711e.
18. Cf. *Cic.* 4; 5.2; 41.8.
19. *Rep.* 372e; cf. *Laws* 691e.
20. *Laws* 706c.
21. For details see R. M. Errington, *Philopoemen* (1969), p. 102f.
22. Plato, *epist.* iv 321b.
23. *Ant.* 29.1; cf. Plato, *Gorg.* 464c.
24. *Dion* 17.1–4, where Dion's friendship with Speusippus is mentioned.
25. For his philosophical works see H. Bardon, *La Littérature Latine Inconnue*, i (1952), pp. 209 and 228.
26. He claimed to revive the old Academy; cf. *RE* Antiochos no. 62.
27. *Brut.* 1.7; 9.7.
28. At *Brut.* 37 Cassius uses Epicurean theory in order to calm Brutus' perturbation at his dream.
29. He wrote on the Spartan state; cf. von Arnim, *Stoicorum Veterum Fragmenta* i 620.
30. See D. R. Dudley, *JRS*, xxxi (1941), pp. 94–99; and J. B. Becker, *Parola del Passato*, xix (1964), pp. 125–134.
31. Plutarch makes rhetorical play with *meteōrisas* (4.6) and *meteōrologia*. On buffoonery (*bōmolochia*) see D. A. Russell, *Plutarch* (1973), p. 155.
32. Cf. above, ch. 3.2, p. 89.
33. See Polybius x 22.2; Pausanias viii 49.2. The form of the names is in doubt, since they also occur as Ecdemus and Megalophanes.
34. For Aratus' dealings with Aristippus see F. W. Walbank, *Aratos of Sicyon* (1933), p. 58f.
35. See *Cato i* 2; Nearchus is mentioned in Cicero, *De senectute* 41.
36. On his retirement cf. J. van Ooteghem, *L. Licinius Lucullus* (1959), p. 166f.

37. Plutarch gives the traditional picture of Aristotle; cf. J. R. Hamilton, *Plutarch, Alexander, ad loc.*
38. See G. W. Bowersock, *Augustus and the Greek World* (1965), pp. 33 and 39.
39. *RE* Philostratos no. 7.
40. Plato, *Gorgias* 487d–e, answering Callicles at 484c.
41. For this cf. R. MacMullen, *Enemies of the Roman Order* (1967), p. 18f.

CHAPTER 7

1. In general see R. Jeuckens, *Plutarch und die Rhetorik* (1907).
2. Malcovati, *ORF*³ i, n. 3.
3. Plato, *Phaedrus* 271c.
4. He reminds his readers that Pericles left no written works and that favourable judgment on his oratory was passed by the comic writers. He remarks that the saying 'the goddess of persuasion was on his lips' could fairly be applied to Xenophon: *IO* x 1.82.
5. For Coriolanus see *Ant.Rom.* viii 5–9 and 47.
6. See e.g. Cic. *Brutus* 185f. For a story about Cicero's power to sway an audience cf. Plut. *Cic.* 13. On the orator's duties see G. M. A. Grube, *The Greek and Roman Critics* (1965), p. 177f.
7. Cf. above, ch. 2.4, p. 75.
8. *Cato ii* 19.9; Ziegler suggests that the reading should be, not 'Catones', but 'pseudo-Catones'.
9. At *Praec. ger. reip.* 801C: Menander fr. 472 (Koch).
10. Cf. *Sert.* 2.2 and *Caes.* 3.2–4.
11. Cic. *de inv.* i 2–3.
12. For Plutarch's collection see *Apophthegmata Laconica* 208A.
13. For brevity as a grace see Ernesti, *Lexicon Technologiae Latinorum Rhetoricae*, p. 40.
14. According to Quintilian *IO* x 1.123, his philosophical works were superior to his speeches. For Cicero's comment see *ad Att.* xiv 1.2; see also A. E. Douglas, *Cicero, Brutus* (1966), p. xxf.
15. Cic. *Brutus* 50.
16. Cf. L. Radermacher, *Artium Scriptores* (1951), p. 6f.
17. Cf. *Mor.* 504A–505F and 354C. On silence see O. Casel, *De Philosophorum Graecorum Silentio Mystico* (1919).
18. See especially Quintilian *IO* vi 3.2.
19. For the joke as a sign of *humanitas* see e.g. Cic. *de oratore* ii 215f., especially 230.
20. Cic. *de oratore* ii 243–244.
21. For his influence see G. M. A. Grube, *The Greek and Roman Critics* (1965), p. 341.
22. For a survey of his criticism see Grube, *op. cit.* p. 207f.
23. Cic. *Brutus* 63.
24. For roughness (*trachutēs-asperitas*) cf. Ernesti, *Lexicon Technologiae Graecorum Rhetoricae*, p. 356.
25. Cic. *Paradoxa Stoicorum* 1.
26. For Gaius' oratory see Malcovati *ORF*³ i, n. 48.
27. Aulus Gellius *NA* x 3.

28. Plutarch is probably referring to the pitch-pipe.
29. Cf. K. Kourouniotes and H. A. Thompson, *Hesperia*, i (1932), especially p. 134.
30. See Cic. *De amicitia* 96. The argument for Licinius seems strong; see E. S. Staveley, *Greek and Roman Voting and Elections* (1973), p. 195 and n. 384.
31. *Essais* ii 32.
32. See H. Erbse, *Hermes*, lxxxiv (1956), p. 398f.
33. See *Thes.-Rom. comp.* 6.
34. T. J. B. Spencer, *Shakespeare's Plutarch* (1964), p. 8.
35. Cf. *Marc.* 3.6.
36. More exactly, he says that Greek words were at first more intermingled with Latin than they were later on: cf. *Rom.* 15.4 and *Numa* 7.10.
37. See H. Erbse, *op. cit.* (n. 32), p. 403f.
38. Plutarch refers here to Sulla's sumptuary legislation and to Lysander's introduction of gold and silver coinage at Sparta; *Lys.* 17.
39. Polybius vi 11 and Dion. Hal. *Ant.Rom.* i 4.
40. As at *De oratore* i 45f.
41. Livy ix 17.19f.
42. See e.g. iii 8 *Ext.* 1; and especially iv 7 *Ext.* 1: 'Haeret animus in domesticis, sed aliena quoque bene facta referre Romanae urbis candor hortatur.'
43. Nepos, *de ducibus, praef.* 1.1–4; cf. Cic. *Tusc.* i 4.


CONCLUSION

1. Montaigne, *Essais* ii 32.
2. See Boswell's *Life of Johnson* (OUP edn), pp. 23–24.

# Select Bibliography

TRANSLATIONS AND EDITIONS

Amyot, Jacques, *Plutarque, Les Vies des Hommes Illustres*, ed. Pléiade, Paris, 1951.
Flacelière, R., *Plutarque, Vies*, vols. i–vii, Paris, 1957 etc.
Perrin, B., *Lives*, Loeb Classical Library, London; Cambridge, Mass., 1914 etc.
Scott-Kilvert, I., *The Rise and Fall of Athens* (Penguin), Harmondsworth, 1960.
Scott-Kilvert, I., *Makers of Rome* (Penguin), Harmondsworth, 1965.
Scott-Kilvert, I., *The Age of Alexander* (Penguin), Harmondsworth, 1973.
Spencer, T. J. B., *Shakespeare's Plutarch* (Penguin), Harmondsworth, 1964.
Warner, Rex, *Fall of the Roman Republic* (Penguin), Harmondsworth, 1958.

*Alexander*; ed. J. R. Hamilton, Oxford, 1969.
*Aratus*; ed. W. H. Porter, Cork, 1937.
*Aristeides*; ed. I. C. Limentani, Florence, 1964.
*Brutus*; ed. R. del Re, Florence, 1948.
*Caesar*; ed. A. Garzetti, Florence, 1954.
*Cicero*; ed. D. Magnino, Florence, 1962.
*Demetrius*; ed. E. Manni, Florence, 1953.
*Dion*; ed. W. H. Porter, Dublin, 1952.
*Gracchi*; ed. E. Valgiglio, Rome, 1963.
*Marius*; ed. E. Valgiglio, Florence, 1965.
There are editions of several Lives by H. A. Holden, Cambridge: *Gracchi* (1885); *Sulla* (1886); *Timoleon* (1889); *Themistocles* (1892); *Demosthenes* (1893); *Pericles* (1894).


ARTICLES AND BOOKS ON PLUTARCH

Aulotte, R., *Amyot et Plutarque*, Geneva, 1965.
Babut, D., *Plutarque et le Stoicisme*, Paris, 1969.
Barbu, N. I., *Les procédés de la peinture des caractères et la vérité historique dans les biographies de Plutarque*, Paris, 1934.
Barrow, R. H., *Plutarch and his Times*, London, 1967.
Berry, E. G., *Emerson's Plutarch*, Cambridge, Mass., 1961.
Bowersock, G. W., *Augustus and the Greek World*, Oxford, 1965.
Brower, R. A., *Hero and Saint: Shakespeare and the Graeco-Roman Heroic Tradition*, Oxford, 1971.

# Plutarch's 'Lives'

Clifford, J. L., *Biography as an Art*, Oxford, 1962.
*Congrès de Paris*, Association Budé, 1969, pp. 481–594 (Contributions by R. Flacelière and others).
Dihle, A., *Studien zur Griechischen Biographie*, Göttingen, 1956.
Erbse, H., 'Die Bedeutung der Synkrisis in den Parallelbiographien Plutarchs', *Hermes*, lxxxiv (1956), pp. 389–424.
Fuhrmann, F., *Les Images de Plutarque*, Paris, 1964.
Gomme, A. W., *A Commentary on Thucydides*, i, Oxford, 1945, pp. 54–84.
Gossage, A. J., 'Plutarch' in *Latin Biography* (ed. Dorey), London, 1967, pp. 45–78.
Helmbold, W. C., and O'Neil, E. N., *Plutarch's Quotations*, Baltimore, 1959.
Hirzel, R., *Plutarch*, Leipzig, 1912.
Jeuckens, R., *Plutarch von Chaeronea und die Rhetorik*, Strassburg, 1907.
Joly, R., *Le Thème Philosophique des Genres de Vie*, Brussels, 1955.
Kirn, P., *Das Bild des Menschen in der Geschichtsschreibung von Polybius bis Ranke*, Göttingen, 1956.
de Lacy, P., 'Biography and Tragedy', *AJP*, lxxiii (1952), pp. 159–171.
Legrand, P. E., 'De la "Malignité" d'Hérodote', *Mélanges Glotz*, ii (1932), pp. 535–547.
Leo, F., *Die Griechisch-Römische Biographie nach ihrer literarischen Form*, Leipzig, 1901.
Levi, M. A., *Plutarco e il V Secolo*, Milan, 1955.
MacCullum, M. W., *Shakespeare's Roman Plays*, Oxford, 1910.
MacMullen, R., *Enemies of the Roman Order*, Harvard, 1967.
Martin, H., 'The Concept of Prāotēs in Plutarch's *Lives*', *Greek, Roman and Byzantine Studies*, iii (1960), pp. 65–73.
  'The Concept of Philanthropia in Plutarch's *Lives*', *AJP*, lxxxii (1961), 326–339.
  'The Concept of Philanthropia in Plutarchc's *Lives*', *AJP*, lxxxii (1961), p. 164f.
Meinhardt, E., *Perikles bei Plutarch*, Frankfurt, 1957.
Misch, G., *A History of Autobiography in Antiquity*, London, 1950.
Momigliano, A., *The Development of Greek Biography*, Cambridge, Mass., 1971.
Peter, H., *Die Quellen Plutarchs in den Biographien der Römer*, Leipzig, 1865.
Renoirte, Th., *Les 'Conseils Politiques' de Plutarque*, Louvain, 1951.
Russell, D. A., 'Plutarch's Life of Coriolanus', *JRS*, liii (1963), pp. 21–28.
  'On Reading Plutarch's *Lives*', *Greece and Rome*, xiii (1966), pp. 139–154.
  'Plutarch, *Alcibiades* 1–16', *Proceedings of the Cambridge Philological Association* (1966), pp. 37–47.
  *Plutarch*, London, 1973.
Schläpfer, H., *Plutarch und die Klassischen Dichter*, 1950.
Soury, G., *La Démonologie de Plutarque*, Paris, 1942.
Stadter, P. A., *Plutarch's Historical Methods*, Cambridge, Mass., 1965.
Stauffer, D. A., *The Art of Biography in eighteenth-century England*, Princeton, 1941.
Theander, C., *Plutarch und die Geschichte*, Lund, 1951.
  'Plutarch's Forschungen in Rom', *Eranos*, lvii (1959), pp. 99–131.
Uxkull-Gyllenband, W. G., *Plutarch und die Griechische Biographie*, Stuttgart, 1927.
Wardman, A. E., 'Description of Personal Appearance in Plutarch and Suetonius', *CQ*, xvii (1967), pp. 414–420.

## Select Bibliography

'Plutarch's Methods in the *Lives*', *CQ*, xxi (1971), pp. 254–261.

Westlake, H. D., *Individuals in Thucydides*, Cambridge, 1968.

Ziegler, K., *Plutarchos* in *Real Encyclopädie für Altertumswissenschaft*; also separately published in 1949 and 1964.

# Index of Passages from Plutarch

# Index of Passages from Plutarch

264

(b) THE MORALIA

# General Index

269